THE CISTERCIAN SPIRIT

CISTERCIAN STUDIES SERIES

CISTERCIAN STUDIES SERIES: NUMBER THREE

THE CISTERCIAN SPIRIT
A SYMPOSIUM

In Memory of Thomas Merton

edited by

M. Basil Pennington ocso

CISTERCIAN PUBLICATIONS
Spencer, Massachusetts
1970

Ecclesiastical permission to publish this book was received from Bernard
Flanagan, Bishop of Worcester, April 23, 1969.

Printed in the Republic of Ireland by
Cahill & Co. Limited, Parkgate Printing Works, Dublin

CONTENTS

IN MEMORIAM: THOMAS MERTON, 1915-1968

THOMAS MERTON is dead. For those of us who knew him, the man of humor, of charm, the man so highly gifted, so intensely alive, it is hard to believe that he is gone. But this is not especially remarkable; the sudden death of any man in the prime of life always comes as a shock. What endures in this case is the slowly growing awareness of an irreparable loss, a sense of the many paths that had just been opened before him, paths along which he himself would have walked securely while he led the many others who were always ready to follow him. His last journey was a pledge of this: all the way from Kentucky to Bangkok he left a trail of visits and talks filled with confidence, life and hope.

But Merton would never have wanted to provoke sadness and mourning. Even when marked by struggle and trial, his life was essentially a celebration, and in death he should be remembered with joy. He is of course remembered for an extraordinarily large and varied body of writings, and sooner or later somebody is going to bring out the complete works, an enterprise that would doubtless amuse the author if he knew of it, but which will certainly be of great value to students of literature and religion alike. Nevertheless, if there is anything for which Merton should be remembered it is his life as a monk. He produced many studies on monastic life and subjects closely related to it, especially prayer. But he could only write as he did about monasticism because he lived it first.

Although he belonged to a strictly enclosed contemplative order, Merton's life seems to have been lived very much in the public gaze

His autobiography was a best-seller and has long since entered the ranks of the classics of its type. He wrote ardently and voluminously on the contemplative life, and there can be no question about the influence he exercised over the mental and spiritual climate of the generation that was growing up in this country after the second world war. In the last decade of his life he openly expressed his increasing concern over the spiritual bankruptcy of modern man, whom he saw as the slave of a bastard society spawned of political unscrupulosity and technological overkill and producing in its turn the fruits of atomic war and racial hatred. He unerringly perceived and tirelessly denounced hypocrisy and demagoguery whether in religious or civil life. And yet his relentless realism never turned bitter and he retained a basic optimism in the power of man to be converted and live: the result of a vision that was radically biblical, and monastic in focus, but expressed in human terms that touched not only the heart of the matter he was dealing with, but the heart of his reader or listener as well, and caused thousands who never knew him personally to admire and look up to him.

In spite of all this—the publicity, the correspondence (which he would have preferred to avoid, but which he generously carried on for the sake of others), the years of teaching novices and scholastics in his monastery—there was something of Thomas Merton that remained hidden and secret; there were inmost depths of the man that could not be reached by the curiosity seekers, perhaps not even by those who thought they knew him well. He once wrote, "They can have Thomas Merton if they want him; he's dead. They can have Father Louis too for that matter; he's also dead." He liked to describe the Virgin Mary as the most hidden of all the saints, externally given the most reverence, but in her deepest reality known only to God; it was in this respect more than in any other that he took her for his patron. No matter how much he wrote about himself, expressed his views and opinions, made his unique contribution to the world around him, his was basically a life hidden with Christ in God.

And yet he knew that he was like a city on a mountain, and that he had no right to hide the light that had been given him. He shared himself and his talents unstintingly, only reserving for himself the time and the solitude he felt were indispensable for his monastic vocation. The present writer and many like him can testify to Merton's constant generosity in contributing articles and book reviews to a variety of publications. He knew that his name lent enormous prestige to any book or magazine in which it appeared, and he always came gladly to the aid of struggling editors; yet he did it with unsophisticated simplicity and humor. No matter how serious his work, he never took himself too seriously, and this of course only increased the depth and importance of his work. And so it is that paradoxically enough something of the hidden depths of the man necessarily came to the surface. Like every human life, and especially a life intentionally immersed in God, his existence was a mystery, but a mystery at least partially revealed; a light, small but burning brightly in the heart of darkness: "as unknown and yet well known . . . as sorrowful yet always rejoicing, as poor yet enriching many, as having nothing yet possessing all things" (2 Cor 6: 8–10).

And now the light has gone out. Or has it? There is room for regret that he could not do still more, but how much should we demand of someone who gave so much? What he gave is still with us and will remain. And he himself is still with us. Those who took part in the symposium recorded in these pages can bear witness to the fact of his presence during the days we were together. We had hoped he would be with us to tell us about the Bangkok journey and make still another inestimable contribution to the renewal of his order and of monastic life as a whole. It was not to be as we had hoped, but that he was really there, exercising a special influence in his own way is beyond question. And there is every reason to believe that his influence will continue to be felt, in the monastic order, in the church as a whole, and perhaps much farther afield. Genius is rare, holiness is even rarer, but when they make their appearance as they unquestionably did in Merton, they have the power to pass beyond the last frontier; death itself can lay no claim on them. And when they appear in a man whose whole life is dominated by love, they are joined with the power of love which is stronger than the grave and already participates in the life of the resurrection. Thomas Merton is still with us in the love of Christ which surpasses all understanding. He is more hidden now, but at last he is one with the waters of Siloe that flow in silence and bring richness and healing to the soil of the world.

Basil De Pinto OSB

Mount Savior,
Pine City, New York

INTRODUCTION

T HE PRECISE TITLE of this Symposium was: *Towards
discerning the spirit and aims of the founders of the Order of
Cîteaux.* This title is quite exact; there was no expectation
that this Symposium could in itself establish or discern the precise
spirit and aims of the founders. Rather, its hope was that it might
take at least a first step towards that goal. The aim was to survey,
in a general way, the area and the matter to be studied and, as it
were, establish the state of the question.

Our times might be called: The day of the question. Often
meetings such as this are devoted exclusively to questions and many
times pseudo-questions. One leaves them in a sort of cloud of
unknowing. Happily, this meeting took instead a very positive
outlook. There was no hesitation to affirm fundamental realities,
realities which need not be called into question even though they
can always be studied and understood with greater depth and
awareness. Yet, at the same time, the Symposium did not sidestep
real questions, and much of its time was given to grappling with
them. It had been suggested by one of the participants that we
should make an inventory of the questions that confronted us. This
would have been helpful if done, but unfortunately time did not
allow for this at this meeting.

There were some questions that emerged very clearly. Our need
for critical editions of the primitive documentation of the Order
was very keenly felt. Only when their chronological order and
authenticity are established will we have some of the basic tools very

much needed in this area of study. Furthermore, we realized our inability to affirm with any degree of certitude just who are the founders of the Order of Cîteaux. While factually we know the men who started the monastery, and the men who ratified the Charter of Charity, it is a theological reality we are considering here and this is a theology which needs to be more fully explicated and understood. There is also a sociological question, for a religious order is necessarily a social structure. A first attempt was made in the course of the Symposium to explore this aspect. However, it was only a beginning and a future symposium will hopefully devote its attention to this much more extensively. There was an awareness that some questions and areas were hardly touched upon at all: the role of Mary in the life and spirituality of the Cistercians; the primitive origins of the Cistercian Nuns; and the full consequence and significance of the seventeenth-century divisions which lead to the establishment of the two Orders in the end of the nineteenth century. Undoubtedly, much work remains to be done: research, interpretation, synthesis, communication, and prayer. But we can hope that the Symposium of 1969 along with the publication of these papers will prove to be a contribution to this work.

Our survey of the matter followed a somewhat chronological order. After the presentation of the theme on the opening evening, the papers of the following day were devoted to studying the context in which the founding of Cîteaux took place. First there was a consideration of the historical situation which prevailed in the Church and society in the eleventh century. It was a period of great reform movements, not to speak of revolutionary developments, that profoundly affected the lives and thinking of men and nations and set the stage for the possibility of such a widespread monastic movement as Cîteaux. Then there was considered the place that a rule should have in the life of a monastic community. For the monastic developments of that time found it necessary to relate themselves to the almost universally accepted Rule of St Benedict. The Cistercian renewal also had to relate itself to the dominating monastic influence of the time, with which it soon found itself in open conflict—the impressive and extensive Cluniac system and its affiliations. Further light was thrown on this relationship by studying in particular the relationship between the two great figures who, as it were, incarnated the respective movements—Peter the Venerable of Cluny and St Bernard of Clairvaux.

The context having been established, attention was then turned to the primary source of our knowledge of the early Cistercians in a study of the primitive documents. After a presentation by a canonist, an extremely fine and profound analysis was undertaken by one of the outstanding monastic scholars of our times: Father Jean Leclercq OSB. After his thorough historical and theological analysis of these documents, Father Leclercq opened the way to another approach by exploring briefly the sociology of religious orders. Hence there are included in this collection two papers by Father Leclercq.

It was said several times during the Symposium that the Cistercian fact was a complexus of ideals, structures, and outstanding men. To understand this truth more fully, it was necessary to study it as incarnated in some of Cîteaux's great men. Thus, a group of papers were presented giving the witness of the Cistercians of this period. Dom Jean Leclercq's paper had presented Bernard as the theologian of Cistercian life. An excellent paper was presented on William of St Thierry giving his witness to the spirit and aims of the early Cistercians. Another paper explored more generally the witness of the early English Cistercians and was followed by a special study on the "Bernard of the North"—Aelred of Rievaulx.

Often it is in the concrete situation or problem that we see most clearly the principles that are at work, the ideals that are struggling for realization. In our Symposium this was the case when Father Chrysogonus Waddell shared with us the fruit of his years of research on the problem of the reform of the Cistercian Antiphonary. Also, it is undoubtedly true that something can often be seen much better when one steps back a bit from it and looks at it from a different perspective. For this reason, we were interested in the witness given by those who came after the founders in the course of the following century. Dom Jean Leclercq gave the general overview of this, while the final paper of the Symposium explored the developments among the nuns of the Order.[1]

At this Symposium the papers were largely historical in content and concerned for the most part with the eleventh, twelfth, and early thirteenth centuries. They did at times enter into theological considerations and touch upon the relevance of these facts and realities to our times. This was carried through much more extensively in the lengthy discussions (usually an hour and a half) which followed each paper. This is all that an initial Symposium could hope to do. Undoubtedly, much more remains to be done not only in the area of history but also in theology, sociology, psychology, and above all in relating the fruit of all this study to today's renewal efforts.

In presenting these papers we hope that they will stand as a witness to the vitality which exists today within the monastic order and in particular within the Order of Cîteaux. We hope they will encourage the renewal efforts of the Cistercian Order and of monasticism in general, and inspire other undertakings of a complementary nature. The work to be done is so vast that there need be no rivalry, for there is certainly no dearth of material to be studied and areas to be explored. Such meetings undoubtedly demand considerable work and sacrifice on the part of the monks and nuns participating. This is especially true for those dedicated to the contemplative way of life. The more the labors can be shared, the lighter the burden will be for each.

In concluding this brief introduction, I hope it will not be out of place for me to express my very deep and sincere gratitude to all those whose generous cooperation and collaboration made this Symposium a possibility and, I believe, a success. It was a very

1. In an effort to keep this volume within manageable proportions three of the papers read at the Symposium have not been included: Basil De Pinto OSB, The Twelfth-Century Benedictines and Cistercian Monasticism; Bernard Johnson OCSO, Discerning the Spirit and Aims of our Fathers and Founders in Three Early Documents: *Exordium Parvum—Carta Caritatis—Exordium Cistercii*; Roger De Ganck OCSO, The Cistercian Nuns of Belgium in the Thirteenth Century: The Second Wave of Cistercian Spirituality. It is hoped, however, that these interesting and valuable papers will appear elsewhere.

fruitful and encouraging sign of the times to see sit down together, monks and nuns, Benedictines and Cistercians, Cistercians of both observances. Significant too was the presence of many Cistercian abbots who came to "listen and learn." We are grateful for their support. Above all and before all, we would express our humble gratitude to God our Father who through his Son, Jesus Christ, sent into our midst his Spirit of Love and Light to guide us in our search for Truth.

M. Basil Pennington ocso

St Joseph's Abbey,
Spencer, Massachusetts

TOWARDS DISCERNING THE SPIRIT AND AIMS OF THE FOUNDERS OF THE ORDER OF CÎTEAUX

FIRST OF ALL we might well ask why should we be concerned with this matter. What is meant by the spirit and aims of our founders and why should we seek to discern them?

Spirit

It is difficult to define exactly what is meant by spirit. The term is being used analogically or even metaphorically.

Spirit is the life principle in a living organism, that which animates it. Though it is distinct from the body, it is intimately united with it. In an institution the spirit is what makes it "to be alive," to fulfill its functions with vitality. In the final analysis, this spirit lives in the men who constitute the institute. In our present context it is the driving inspiration which moved our founders as they brought a new monastic order into existence.

When this spirit has been embodied in writing, often it is later set in opposition to its very body, the "letter." In reality, the spirit will be found deep within the letter. We have to consider then the writings and the actions of our founders to discern their spirit, we have to probe these to their very heart and discover the ultimate criteria for the choices they made. These ultimate criteria are what constitute the spirit.[1]

---

1. Cf. Paul Molinari sj, "Religious Renewal and the Founder's Spirit" in *Review for Religious*, 27 (1968), p. 801.

Aims

The concept of aims is less difficult to define, although in the concrete it might be just as difficult to discern. The aim is that toward which the founders directed their efforts, the goal they set themselves. The aims of an institute need not be unique, something which distinguishes it from all other institutes. Indeed, many religious families have somewhat the same aims. It is more properly the spirit that distinguishes them. On the other hand, it is possible for the same spirit to inform diverse aims. St Dominic's spirit of truth sends the Dominican professor into the lecture hall of a university and the Dominican missionary into the barrio or the inner city; the spirit which animates the labor is the same but the immediate aim is quite diverse.

Founders

This concept is relatively simple and most religious institutes have little difficulty in identifying their founders. (However, as we shall see below, in our Order the question is not so easily resolved.) The founders might be defined as those who took the first steps to establish an institute, giving it a spirit, purpose, and the essential means for carrying out its mission.

It might be well to note here that every religious family shares a certain heritage from founders other than the immediate, particular founders of the institute. The spirit of these founders can actually be of greater importance though it comes to the institute mediated and specified by the spirit of the proper founders. Ultimately, Jesus Christ, the Son of God, is *the* Founder; his Gospel, the ultimate Rule. Within this total context of Christianity we look to the founders of monasticism as determining a special way of living the Christian response. St Benedict, for us, has given further precision to the monastic charism. And then the founders of the Order of Cîteaux specified in what spirit we as Cistercians are to live the Christian, monastic life according to St Benedict's Rule for Monasteries.

Order

The word "order" or "*ordo*" has gone through an evolution and still possesses more than one meaning for us. Order can refer to established relationships between people and things or their proper arrangement.[2] In the early Church it was regularly attributed to particular functional groups within the Church, and this usage is still familiar to us.[3] Order again can refer to the whole ordering of a life—a discipline or way of life. Thus we speak of the *ordo monasticus*.[4] Finally, it was only in the era when our own Order was being founded that order began to signify a religious institute.[5] Therefore, when we come to the consideration of the founders of our Order, we can perhaps distinguish between those who are the founders of the Cistercian way of life and those who are the founders of the Order as an institute. The norm given for the implementation of the Conciliar decree *Perfectae caritatis*, which has inspired our search, refers to the founders as founders of the institute.[6] However, the two cannot be wholly divorced, for it is a question

2. This use of *ordo* is quite frequent in St Benedict's Rule for Monasteries (Hereafter RB), e.g., 2:19; 11:4, 5, 7; etc. (For citations of RB we use the division of chapter and verse of E. Manning [Westmalle: Typis Ordinis Cisterciensis, 1962], who follows Lentini.)

3. E.g., RB 60:1: *de ordine sacerdotum;* 65:20: *de ordine praepositurae.*

4. E.g., RB 11:11; *Charter of Charity* (Hereafter CC), c. 4, ed. J.-B. Van Damme, *Documenta pro Cisterciensis Ordinis Historiae ac Juris Studio* (Westmalle: Typis Ordinis Cisterciensis, 1959), p. 17; trans. D. Murphy, in L. Lekai, *The White Monks* (Okauchee, Wis.: The Cistercian Fathers, 1952), c. 3, p. 269.

5. Cf. J. Hourlier, "Cluny et la Notion d'Ordre Religieux," in *A Cluny: Congrès Scientifique* (Dijon, 1950), pp. 219ff. We find it used in this sense in CC, c. 10f. p. 20; Murphy, cc. 11f., pp. 272f.; St Bernard, Epistle 4, PL 182:90; trans., B. James, *The Letters of St Bernard of Clairvaux* (London: Burns Oates, 1953), p. 21. In some instances there is real ambiguity whether the word signifies a way of life or an institute, e.g., CC, cc. 7, 8, 9, pp. 17f.; St Bernard, Epistle 6, 1, PL 182:92; James, Letter 7, p. 25 (The English translation invariably translates "*ordo*" as though it signified institute).

6. Cf. the Apostolic Letter, *Ecclesiae sanctae,* August 6, 1966 (implementing four decrees of the Second Vatican Council), Part II, n. 12a: "The spirit of the founders and their specific aims and the healthy traditions, all of which constitute the patrimony of each institute. . . ."

of the *spirit* of the founders, and this is, of course, closely related to the observances of the life.

Cîteaux

Cîteaux is the New Monastery which was founded by Robert of Molesme and his twenty companions on the Feast of St Benedict in the year 1098. At first it was called the New Monastery to distinguish it from the old monastery of Molesme.[7] It was the founding of this New Monastery and the events which took place in it in the succeeding decades that led immediately to the founding of the order which properly bears the name of the Order of Cîteaux.

Discernment

Our quest, then, is to discern the spirit and aims of the founders of the Order of Cîteaux. But what does it mean, to discern? Etymologically, to separate or to distinguish one thing from all others. To do this we must have true insight into the reality which we wish to discern or distinguish.

The word, "insight," almost naturally brings to our minds the name of Father Bernard Lonergan sj. I believe his methodology can be applied fruitfully to our undertaking.[8]

Father speaks of eight specific functions. First of all there must be *research*. We must seek to know as clearly as possible what our Fathers said, thought and did. Then there must be an accurate *interpretation or exegesis* of this data. Next, the historian must place

---

7. The documents not infrequently refer to the New Monastery as a hermitage, *"heremum,"* Little Exordium, ed. Van Damme, *op. cit.,* c. 3, p. 7; c. 7, p. 9; etc.; trans., R. Larkin, in Lekai, *op. cit.,* pp. 253ff. But the same document also gives it the name "Cîteaux," e.g., cc. 3, 9, as well as referring to it as the New Monastery, e.g., cc. 7, 8, 14. For a brief study of the historical evolution of the name of the New Monastery, cf. J. Marilier, *Chartes et Documents concernant l'Abbaye de Cîteaux,* 1098-1182 (Rome: Editiones Cistercienses, 1961), pp. 24ff.

8. I hesitate to attribute to Fr Lonergan the methodology suggested here, for I am sure it in no wise does true justice to his genius. However, I do have to acknowledge a true dependance on his invaluable studies.

all this in its proper *historical context* and perspective.[9] It would seem to me that these three functions could be further divided according to the more common divisions of labor, namely that of field and of subject. For example, research, interpretation and study must be done in the different fields of archeology, spiritual writings, documents, liturgy, economy, etc.; the same functions need to be carried out in regard to the different subjects: Robert, Stephen, Bernard, Isaac, etc.[10] After all the material has been drawn together, the function is that of *dialectics*.[11] The complementary and conflicting factors must be critically evaluated so that we can see how the different elements complement one another to make an intelligible whole or where one line of thought or action stands in irreducible conflict with another. Reflection upon this leads us to the fifth function of *establishing the foundations*, of objectifying the great themes which guided the whole thrust of Cîteaux and which must serve as the foundation for the renewal of Cistercian life. Within the horizons of these foundations there must be established the

---

9. "Only ideal republics spring in full stature from the mind of man. The civil communities that exist and function know only a story of their origins, only an outline of their development, only an estimate of their present complexion."—B. Lonergan, *Insight* (New York: Philosophical Library, 1965), p. 211.

10. "For the practical common sense, operative in a community, does not exist entire in the mind of any one man. It is parceled out among many, to provide each with an understanding of his role and task, to make every cobbler an expert at his last, and no one an expert in another's field. So it is to understand the working of life and, as best one can, discover the functional unity that organically binds together the endlessly varied pieces of an enormous jigsaw puzzle."—Lonergan, *ibid.*

11. "Dialectic is pure form with general implications; it is applicable to any concrete unfolding of linked but opposed principles that are modified cumulatively by the unfolding; . . . it is adjustable to any course of events, . . . it constitutes a principle of integration for specialized studies that concentrate on this or that aspect of human living and it can integrate not only theoretical work but also factual reports. . . . It is perhaps unnecessary to insist that dialectic provides no more than the general form of a critical attitude. Each department has to work out its own specialized criteria, but it will be able to do so by distinguishing between the purely intellectual element in its field and, on the other hand, the inertial effects and the interference of human sensibility and human nerves."—Lonergan, *ibid.*, p. 244.

guiding principles of the life. This is the work of the sixth function of *doctrine*. Finally, all these different principles of the life must be brought together into a system. This would correspond to *systematics*. When this is achieved there yet remains the final function of communication, finding the adequate way to express the foundations, doctrine and system.[12] This is discernment in the fullest sense of the word.

It is readily seen from this how the work of discerning the spirit and aim of the founders of Cîteaux must indeed involve teamwork, cooperation, and extensive participation not only on the part of members of our Order, but also with capable and qualified scholars from outside the Order.[13] It is only through the corporate effort of men working in the different fields and subjects, according to the different functions, that we can hope to attain to that solid and sure knowledge which will allow us to go forward confidently in the work of renewal and to express "in suitable and clear words 'the spirit of the founders and their specific aims and the healthy traditions, all of which constitute the patrimony of the institute.' "[14]

12. Drawing from Fr Lonergan's thought we might point out here that if the leaders of the renewal of our Order share a common bias, if they harbor rationalizations and myths, then they cannot but communicate these to the other members of the Order. "Then the blind will be leading the blind and all will head for a ditch. There is needed, then, a critique of history before there can be any intelligent direction of history. There is needed an exploration of the movements, the changes, the epochs of a civilization's (read: the Order's) genesis, development, and vicissitudes. The opinions and attitudes of the present have to be traced to their origins, and the origins have to be criticized in the light of dialectic."—Lonergan, *ibid.,* pp. 240f.

It can be readily seen how these eight functions apply to the work of Cistercian Publications. First the critical text must be established. This is the work of *research*. Translation involves, indeed, a good bit of *interpretation*. Introductions to the writings of our Cistercian Fathers and also the *Cistercian Studies Series* will endeavor to place these documents and writings in their proper *historical context*. Furthermore, these studies will seek through *dialectics, foundations, doctrine* and *systematics* to bring out the Fathers' full significance and importance to us today. And, of course, the ultimate purpose of Cistercian Publications is to communicate this information to all the members of our Order, as well as to all interested parties within and without the Church.

13. Hence the importance of the Symposia which Cistercian Publications is sponsoring.

14. *Ecclesiae sanctae, loc. cit.*

Why?

Let us turn now to the question of why we should seek to discern the spirit and aims of the founders of our Order.

As Fr Lonergan has brought out, it is of the very nature of the human mind to make such inquiry.[15] The most obvious witness of this is the little child who ceaselessly asks, as his eyes open to the wonders of the world, "Why?"

But also, I think we will agree with Mabillon when he says, that "among those who follow the monastic life it is a sort of truism that the more devout one becomes, the more he will be concerned with the spirit of his Rule . . . the more he will seek to plumb the mind of the legislator. . . ."[16] Whenever one speaks to our monks or nuns about our Fathers or the early documents of the Order, he immediately finds a keen and positive response. Why is this? It seems to me it is because he is mentioning something that the Holy Spirit has already put into the hearts of his listeners. The monk, in the lives and doctrine of the founders, is finding explicated in a meaningful way that which had already more or less consciously led him to embrace this particular form of monastic life. The Spirit gives him, as it were, an interior sensitivity and a spontaneous inclination to the spirit of the founders.[17] It is faith in the reality of the spirit of our founders living in the minds and hearts of the monks and nuns of the Order which has guided the commission preparing the New Charter of Charity to seek the active collaboration of all.[18]

A Mandate

However, even apart from these desires flowing from nature and grace there stands an imperative for us to undertake this study. The Church, not only in our own times but always, has called upon men walking in the footsteps of others and sharing in their charism to look to their Fathers for inspiration, guidance and paternal assistance:

15. Lonergan, *op. cit.,* pp. 4, 173f., 348.

16. *S. Bernardi Opera Omnia,* ed. nova (Paris, Migne, 1862), col. 857f.

17. Cf. Molinari, *op. cit.,* p. 802.

18. In this it is only following an insight of the Church; cf. *Ecclesiae sanctae,* II, nos. 2, 9, 18.

Look, I ask you, to your Fathers who established our holy Order.
How leaving the world and contemning all created things, leaving
the dead to bury their dead, they fled into solitude. . . . Indeed
they received the firstfruits of the Spirit, and the oil of their
sweetness has flowed down even to us. You must think and act
with greater care that you do not degenerate from their virtue,
but rather that what you were in root you may also be in branch,
and that you who have received from them this seed of life may
bear with them the same flower and fruit. . . . Keep in your mind's
eye the institute of your Fathers, holding on to their prophetic
example. . . .[19]

In recent times this message of Pope Eugene III has been frequently
reiterated as his successors have called upon all religious to look to
their founders. To cite a few examples:

Religious of every age, whether young or old, lift up your eyes
to your illustrious founders. Their maxims speak to you, their
statutes are your guides, their example shows you the way. May
it be at once your fondest and most saintly preoccupation to
listen to their words, to follow their Rules, to imitate their
example. . . . It is thus that you will secure the greatest benefits
for yourselves, for the Church and for society.—Leo XIII,
June 29, 1901.[20]

We exhort all men who are religious to contemplate the
example of their respective Founder, Father and Lawgiver, if they
wish to share in a secure and abundant way in the graces which
flow from their vocation. For, what else were these eminent men
doing when they founded their institutes but obeying a divine
inspiration?—Pius XI, March 19, 1929.[21]

It is not only past ages which are indebted for innumerable
benefits to this Patriarch (Benedict) and the institute which he
founded . . . the members of the great Benedictine family should
learn to follow with ever greater zeal his splendid example and to

19. Eugene III. The whole of this beautiful letter should be read. It is
prefixed to St Bernard's Epistle 273, PL 182:477f.

20. *The States of Perfection*, ed. G. Courtois (Westminster, Md.: Newman
Press, 1961), n. 51, p. 22.

21. AAS, 16 (1929), p. 135.

give effect, each in his own life, to the principles and the models of his virtue and sanctity.—Pius XII, March 21, 1947.[22]

The Council, too, directed the minds of religious to a serious consideration of the spirit of their founders:

> Submissively following the promptings of the Holy Spirit, the hierarchy also endorses rules formulated by eminent men and women. . . . Moreover, by its watchful and shielding authority the hierarchy keeps close to communities established far and wide for the upbuilding of Christ's Body, so that they can grow and flourish in accord with the spirit of their founders.[23]
>
> It redounds to the good of the Church that institutes have their own characteristics and work. Therefore, let their founders' spirit and the special aims they set before themselves as well as their sound traditions—all of which make up the patrimony of each institute—be faithfully held in honor.[24]

This teaching of the Council was derived in part from the norms which Pope Paul VI gave to religious in regard to the work of the general chapters:

> The principal task of the general chapter is, as time goes on, to keep intact those norms of the religious family which were set up by its founder and lawgiver. . . . Moreover, with respect to undertaking new projects or activities, you should refrain from taking on those which do not entirely correspond to the principal work of your institute or to the mind of your founder. For religious institutes will flourish and prosper so long as the integral spirit of their founder continues to inspire their rule of life and apostolic works as well as the actions and lives of their members.[25]

22. Courtois, *op. cit.,* n. 263, p. 115. Cf. G. Kramer, "Return to the Founders: a Vatican II Appraisal" in *American Ecclesiastical Review* (Washington: Catholic U. Press) vol. 157 (1967), pp. 294ff.

23. *Lumen gentium,* n. 45.

24. *Perfectae caritatis,* n. 2.

25. Paul VI, Address to all Religious, May 23, 1964, NCWC translation pp. 10f. The Holy Father has recently reiterated this when speaking to the General Chapter of the Society of the Divine Word, January 22, 1968 (AAS, LX [1968], pp. 199ff.).

We were specifically set to our present task of seeking to discern the spirit and aims of our founders by the same Holy Father's *Motu Proprio* implementing the conciliar decrees where it lays down the norms for preparing the new constitutions of the Order:

> The general laws of each institute (Constitutions, Typika, Rules or whatever name they bear) should ordinarily include these elements: *a*) The evangelical and theological principles of the religious life and its union with the Church and suitable and clear words in which "the spirit of the founders and their specific aims and the healthy traditions, all of which constitute the patrimony of each institute, are acknowledged and preserved."[26]

It is evident, then, that the Church does want us to discern, in the full sense of that word, the spirit and aims of the founders of our Order.

For the Church

But one might legitimately ask why does the Church place such emphasis on these.

As was indicated in the conciliar text above, the Church sees in this variety of charisms a good for the whole Body of Christ.[27] Earlier in the same Constitution it was stated:

> It has come about, that, as if on a tree which has grown in the field of the Lord, various forms of solitary and community life, as well as various religious families have branched out in a marvelous and multiple way. . . . Such a multiple and miraculous growth augments both the progress of the members of these various religious families themselves and the welfare of the entire Body of Christ.[28]
>
> Religious should carefully keep before their minds the fact that the Church presents Christ to believers and non-believers alike in a striking manner daily through them. The Church thus portrays Christ in his contemplation on the mountain, in his

26. *Ecclesiae sanctae*, II, n. 12.

27. *Lumen gentium*, n. 45.

28. *Ibid.*, n. 43.

proclamation of the Kingdom of God to the multitudes, in his healing of the sick and maimed, in his work of converting sinners to a better life, in his solicitude for youth and his goodness to all men, always obedient to the will of his Father who sent him.[29]

For Ourselves

But this emphasis on the founders' spirit is not only for the good of the Body of Christ as a whole but also for the good of the individual who is called by the same Spirit to share and to live in the charism of the founders. A religious vocation, a monastic vocation, is essentially this call of the Spirit. In responding to such a vocation, holiness can be found only insofar as one does fully live in the spirit of this shared charism.

Today we make much of the discernment of spirits. And this is right. Happily we can be certain that our founders were acting under the impulse of the Holy Spirit. In approving them and their way of life the Church has given us assurance of this. We are called to participate in the same impulse of the Spirit. The better we discern and understand it the more we can enter into a full living of it.

It is incumbent that we ourselves study the spirit of our founders and not be content with what has been passed on to us by our predecessors. For in a manner similar to that in the field of biblical exegesis and dogma, understanding of the spirit of the founders is subject to progressive evolution. We can progressively understand more and more what the Holy Spirit initiated in them and what is to continue in us for the good of the Church.[30]

What we are seeking to discern is something of God's wonderful work in the souls of the founders. Therefore, a deep appreciation

---

29. *Ibid.*, n. 46. The *Motu Proprio* for implementing *Perfectae caritatis* further stresses that this is for the good of the Church: "To achieve the good of the Church, the institutes should strive for a genuine knowledge of their original spirit, so that faithfully preserving this spirit in determining adaptations, their religious life may thus be purified of alien elements and freed from those which are obsolete."—*Ecclesiae sanctae*, II, n. 16 (3).

30. "Troubled times of crisis demand the discovery and communication of new insights and a consequent adaptation of spontaneous attitudes. . . ."—Lonergan, *op. cit.*, p. 216.

of God's work, as well as love for the Church and reverence for our own vocation, should inspire us to do this and to do it with the fullest possible objectivity.[31]

For Others

Finally, in this time of renewal, I think there is a very special reason why the Cistercians in particular should seek to discern and clearly set forth the spirit and aims of their founders for all to see and study. The dynamism of the spirit of the founders of Cîteaux exemplifies the spirit of renewal which the Church is today trying to bring to life in all religious institutes. Father Claude Peifer brought this out in a paper he delivered at a meeting of the Social Science and Education and Psychology Sections of the American Benedictine Academy:

> It is here that we meet a real renewal in twelfth-century monasticism. Their purpose was a return to sources, a rediscovery of the meaning of monastic life, and the translation of their discovery into structures adapted to the age in which they lived. This is the achievement of Cîteaux. . . . Thus their return to sources did not hesitate to go back beyond the Rule to rediscover the life situation out of which the Rule grew. The white monks were representative of the new mentality of the times: they were not satisfied with compromises and accommodations. They wanted the original form in its purest state. But it was the essential values which concerned them, not merely archeological reconstruction of the past; and, when occasion demanded it, they did not scruple to innovate if this was required to achieve authenticity. This was the finest realization of the twelfth century and, I submit, of the whole of Benedictine history. It involved coming to grips with the problem of rethinking the whole Benedictine ideal from the beginning, and then creating structures in which it could be suitably incarnated and lived in the contemporary world. These are exactly the two things which Vatican II lays down for renewal of religious institutes: *ressourcement* and *aggiornamento*. That is why I believe that the twelfth century offers the clearest analogies to the contemporary situation, and was the only reform

31. Cf. Molinari, *op. cit.,* p. 800.

in Benedictine history which actually achieved for its time what is demanded of us today.[32]

Father Peifer brings out well how the spirit and aims of our Cistercian founders correspond to the present day concern and thrust of the Church. That mentality which "examines the structure itself and the value of the system upon which it is based and undertakes to revise and reformulate the theory and to rebuild the structure in a form which will effectively communicate the theory to the contemporary world,"[33] is one of the precious facets of the spirit of our founding Fathers and one that can stand as an exemplar to all religious who seek to respond to the call of the Council. Father also touches upon what is perhaps one of the greatest problems we have in trying to establish and work out the principles of our renewal, and at the same time he places it in a broader context which gives us some insight into the solution of that problem.

The Rule

The problem is that of the attitude of our founders toward the Rule of St Benedict. The Little Exordium emphasizes their great desire to live the Rule which they had professed, their sorrow at seeing it transgressed, their attempt to abandon everything that was contrary to the Rule or superfluous to its observance.[34] The Rule was to be obeyed in everything, just as it was in the New Monastery.[35] While it is true that they do not speak in these early documents of a literal (*ad litteram*) observance of the Rule,[36] they were nonetheless preoccupied with precision and intensity in

32. C. Peifer, "Monastic Renewal in Historical Perspective" in *American Benedictine Review,* vol. 19 (1968), pp. 14f.

33. *Ibid.,* p. 2.

34. This can be found expressed in almost every chapter of the Little Exordium.

35. CC, c. 2, p. 16; Murphy, p. 268.

36. P. Salmon, "Monastic Asceticism and the Origins of Cîteaux" in *Monastic Studies,* n. 3 (1965), pp. 131ff., fn. 25.

returning to the purity of the Rule. When confronted with this
great emphasis on the careful observance of the Rule we sometimes
attempt to water it down by pointing out as many exceptions as
we can, e.g., the sweeping simplicity in the liturgical accoutrements
that is found in chapter seventeen of the Exordium, the institution
of the lay brothers, the omission of deans and oblates, and the
confederation of the monasteries. However, in all frankness it has
to be admitted that these are at most *praeter regulam* rather than
contra regulam. Nevertheless, they are realities and they do show
some real adaptation to the social and economic conditions of the
times. This cannot be denied. Yet neither can it be denied that in
their mind these innovations were directly ordered to a fuller living
of the Rule.[37]

This desire to live the Rule of St Benedict more integrally and
fully was not unique to Cîteaux. It was an inspiration common to
many of the monastic foundations being made in that period. We
might note in particular the foundation of Savigny, which was one
day to consolidate with the Cistercians, and Bernard de Abbeville's
foundation at Tiron.[38] More notable is the earlier foundation of
Molesme in the Alps. In its Foundation Charter, drawn up in 1097,
we find terminology which will again appear in the Little Exordium:
"*Deo inspirante Sancti Patris nostri Benedicti praeceptis actibus
inhaerentes.*"[39]

---

37. E.g., in the case of the lay brothers: "since they realized that without
their help they would be unable to fulfill perfectly the precepts of the Rule
day and night, they decided to admit unlettered men as lay brothers with the
approval of the bishop and treat them in life and in death as themselves
except for the rights reserved for monks."—Little Exordium, c. 15, p. 13;
Larkin, p. 263.

38. P. Cousin, *Précis d'Histoire Monastique* (Paris: Blond & Gay, 1956),
pp. 287 ff. We might indicate also St Stephen's foundation at Grandmont and
the foundation of Géraud at Sauve-Majeure and the double monastery
founded by Robert d'Arbrissel, Fontevrault. See also, D. Meade, "From
Turmoil to Solidarity: the Emergence of the Vallombrosan Congregation"
in *American Benedictine Review*, vol. 19 (1968), pp. 323ff., especially p. 330;
R. Duvernay, "Vallombruse, Cîteaux et Etienne Harding" in *Analecta
S.O. Cisterciensis*, vol. 8 (1958), pp. 428ff.

39. *Documenta*, p. 3.

The Union of the Abbeys

What was the most distinctive innovation and perhaps the greatest departure from the Rule was the federation of the monasteries worked out and established in the Charter of Charity. The Cistercians rightly pointed to the centralized Cluniac system as being something contrary to the Rule of St Benedict which made the local abbot very much the lord and master of his monastery.[40] They assert as part of their renewal the reestablishment of the autonomy of the local community.[41] However, in practice, while safeguarding to a great extent the juridical and economic independence of the monasteries, they formed a bond of social charity which to some degree restricted the full autonomy of the local abbot.

The Founders of the Order of Cîteaux

Here it might be opportune to raise the question, who *in concreto* are the founders of the Order of Cîteaux.

There can be no doubt that Robert of Molesme, Alberic and Stephen Harding, along with their companions, are the founders of the New Monastery which in a short while came to be called the Abbey of Cîteaux.[42] But if they had it in mind that the New Monastery should become the center of a federation of abbeys they nowhere express this. Nor did Robert's early return to Molesme leave him much time to develop such an idea. Alberic, too, passed quietly off the scene in death while the very survival of the dwindling group was still in question.[43] If the title of founder of the

---

40. Cf. RB, cc. 2, 3, etc.

41. Little Exordium, c. 14, *op. cit.,* p. 14; Larkin, p. 264. Cf. J.-B. Van Damme, "Formation de la Constitution Cistercienne" in *Studia Monastica,* vol. 4 (1962), p. 127: "Mais il y eut un statut arrêté par les moines venus de Molesme: les monastères qu'ils fonderaient un jour, devaient être tous des abbayes. C'était une position de principe, rien de plus, mais le principe était défini, et il était de grande importance!"

42. Cf. Marilier, *op. cit. (supra,* fn. 7), pp. 24f.

43. Cf. Little Exordium, cc. 14ff., *op. cit.,* pp. 14f.; Larkin, p. 264.

Order of Cîteaux can be claimed for any single man, Stephen Harding would be that man.[44]

However, I do not think any one man *can* be the subject of such a claim. I would submit that in reality the actual founders of the Order of Cîteaux were the abbots gathered in the General Chapter of 1123. When they ratified the Charter of Charity they created "a new society endowed with a democratic authority having its own proper end and laws which were to be established by a supreme authority within the Order, the General Chapter.[45] With this, the Order of Cîteaux was born. When these abbots abdicated some of the autonomy which was natively theirs as superiors of *sui iuris* abbeys, to establish a corporate body, they brought into existence a true order. Up to this time the Order of Cîteaux was an order only in the earlier sense of the word. It signified a particular mode of life or discipline. It was at this moment that the Order of Cîteaux became a true institute within the Church. And these abbots assembled were the founders of this institute, the founders of the Order of Cîteaux as an institute.

St Bernard: One with the Founders

If this thesis that the founders of the Order of Cîteaux are the twenty abbots who assembled for the General Chapter of 1123 is granted, then there was included among the founders a number of the so-called "second generation," and most significantly, Bernard of Clairvaux.[46]

44. We could hardly consider the group as a whole to be the founders of the Cistercian Order for there was evidently a lack of unanimity among them as to their ideal and aims and some of them freely withdrew to return to Molesme with Robert. Cf. Little Exordium: "And some of the monks who did not love the desert returned with him (Robert)."—c. 7, *op. cit.,* p. 9; Larkin, p. 257.

45. J.-B. Van Damme, "Formation de la Constitution Cistercienne," p. 135; cf. also, J.-B. Mahn, *L'Ordre Cistercien et son Gouvernement,* 2 ed. (Paris: Boccard, 1951), pp. 61f.

46. Aside from Stephen Harding, Bernard of Clairvaux and Arnold of Morimond (who shortly after withdrew irregularly from his abbey) most of the names would be unfamiliar to most, e.g., Blessed Peter I of La Ferté and Hugh of Macon, abbot of Pontigny.

However, the fact that Bernard and the other great leaders of the "second generation" are technically founders would not make a great difference. For certainly, their doctrine and example pertain to the constitutive tradition of the Order of Cîteaux[47] and are the fullest expression of the spirit of the founders.[48] As Dom Salmon has well put it:

Although St Bernard is not one of the founders of Cîteaux (sic) *he is the incarnation of its spirit.* He entered the monastery fifteen years after its foundation and received his formation from St Stephen Harding. With Bernard the new Order matured and entered a new era of unprecedented fruitfulness. In him the new-born institute received a genius and saint who would give the Cistercian ideal its definitive form.[49]

St Stephen recognized in Bernard the flowering of his own spirit and ideal. After Bernard had been only a few years under his guidance he did not hesitate to send him as the spiritual father and guide of his third foundation. With his great gifts of mind and his unsurpassable art of expression Bernard has incarnated for us in written word the spirit of Cîteaux.[50]

Some have proposed that there is a marked difference between the outlook of the actual founders of the New Monastery and that of the "second generation," and of St Bernard in particular. In

47. The Council has not hesitated to put on an equal par the spirit and aims of the founders and the sound traditions of an order: "Therefore, let their founders' spirit and special aims that they set before them as well as their sound traditions—all of which make up the patrimony of each institute—be faithfully held in honor."—*Perfectae caritatis,* n. 2 b.

48. It is noteworthy that in the dialogue between a Cluniac and Cistercian written in a Morimond filiation not long after the death of Bernard, it is he who is most frequently cited to give expression to the Cistercian ideal. See *Dialogus inter Cluniacensem Monachum et Cisterciensem de Diversis Utriusque. Ordinis Observantiis,* Martène and Durand, *Thesaurus Novarum Anecdotarum* V, 1569ff.; also, W. Williams, *Monastic Studies* (Manchester: University of Manchester Press, 1938), c. 6, pp. 61ff.

49. Salmon, "Monastic Asceticism," p. 133.

50. Very aptly does Dom Jean Leclercq speak of him as the "Theologian of the Cistercian Life." Cf. *infra,* pp. 101ff.

C

support of this they point to ideas on art,[51] and music,[52] and to a number of the particular provisions of the early General Chapters. These enactments have a certain strictness or narrowness about them which, they say, are due to Bernard's influence.[53]

I do not know in actual fact to what extent we can with certitude attribute different decisions of the General Chapter to St Bernard's influence. I would agree with Dom Salmon that "Bernard's ideas on the problem we are dealing with are not easy to assess because they are usually expressed in connection with the dispute with Cluny in which feeling and eloquence had a greater role than objective description."[54] In any case it may well be asked whether these particular and relatively minor observances really do reflect

51. Cf. C. Oursel, *Miniatures Cisterciennes* (1109–1134) (Macon: Protat, 1960), pp. 19f.

52. Cf. S. Marosszéki, "Les Origines des Chant Cistercienne," in *Analecta S. O. Cisterciensis,* vol. 8 (1952), pp. 1–137; especially, c. 2, pp. 10–14; p. 23; p. 72; and the conclusion, pp. 129ff.

53. E.g., *Instituta Generalis Capituli,* 13: no gold and silver clasps on liturgical books; 14: no white bread, not even on feasts; 20: no statues or pictures, only painted wooden crosses (It must be noted that this is only a repetition of what is already found in the Little Exordium which in the seventeenth chapter prescribes very extensive austerity and simplicity in the liturgical ornamentation just as in chapter fifteen it called for great simplicity and poverty in food and clothing. While some of the later prescriptions of the General Chapters seem to us to descend to too many details and be perhaps petty, they do find a certain precedent in the basic prescriptions of the Little Exordium); 22: no pets, at least not unusual ones; 25: no cheese or eggs for guests on fast days; 27: only two externs with their wives may be buried in the monastery; 29: monks are not to baptize or be sponsors at baptism (This has been incorporated into Canon Law); 52: the monks are not to sell wine to taverns; 54: the measure of the bread and wine, and also of vegetables is to be the same in all abbeys and granges; 58: the monks need permission of the General Chapter to write books; 59: detailed regulations for shepherds; 61: detailed regulations for bishops of the Order; 63: pepper and cinnamon and other imported spices are forbidden; 64, 65, 76, 88: detailed penal regulations; 73: monks are to sing with manly voices; 80: the letters in choir books are to be in one color and only white glass is to be used in windows with no crosses or pictures; 83: the monks when riding are not to use leather chaps; 84: the monks are not to prostrate in prayer in church.—*Nomasticon Cisterciense,* ed. Paris-Séjolon (Solesme: St Peter's, 1892), pp. 212ff.

54. Salmon, "Monastic Asceticism," pp. 133f.

the basic spirit of the man or the institute. Certainly, in approaching the question of the observance of the Rule no one could be more benign and discreet than Bernard:

> He who thinks it perjury not to observe the Holy Rule to the exact letter has, I think, paid scant attention to what he has actually promised. No one really promises "the Rule" but specifically that he will act "according to the Rule" in the inception and pursuit of his holy undertaking. . . . This form of profession formula has in our day been adopted by almost all orders of monks. However, despite this common point of departure, God is served in many diverse ways in the various orders and houses. So long as one is guided by the sound and legitimate customs of his house, he is beyond any doubt, living according to the Rule. For the Rule admits of variations and local customs. . . . Even if they do not keep it all "to the hair" (as the saying goes), and even if they change or omit certain details according to the customs of their house, as long as they are faithful to what is locally accepted as "a just and pious life" they are truly living the Rule. Such conduct is, in fact, recommended by the Rule itself in the eighth degree of humility: "that a monk do nothing that is not sanctioned by the custom of the house or the example of the seniors."[55]

It is, however, true that St Bernard holds up a particular ideal for his Cistercian brethren. He goes on to say in the same place:

> Of course, it is a different matter for the Cistercians and for those who, like them, have promised an integral and literal observance of the Rule, rather, than a life according to the Rule, since such is their interpretation of monastic profession.[56]

The Primacy of Charity

However, this statement, strong though it may be, must be

55. *De Praecepto et Dispensatione*, n. 48, in *S. Bernardi Opera Omnia*, III (Rome: Editiones Cistercienses, 1963), p. 286; trans. C. Greenia, *Monastic Obligations and Abbatial Authority: St. Bernard's Book on Precept and Dispensation*, in *The Works of Bernard of Clairvaux*, vol. 1, The Cistercian Fathers, I. Compare this with the letter of Peter the Venerable to Bernard, among the Letters of St Bernard, Epistle 229, PL 182:398ff.

56. *Ibid.*, n. 49.

understood in the whole context of Bernard's thinking. In his famous *Apologia* he very frankly says to his Cistercian brethren:

> If you think that all those who profess the Rule are bound to keep it literally (*ad litteram*) without any possibility of dispensation, I dare to say, that neither you nor the Cluniac are doing your job. . . . But if you grant that there are some things that can be changed by dispensation, then surely both you and the Cluniac are keeping the Rule, though each in his own way. You keep it more strictly (*districtius*) and he perhaps more discreetly.[57]

In the *Book on Precept and Dispensation*, Bernard expresses his thought more fully in regard to changing the Rule by dispensation. Speaking of the Rules of Sts Basil, Augustine and Benedict, as well as those of the Canons Regular, he says:

> These Rules were devised or ordained not because it is not lawful to live in a different manner but because this manner of life was found to be expedient, expedient, that is, for the gaining or the preservation of charity.[58]

Bernard, then, places the end of all the Rules in charity. In this he is clearly giving voice to the thought of St Benedict who expresses the same idea in the Prologue to his Rule for Monasteries:

> But if a certain strictness results from the dictates of equity for the amendment of vices or the preservation of charity, do not be at once dismayed and fly from the way of salvation, whose entrance cannot but be narrow. For as we advance in religious life and faith, our hearts expand and we run on the way of God's commandments with unspeakable sweetness of love.[59]

Again, in the seventh chapter on humility, which is the heart and center of Benedictine spirituality, St Benedict points toward the

57. *Apologia ad Gueielmum*, n. 14, *Opera S. Bernardi Omnia* III, pp. 93f.; trans. M. Casey, *Cistercians and Cluniacs: St Bernard's Apology to Abbot William*, in *The Works of Bernard of Clairvaux*, vol. 1, The Cistercian Fathers I.

58. *De Praecepto*, n. 5, p. 257.

59. RB, Prologue, 47ff.

goal of this way of life: "Having climbed all these steps of humility therefore, the monk will presently come to that perfect love of God which casts out fear."[60] As Dom Salmon sums it up: "In St Benedict's mind, all the observances it (the Rule) prescribes have no other purpose than that of preparing for the expansion of charity and union with God."[61]

St Bernard conceives the matter in no other way. The end of the life is love. The purpose of a return to the Rule, a fuller living of the Rule, is a growth in charity. Therefore St Bernard very logically concludes:

> It is right that what was established for the sake of charity should be omitted, discontinued or changed for something better when charity calls for it. On the other hand, it would be erroneous to wish to maintain contrary to charity something that has been established for its sake.[62]

That this primacy of charity is a central facet in the spiritual heritage of the founders of Cîteaux hardly needs to be argued. The very name which they have given to their fundamental charter bespeaks it: Charter of Charity. And they themselves make it clear why they have chosen this name:

> . . . the mode of their agreement, it was charity by which the monks in their abbeys, though separated in body in different countries of the world, would be indissolubly united in spirit. They had a good reason to name this decree the Charter of Charity because . . . it had for its object charity alone and the good of souls in regard to divine and human affairs.

> We wish to retain in the spirit of charity the care of their souls . . . that we may live united by one charity, one Rule. . . .[63]

This theme is common in the writings of the Cistercian Fathers but

60. RB 7:67.
61. Salmon, "Monastic Asceticism," p. 136.
62. *De Praecepto*, n. 5, p. 257.
63. CC, Prologue and c. 1, *op. cit.*, pp. 15f.; Murphy, pp. 267f.

it is most eloquently developed in the book written at the request of St Bernard by the novice master of Rievaulx, St Aelred.[64]

The Role of Observances

In establishing the primacy of charity we do not seek, nor did our Cistercian Fathers seek, to deny the importance to be placed on external observances, especially those observances outlined in the Rule of St Benedict. Our Fathers would not readily subscribe to the tendency which has been found in more recent centuries to spiritualize the Rule; to place all the stress on the inner spirit, maintaining that that is all that matters and giving little importance to the external.[65] Here we have another element of the spirit of Cîteaux which we must readily admit, namely, a real importance is given to the observances of the monastic life, specifically to those of the Rule of St Benedict, since this is the Rule we profess. It is a ready and realistic acceptance of the fact of each man's personal incarnation, that body and soul must work together. St Bernard expressed it thus:

> I am not saying that external means can be overlooked nor that the man who does not use them will very quickly become spiritual. Spiritual things are higher, but there is little or no hope of winning them or receiving them without making use of physical means. . . . The man in the best position is he who uses both . . . harmoniously and with discernment.[66]

Today we may need quite different observances,[67] we may need

64. *Speculum Caritatis*, PL 195:503–620; trans., A. Walker & G. Webb, *Mirror of Charity* (London: Mowbrays, 1962).

65. Cf. Salmon, "Monastic Asceticism," pp. 119ff.

66. *Apologia*, n. 14, *op. cit.*, p. 94.

67. "The manner of living, praying and working should be suitably adapted everywhere . . . to the modern physical and psychological circumstances of the members, as required by the nature of each institute. . . ."— *Perfectae caritatis*, n. 3. "The special penitential practices of institutes should be revised insofar as it is necessary so that taking into account traditions whether of the East or West, and modern circumstances, the members may in practice be able to observe them, adapting new forms also drawn from modern conditions of life." *Ecclesiae sanctae*, II, n. 22.

even greater simplicity than the founders of Cîteaux. But it pertains to the spirit of Cistercian life that it be wholly ordered to love and that there be certain observances in the life which follow on the Rule of St Benedict, and are lived with a certain intensity to foster growth in love. Then and today, a man is called to enter the Cistercian Christian community to live together in community with observances structured to foster a disciplined human and Christian freedom for a maximum response to God and his brethren in love.

The Experience of God

We see, then, that the central facet of the spirit of the founders of Cîteaux is that of giving a primal place to charity in a life which is structured according to the order (and I use "order" here in the older sense of a way of life or discipline) of St Benedict's Rule insofar as that order truly serves the primacy of love. Undoubtedly other facets of the spirit of the founders are to be explored in serious studies. They certainly set for themselves an ideal of poverty, to be "poor with the poor Christ,"[68] uniting it with a remarkable simplicity.[69] Solitude was important to them, and effective separation from the world.[70] Another aspect of Cistercian spirituality or asceticism was manual labor.[71] Indeed, this, if anything, seemed to be one of the distinguishing marks which set the Cistercian renewal apart from all the other renewals taking place contemporaneously with it. Another note which responds very much to our times was the founders' authenticity.[72] They vowed to live according to the Rule of St Benedict and this they determined to do. They did not want to promise one thing and do another.[73]

68. Little Exordium, c. 15, *op. cit.*, p. 13; Larkin, p. 263. Duvernay has assembled several pages of texts showing this; *op. cit.*, pp. 397–404.

69. Cf. Little Exordium, cc. 15, 17, *loc. cit.*, pp. 13ff.; Larkin, pp. 262ff.

70. *Ibid.* For other texts see Duvernay, *op. cit.*, pp. 389ff.

71. *Ibid.*, c. 15. Cf. also Duvernay, *op. cit.*, p. 404.

72. This word "authentic" had a somewhat different or more restricted meaning for our founders, primarily, conformity of texts. I am using it in our present day sense.

73. This is evident throughout the documents.

But I would like to bring forward here only one other facet of the Cistercian spirit, one which is very closely connected with its central facet, the primacy of love, and that is, the emphasis placed upon the experience of God. In a later terminology this might well be referred to as mystical experience, or the mystical element, mysticism, but as the idea of "mystic" has come to have many connotations it is perhaps best for us to stay with the simple expression, the experience of God.

Father Amedeus Hallier, in his excellent work, *The Monastic Theology of St Aelred*[74] brings out clearly the fundamental and dominating role this element of experience plays in the thought and spirituality of St Aelred. Examples can readily be drawn from many other early Cistercian Fathers.[75] Here I will content myself with indicating very briefly its presence in the writings of the "Theologian of the Cistercian Life."

St Bernard in tracing out the stages of the spiritual life uses many and varied analogies. But whether his image be three kisses[76] or three ointments[77] or seven infusions of the Spirit,[78] or any other, it always leads to "the quiet of contemplation after the painful fatigues of action," to the fullness of love where God "is not so much perceived as vaguely felt and apprehended and that in a passing way and by the light of a sudden and momentary blaze of glory so that a great flame of love is enkindled in the soul."[79]

When he comes to the central theme of Benedictine spirituality

74. A. Hallier, *The Monastic Theology of St Aelred: An Experiential Theology*, trans. C. Heaney, Cistercian Studies Series, II.

75. E.g., William of St Thierry, *Exposition on the Song of Songs: The Works of William of St Thierry*, vol. 2, Cistercian Fathers, nos. 4, 20, trans. C. Hart.

76. Sermon 3, *Sermones super Cantica Canticorum, S. Bernardi Opera Omnia*, (Rome: Editiones Cistercienses, 1957), pp. 14ff.; trans. K. Walsh, *The Sermon on the Song of Songs, The Works of Bernard of Clairvaux*, vol. 2, Cistercian Fathers, IV.

77. Sermon 10, nn. 4ff., *op. cit.*, pp. 50ff.

78. Sermon 18, *op. cit.*, p. 103ff.

79. Sermon 18, n. 6, *op. cit.*, p. 107.

in his commentary on chapter seven of the Rule this characteristic thrust of the Cistercian spirit is much in evidence.[80] For Bernard, Benedict's ladder leads directly to perfect love, to the banquet of King Solomon, to the delights and joy of contemplation.[81] It leads to the chamber of the king where the soul "rests securely in the king's embrace. While in this chamber the soul sees things that man's eye cannot see and hears mysteries that no tongue can repeat. . . ."[82]

Here we see that this "mystical" element of the Cistercian spirit is nothing more than an explication of elements to be found in the Rule itself, the full flowering of the seeds sown by the Legislator of Monte Cassino. For he too would have his monks "run the way of God's commandments with an unspeakable sweetness of love,"[83] and "come to that perfect love of God which casts out fear."[84] He would have them "attain to the loftier heights."[85]

From this we can perhaps glean this insight: when our Fathers, the founders of the Order of Cîteaux, aspired to live the Rule in a fuller and more perfect way: *arctius, perfectius, pure, simpliciter, ex integro*, their concern was not only and indeed not even primarily to live all its particular observances. Their concern was to live the Rule in its fullness and to come to the fullness of the life of the Rule. A full observance for them meant truly striving to attain the ultimate goal which the Rule set before them, the perfection of love in the experience of God.

Conclusion

This study does not propose any apodictic conclusions. It is an effort which seeks to clarify a little more the state of the question, to outline a possible methodology for comprehensive study and fruitful collaboration, and to bring forward a few considerations which seem to demand our attention before we can arrive at any ultimate answers.

80. St Bernard, *The Steps of Humility*, G. Webb and A. Walker (London: Mowbrays, 1957).

81. *Ibid.*, c. 2, pp. 24ff. 82. *Ibid.*, c. 7, p. 43.

83. RB, Prologue, 49. 84. RB 7:67. 85. RB 73:9.

The methodology of Bernard Lonergan, especially as he proposes to apply it to theology can be, I believe, of great help to us.[86]

In regard to the actual founders of the Order of Cîteaux, I submit that they are the members of the 1123 General Chapter, and this includes St Bernard. In his writings and those of the other great writers of the "second generation" we have the fullest expression of the spirit of our founders. This spirit essentially is seeking God, the experience of God through perfect love. It is but an explication of the goal repeatedly proposed in the Rule of St Benedict. While its thrust toward the ultimate makes it impatient of anything that does not truly contribute to its quest, intense realism makes it aware of the need of incarnational observances and the structures of an order bonded by charity. This leads it to seek an authentic living of the Rule professed, in simplicity and poverty, in solitude and effective separation from the ways of the world. None of these elements is necessarily exclusively or uniquely Cistercian, but a balanced blending of them produced and can still produce a monastic life that is eminently attractive and fruitful.

M. Basil Pennington OCSO

St Joseph's Abbey,
Spencer, Massachusetts

---

86. Fr Lonergan developed this in a series of lectures at Boston College in June, 1968, and is presently preparing a book on it.

MOTIVES AND IDEALS OF THE ELEVENTH-CENTURY MONASTIC RENEWAL

EACH TIME the auspicious beginnings of the second Christian millennium come up for discussion the laws of association carry my memory back to the dramatic details of one of my boyhood readings that impressed me then very deeply. It was a story of the *Historical Miniatures* of August Strindberg about the universal expectation of the end of the world, coming to a spectacular climax on New Year's Eve in 999. In Rome a tremendous throng converged upon St Peter's basilica. As the last minutes of the day were ticking away all wanted to hear the blare of heavenly trumpets. Then the big clock (?) started to strike midnight: one, two, three . . . and finally the sound of the twelfth bell floated away over the frozen multitude. Some could bear the tension no longer and fell lifeless to the ground, but nothing more striking happened. A few anguished moments later the aging Pope Sylvester rose, turned to the crowd and with an indulgent smile on his lips blessed and dismissed the delirious people. He, of course, the wise old monk, knew all along that history was not to be closed but to be continued with another eventful century.

The purpose of our gathering here is the discernment of the spirit and aims of our founding fathers so that, inspired by them, our work toward a necessary Cistercian renewal might be carried out with proper regard for our precious inheritance. The founders of Cîteaux were undoubtedly children of their age. All grew up in the intellectual and spiritual environment of the late eleventh century; and when they set out in 1098 toward that new and

27

exciting venture, they wished to materialize an ideal shared with
their less successful predecessors.

It is only logical, then, that the discussion of the aims of St Robert
and his companions be preceded by the consideration of the
troubled monastic scene of the eleventh century. Without the
proper understanding of this background we could hardly contemplate in valid perspective the builders of the New Monastery. In
this endeavor we must rely on the methods offered by sound
historical scholarship, the cornerstone of which is a sincere devotion
to objectivity. Yet, we are not studying, thinking and writing in a
serene atmosphere of detachment but under the pressure of an
emergency. Moreover, at least instinctively, we all have specific
ideas on how to insure the safe survival of our Order; perhaps we
even feel already committed to a course of action which, in our
judgment, should be the most appropriate and effective. When we
turn to the past, therefore, we wish to see our notions verified, our
intentions supported; we want to make the great figures of monastic history speak in our behalf. To put the problem into a more
concrete form: In a world crying for active apostolate, involvement
and social commitment, can we afford to prove that our founding
fathers yearned to live in a complete detachment from all such
cares?

Another related and equally grave problem lies in the tremendous
difference that separates us from the world of our holy founders.
The understanding that both our century and theirs feature revolu-
tions brings little comfort, for the motion in each seems to point to
diametrically opposite directions. Let me give a few examples:
The eleventh century made great strides toward an institutionalized
Church, a development that many of us deplore. Bureaucratic
centralization made then its beginnings, while now we would
rather de-centralize. In that century papal authority rose to an
unprecedented height, but today we like to talk about collegiality.
The clergy was then successfully forged into a distinct class alien
from the world, while now we feel that we must be integrated with
the rest of society. The eleventh century witnessed the first triumphs
of Canon Law, a book that some embarrassed members of our

generation would rather hide. Then the celibacy of the clergy was finally achieved; now clerical marriage is often proposed for serious consideration. I could easily add to this list but I hope I have managed to illustrate my point.

Anyone who tries today to fathom the minds and hearts of people who lived 900 years ago is faced with a difficulty similar to that of the hunter who rides in a fast-moving car and aims his gun at a bird in full flight. To understand our distant ancestors with a reasonable margin of correctness takes not only a clear and disciplined mind but first-rate scholarship. Since I am well aware of my shortcomings on both counts, I present the following only as a tentative approximation, subject to further comments, adjustments and corrections.

The year 1000 can justly be considered a turning point in the history of Christian Europe for weightier reasons than its conveniently round figure. The first attempt to establish peace, prosperity and civilized order over the ruins of the Roman Empire, i.e. the so-called Carolingian Renaissance, had failed. The proud empire of Charlemagne fell apart under his feuding grandchildren, and the flickering lights of monastic learning and piety were snuffed out by a new storm of barbarian invasions. The Vikings attacked from the north, the Saracens from the south, the Hungarians from the east. By the end of the ninth century, the question was no longer the preservation of Christian civilization but the survival of Christianity itself. The barbarians rode or sailed again at will throughout the continent. Rome or Paris became just as unsafe as Bordeaux, Marseilles or Naples. Smoking ruins of once mighty abbeys dotted the devastated landscape everywhere, while the papacy sank to the level of a degraded institution of purely local significance.

By the middle of the tenth century, however, hopeful signs began to multiply. The fury of invading barbarians abated. Both the Northmen and Hungarians settled down in their newly acquired lands, embraced Christianity and turned out to be constructive partners in the slow process of recovery. The Saxon Otto I created a semblance of order in the German lands, renewed the Empire and rescued the papacy from the clutches of the Theophylacts. Meanwhile the fast growing Cluny restored confidence and respect for monasticism in the consolidating Capetian kingdom.

As the turning of the century approached, an elementary degree of order and security from invasion was achieved. This modest success set the stage for a spectacular outburst of creative energies responsible for the rise of the new civilization of the High Middle Age. It was in the eleventh century that the institutions of Feudalism reached full development. The same era witnessed the emergence of medieval cities featuring a remarkable revival of international trade and commerce. The new cathedral and municipal schools soon outshone the earlier monastic centers of learning and prepared the way for the establishment of universities. The laity eagerly seized the new opportunities, and professionally trained bureaucrats (*ministeriales*) began to replace bishops and abbots in administrative positions of government. Artists, scholars and poets were no longer humble admirers and imitators of classical antiquity. The new Romanesque architecture exhibited amazing originality in both engineering and decorative details. St Anselm can justly be considered the Father of Scholasticism; and his contemporary, Duke William IX of Aquitaine, a pioneer of courtly (troubadour) poetry. In Lombardy the study of Roman Law was resumed, which, in turn, inspired the rise of Canon Law. But there is nothing more dramatic as an illustration and proof of the enormous vigor and self-confidence of this new Europe than the successful counterattack against the infidels: the heroic *reconquista* in Spain and the First Crusade which took French knights thousands of miles away for the recapture of Jerusalem.

The reason, however, for which modern historians unhesitatingly call the eleventh century an era of revolution, comparable in its impact to the Reformation or the French Revolution, is the sudden reversal that took place in the field of Church-State relations, commonly known as the Gregorian Reform.[1] But "reform" is not the appropriate term. The case was not a simple effort to eradicate

---

1. This view has been generally accepted after Gerd Tellenbach, *Church, State and Christian Society,* trans. R. F. Bennett (Oxford: Blackwell, 1940).

abuses and return to some earlier pattern of Church life, but it was a violent demand for drastic change. It was, in fact, an ideological struggle trying to shake off age-old traditions and establish in the world a new order, better suited to changed circumstances.

After the short-lived experiment in the Carolingian Empire, a seemingly lasting equilibrium in Church-State relations was achieved in the Ottonian and early Salian Empires, characterized by an interpenetration of the *ecclesia* and *mundus*. The emperor was not merely a secular ruler, but *rex et sacerdos* with dual obligations, involving the protection and propagation of the Church as well as wide authority over ecclesiastical appointments and functions. The hierarchy, in a similar manner, was fully integrated with the emerging feudal society, carrying, in addition to the administration of sacraments, a variety of governmental, judicial, even military duties. Over a large area the respective authorities of pope and emperor were left overlapping; moreover, a mild tutorship of the emperor over the papacy was not only condoned but often expected. This state of affairs was never more conspicuous than under Henry III (1039–1056), a stern and pious ascetic, "a monk in worldly garb."[2] He settled in the synod of Sutri (1046) a scandalous schism. This emperor deposed the three competitors for the papal throne (Benedict IX, Sylvester III, Gregory VI) and arranged in succession the election of three popes, the third being his own uncle, Leo IX (1046–1054), the first "Gregorian" reformer.

The drastic change in attitudes manifested itself suddenly in 1059 in the famous decree on papal elections and the publication of the equally epoch-making *Three Books Against the Simoniacs* by Cardinal Humbert of Silva Candida. Under the banner of "freedom of the Church" the fight began both against secular influence in ecclesiastical administration and the involvement of the clergy in worldly affairs. The first can be conveniently simplified as the Investiture Conflict, the second as measures against Simony and Nicolaitism. Both phases of the struggle reached a dramatic climax under the

2. Norman F. Cantor, *Medieval History* (New York: Macmillan, 1963), p. 269.

pontificate of Gregory VII (1073–1085), whose goal evidently included the total readjustment of Christian society, leading to an institutional separation of Church and State. This demanded the stripping of the emperor of quasi-sacerdotal powers, effective and exclusive central control exercised by the papacy over the whole Church, a morally purified clergy set sharply from the world and, in case of conflicts between secular and ecclesiastical interests, a decisive role for the pope. The revolutionary program could not be entirely executed either by Gregory or by his successors, but during the course of fifty years of incessant debates every facet of Christian life, including the role and position of monasticism, came under critical re-examination.

Monastic renewal, then, in the eleventh century can be properly understood only as an integral component of the Gregorian Reform. Renewal became inevitable, but not because of declining morals or lax discipline but because the monks were forced to find a new place in a rapidly changing society. What actually occurred was similar to the optical magic of an old-fashioned kaleidoscope. When the viewer turns the tube all particles are bound to move assuming each time a different pattern of colors in perfect balance and harmony. Those who try to justify this or other monastic reforms of significance by piling up incidents of abuses and misdeeds are banging on the wrong door. Unfortunately, human failings have always been in evidence even in the most perfect monasteries, but the eleventh century showed no conspicuous signs of monastic "decline." On the contrary, under Abbot Hugh the Great (1049–1109) the empire of Cluny, with its countless directly or indirectly affiliated houses, reached the apogee of its history. The swelling wave of criticism directed against Benedictine monasticism in the eleventh century can be explained largely by the fact that Cluny and her associates were tardy to notice the changes around them and even tardier to adapt themselves to the new conditions. In fact, contrary to the still often expressed belief, Cluniac spirituality had no direct role in the launching of the Gregorian Reform. Abbot Hugh was less than enthusiastic about the extreme ideas of Gregory and, instead of supporting them, tried to mediate between the Pope and Henry IV. As it is commonly known, this great Abbot was instrumental in the outcome of the famous confrontation at Canossa.[3]

Criticism toward the traditional forms of monasticism came from various sources, but most often from the monks themselves. The best known and certainly the most influential of them was St Peter Damian who, in spite of his high position in the Curia, referred to himself as *peccator monachus*. He found many abbots of his time guilty of worldly display. They spent more time at royal courts than in their monasteries; they were better versed in politics than in matters pertaining to their office; they were constantly involved in litigations over property and income.[4] He had no admiration for the great builders who embellished their churches and enlarged their abbeys. He could not resist retelling a story according to which someone saw in a vision the famous Abbot Richard of Saint-Vanne in hell, condemned to erect scaffoldings forever in punishment for his extravagant taste for fine architecture.[5] Cardinal Peter had no appreciation for liturgical splendor either and criticised "the unnecessary sounding of bells, the protracted chanting of hymns and the conspicuous use of ornament."[6] On the occasion of his memorable visit at Cluny in 1063, he observed that various offices were so prolonged that in a day's routine there was scarcely half an hour left to engage the monks in conversation. Meanwhile he was outright scandalized over the lack of penance and mortification, particularly in food and drink.[7]

---

3. *Ibid.,* pp. 302, 327–328. Cf. Alberic Stacpoole, "Hildebrand, Cluny and the Papacy" in *The Downside Review,* LXXXI (1963), pp. 142–164, 254–272, and Gerhart B. Ladner, "Reformatio" in *Ecumenical Dialogue at Harvard* (Cambridge, Mass.: Harvard University, 1964), pp. 174–175.

4. *De fuga dignitatum ecclesiasticarum,* PL 145:457–460.

5. Jean Leclercq, "La crise du monachisme aux XIe et XIIe siècles" in *Bolletino dell'Instituto Storico Italiano per il Medio Evo e Archivio Muratoriano,* LXX (1958), p. 23.

6. *De institutis ordinis eremitarum,* quoted in Owen J. Blum, *Saint Peter Damian* (Washington: Catholic University, 1947), p. 127.

7. Blum, *Saint Peter Damian,* p. 16.

D

In addition to the just mentioned points other critics of monasticism, whose numbers could be multiplied at will, spoke against seculars living among the monks under various pretexts; against the disturbing presence of children and other unwanted individuals; against monasteries built so close to cities that their solitude was endangered; against unnecessary traveling and extensive vagrancy among monks. Others pointed out that the clerical status of most monks served merely an excuse for the abandonment of manual labor and that the assumption of pastoral duties led to undesirable competition with the secular clergy. In fact, the critics continued, many abbots usurped episcopal authority and eagerly acquired churches with a variety of other profitable benefices, the holding of which the reformers considered improper for monks.[8]

The dissatisfaction of the secular clergy with monastic standards became evident at a number of provincial synods held in France throughout the eleventh century. In 1031 the synod of Bourges stressed the virtue of obedience and stability and threatened vagrant monks with excommunication. The council of Toulouse in 1056 attacked abbots who disregarded their duties and emphasized the neglected virtue of poverty. In 1059 a similar gathering at Rouen chided the monks for vainly pursuing exalted positions and lofty dignities. At subsequent synods at Toulouse (1068) and Rouen (1074), the clergy enjoined the monks to adhere to the strict observance of the Rule of St Benedict without relaxing its prescriptions concerning silence, vigils, fasting and clothing.[9]

It seems that in the eyes of many contemporaries the root of such abuses was the fact that monks, forgetting their proper vocations, disregarded their divinely ordained role and place in the Church. This came to expression in the writings of William of Volpiano (d. 1031), the reformer of Saint-Bénigne in Dijon, who deplored that in their conduct there was no distinction either between clergy

8. See a long list of such accusations in Bede Lackner, *The Eleventh Century Background of Cîteaux* (doctoral dissertation in manuscript at Fordham University, 1968), pp. 120–147. This fine study will soon appear as No. VIII in the Cistercian Studies Series.

9. *Ibid.,* pp. 160–167.

and people, or between priests and monks.[10] His nephew, John of
Fécamp, placed the same issue in an even sharper light when,
following Gregory the Great, he insisted that there must be a clear
line separating the laity from the clergy and an equally distinct place
for monks, who should spend their lives in penance and solitude.[11]

In spite of their many failings the monks of the time must be
credited with manful efforts to reform themselves along the lines
suggested by their critics. New foundations initiated by zealous
individuals multiplied from Calabria to Brittany, while practically
all older abbeys of some reputation undertook the arduous work of
mending their ranks. Instead of attempting to deal with each, here I
wish merely to analyze briefly the three basic ideas that seem to have
guided the eleventh-century monastic renewal. These were poverty,
eremitism and apostolic life. However, I must admit at once that all
three were mutually overlapping concepts and all had been, to some
extent, already integrated with the Rule of St Benedict; therefore
their reappearance resulted in the revival of older forms of monasticism. The originality of new establishments consisted largely in the
peculiar blend in which the separate elements merged.

Contemporary critics singled out riches and luxury as their prime
targets, while reformers urged the strictest poverty as the first step
toward meaningful renewal. Modern scholars seem to be in agreement with the ancient view linking wealth with decline. Thus Jean
Leclercq asserts in one of his fine essays that "in reality the crisis of
cenobitism was a crisis of prosperity,"[12] created by abbeys amassing
landed possessions and improving them through wise administration. A new stress on poverty, therefore, emerged as a spontaneous
reaction to such prosperity. Although the validity of this line of
reasoning sounds to me somewhat doubtful, the problem was so
keenly felt in the eleventh century that in search for solution,
bypassing the Rule of St Benedict, the reformers reached back to
the poverty of Christ on the Cross, the apostles and their first

10. Leclercq, "La crise . . .," p. 24.
11. *Ibid.,* pp. 25–26.
12. *Ibid.,* p. 24.

disciples. The movement started apparently early in the century in Italy, but spread quickly throughout the rest of Europe. The re-emerging dualistic heresies, looking askance at material things and condemning wealth and possessions, added to the impact of half-naked, weird-looking preachers of poverty roaming in increasing numbers the countryside.[13] Not only priests and monks became fascinated by the idea of absolute poverty but also the laity, as the example of the much researched *Patarini* of northern Italy clearly indicated.

In this light the teaching of St Peter Damian, strict as it was, cannot be regarded extreme. He replaced the Benedictine *sufficientia* with *extremitas* and *penuria* and encouraged his followers to go barefoot, sleep on hard beds and be satisfied with the indispensable necessities in clothing, food and drink. While contending that God must be the monk's sole property, he considered the holding of money outright sinful, a violation of the contract made by the monk when he signed his profession. "Therefore, let us turn back, beloved, to the innocence of the primitive Church, so that we may learn to relinquish possessions and enjoy the simplicity of regal poverty," Damian exhorted his disciples.[14]

Needless to say, no religious body could escape the impact of the trend. *Pauperes Christi* became the stereotyped reference to both monks and Canons Regular and was an often repeated phrase in the correspondence of Gregory VII. Nothing can attest more to the overwhelming power of the idea than the strange attempt of Paschal II, a former monk of Vallombrosa, to reach a solution in the Investiture Conflict. In 1111, to the amazement of Europe, he proposed that in exchange for the total elimination of secular interference in Church matters, the hierarchy of the Empire surrender its landed possessions to the crown.[15]

---

13. See a full list of such characters in Jeffrey Burton Russell, *Dissent and Reform in the Early Middle Ages* (Berkeley: University of California Press, 1965), pp. 101–124.

14. Quoted from *Sermo* 53 in Blum, *Saint Peter Damian*, pp. 92–93.

15. Cf. Cantor, *Medieval History*, p. 319.

The revival of eremitism was closely linked with the new concept of poverty as an idea as well as a historical phenomenon. The hermit not only withdrew from society but lived in total renunciation, in total poverty, both internal and external. As St Jerome put it: *nudos amat eremus.*[16] The roots of the movement reached back to the deserts of Egypt and Syria in the early Christian centuries. As a form of religious life it survived, particularly in the East, in spite of the growing popularity of cenobitism. It seems, moreover, that the continuity of eremitism remained unbroken to the eleventh century even in the West.[17] What appears to be new in the epoch under examination is its enormous popularity, its quick spread geographically and its penetration of all strata of the existing society. In trying to explain the obvious facts various attempts have been made to link the movement with the social and economic problems of the eleventh century. Such conditions were, however, very different from place to place, while the appeal of eremitism must have been universal; therefore any suspected causal link between the two remains ambiguous.[18] Since the revival of eremitism became first visible in Italy, it has been often proposed that the movement might have been inspired by eastern anchorites who settled down in the peninsula after they had been forced out from their original land by the advancing Islam.[19] However, religious contacts between Italy and the Byzantine Empire had never been entirely broken; therefore a few hermits hardly could have imported novelties of great significance. Furthermore, even if the local influence of some Byzantine hermits, e.g. that of St Nilus of Calabria, was significant, such isolated incidents cannot furnish adequate reasons for the spread of eremitism north of the Alps. It is probably safer to state that eremitism, just as

16. Jean Leclercq, "L'érémitisme en occident jusqu'à l'an mil" in *L'eremitismo in occidente nei secoli XI e XII* (Milano: Ed. Vita e Pensiero, 1965), p. 29.

17. Cf. "Erémitisme" in *Dictionnaire de spiritualité*, IV (Paris, 1960), 936–982.

18. Léopold Genicot, "L'érémitisme du XIe siècle dans son contexte économique et social" in *L'eremitismo . . .*, pp. 46–69.

19. E.g., J.-B. Mahn, *L'ordre cistercien et son gouvernement* (Paris: Boccard, 1945), pp. 26–27.

the new and strict interpretation of poverty, emerged as a reaction
to the prevailing standards of monastic life, a spontaneous protest
against the comfort and quiet daily routine of monks of great
abbeys which no longer presented sufficient challenge to souls
yearning for the heroic life of the Desert Fathers.[20]

This attitude clearly implied that in the eyes of the new generation
of reformers eremitic life appeared higher than life spent under the
Rule of St Benedict. Accordingly, the monastery was conceived
merely as a training ground for future hermits. As Peter Damian
put it: "As the priesthood is the goal of clerical education, profici-
ency in the arts is the purpose of attending the schools of the
grammarians, and as brilliant pleading at law is the culmination of
dreary hours of legal study, so monastic life with all its observances
is but a preparation for that higher goal, the solitude of the hermitage."[21] The monastery, he contended, was acceptable for the sick
and infirm; but those who chose to stay there permanently could
only be tolerated.

The lasting influence of individual hermits, as long as they truly
remained in solitude and isolation, poses a peculiar problem.
Obviously such people, no matter how deep or rich their spirituality
might be, would pass away without any specific impression on
others. On the other hand, the presence of disciples might facilitate
the transmission of spiritual values, but would destroy solitude and
involve the hermit in some sort of organization, the very thing he
tried to escape. Individuals are ephemeral; only institutions have
enduring existence. Most great hermits of the eleventh century
solved the dilemma by concessions and wound up as founders of
religious communities, where solitude was blended with elements
of cenobitic life. The example of Camaldoli, Fonte Avellana,
Vallombrosa, Fontevrault, Savigny, Grandmont, Grande Chartreuse, Obazine, are only the best known of many similar foundations of eremitical origin, where institutional frameworks guaranteed the survival of a peculiar spirituality long after the disappear-

20. Jean Leclercq, "Epilogue" in *L'eremitismo* . . . , p. 594.
21. Quoted in Blum, *Saint Peter Damian*, p. 126.

ance of the founding hermits and decline of eremitism as a popular movement.[22]

The third incentive for monastic renewal was the drive to imitate the life of the apostles, or, more specifically, the life of the apostolic community in Jerusalem, in poverty, simplicity and mutual charity. As G. Morin observed long ago,[23] in the eleventh century the word "apostolic" carried no connotation of preaching the Gospel or discharging other duties of the *cura animarum*: therefore the following of the apostles could be well within the program of contemplatives or even hermits. On the other hand, the appeal of the "apostolic life" extended far beyond monastic circles. It inspired Canons Regular, itinerant preachers, poverty movements of the laity and many features of the Gregorian Reform.[24] Nothing demonstrates more eloquently the elementary force of the movement than the difficulty Church authorities experienced in trying to contain the growing number of itinerant preachers within the bonds of moderation and orthodoxy. Even such a renowned character as Robert of Arbrissel, the founder of Fontevrault, was severely reprimanded by the Bishop of Rennes for his bizarre appearance and extravagant behavior.[25]

The influence of the primitive Church on monasticism had been, of course, as ancient as monasticism itself. The novelty consisted in the urgency and extent of the demand to reform religious communities in the light of the books of the New Testament. Peter Damian obliged his followers to "return to the innocence of the primitive Church."[26] At the council of Rome in 1059 Hildebrand

22. Cf. Jean Becquet, "L'érémitisme clerical et laïc dans l'ouest de la France" in *L'eremitismo* . . . , pp. 182–204.

23. Dom Germain Morin, *The Ideal of the Monastic Life* (New York: Benziger, 1914), pp. 67–68.

24. M.-D. Chenu, *Nature, Man, and Society in the Twelfth Century* (Chicago: University of Chicago Press, 1968), pp. 202–238.

25. Jean Leclercq, "Le poème de Payen Bolotin contre les faux ermites" in *Revue Bénédictine*, LXXIII (1958), pp. 68–69. Cf. Ernest W. McDonnell, "The *Vita Apostolica*: Diversity or Dissent" in *Church History* XXIV (1955), pp. 15–28.

26. Blum, *Saint Peter Damian*, p. 93.

used virtually the same phrases demanding the restoration of the
common life of the first century.[27] According to a prominent
"poor of Christ" of the next generation, Stephen of Muret, rules
written by men are of secondary importance; therefore, "if anyone
should ask you to what religious order you belong, tell him the
order of the Gospel, which is the basis of all rules."[28] A treatise of
the early twelfth century, *De vita vere apostolica*, attributed to
Rupert, abbot of Deutz, went even further: "If you wish to consult
the relevant passages of Scripture, you will find that they all seem to
say plainly that the Church originated in the monastic life." St
Benedict's Rule was in fact the adaptation of the *regula apostolica*.
Therefore, he continued, the apostles had been monks, and thus the
monks were the authentic successors of the apostles.[29]

The implications of such thoughts were plain enough. Monks
must free themselves from the entanglements of the feudal society;
they must abandon their splendid surroundings, their elaborate
ceremonials, the ease and comfort that the work of their predecessors made possible. Monks worthy of their apostolic heritage
should turn their backs to the world and seek a renewed life in
simplicity, poverty and charity of kindred souls.

In addition to the just discussed triple motive for monastic
renewal, many authors refer to another movement related to the
same trend: "back to the sources" of Christian monasticism.[30]
While it is undeniable that all reformers attempted to justify their
demands by references to the Bible, the Desert Fathers, or to the
Rule of St Benedict, it remains doubtful that such manifestations
amounted to a "movement" characteristic of the eleventh century.
Reformers of all times and every designation have been employing
the same tactics in vindication of novel approaches. Changes,
innovations, breaking with the past rarely generated universal

27. Chenu, *Nature, Man, and Society*, p. 207.

28. Quoted *ibid.*, p. 239.

29. *Ibid.*, p. 206.

30. Most recently and with renewed emphasis in Claude J. Peifer, "Monastic
Renewal in Historical Perspective" in *The American Benedictine Review*.
XIX (1968), pp. 11–16.

enthusiasm among monks; therefore those who proposed such moves were compelled to disguise their intentions as mere attempts to return to certain ancient and hallowed traditions. On the other hand, institutional reforms are necessitated by radical alterations in the fabric of the surrounding society. These changes often result in a new and unique environment and the initiation of corresponding changes in the institutions in question is a sign of a healthy instinct of survival. In such circumstances a traditional organization cannot insure its sufficient readjustment by simply turning back to observances and procedures that are admittedly old. The problem can be solved by accommodations executed in the light of genuine traditions, but it is doubtful how far the eleventh-century monastic reformers were aware of the nature of their task or how sincerely they were devoted to the past. To be sure, they were scarcely in the position to interpret their sources with sufficient authenticity for the simple reason that they were unaware of the fundamental differences that separated the mentality of the late Roman world from their own.

In my opinion it remains highly questionable that "their purpose was a return to sources, a rediscovery of the meaning of monastic life . . . to go back to the period before the Carolingian reformers . . . and recreate the original Benedictine structure in all its simplicity, purity and strength," and that therefore they "did not hesitate to go back beyond the Rule to rediscover the life-situation out of which the Rule grew."[31] As I can see it, the actual process was far less sophisticated. The purpose of the reformers was the creation of a life of austerity in perfect seclusion. The importance of textual references was secondary. When they quoted some convenient passages taken from available sources, they did so primarily in self-justification. They could not possibly go beyond the Carolingian reformers in any scholarly sense, much less "rediscover the life-situation" of pre-Benedictine times because they were ignorant of them and, for lack of adequate libraries and archives, they were unable to approach them. Medieval authors used the few documents within their reach far more often and far more efficiently as legal

31. *Ibid.,* p. 14.

weapons rather than as tools for the painstaking research of the mysterious past. The supposition that men of the eleventh century intended to execute or could, and in fact did, execute the above quoted and exceedingly ambitious scholarly tasks smacks of anachronism.

In the actual use of available sources the reformers followed their instincts and handled them with amazing liberty. Here I wish merely to refer to the variety of contradictory interpretations to which the Rule of St Benedict was subjected. Its text, in basically identical form, was certainly available to all monks from Benedict of Aniane to Robert of Molesme. Its authority was such that, to the best of my knowledge, none dared to reject it. Few, such as Stephen of Muret, practically ignored it; others, such as St Bruno, embraced only certain elements of it; but the majority of reformers, while professing the utmost devotion to the Rule, proceeded to interpret it with less than hermeneutic scrupulosity. This made possible a wide range of foundations: the Roman "Basilica Abbeys," the Anglo-Saxon "Mission Abbeys" and "Cathedral Abbeys," the German "School Abbeys" and "Culture Abbeys," the Carolingian "Prayer Abbeys" and "Pilgrimage Abbeys," the Cluniac "Cult Abbeys," and the eleventh century "Solitude Abbeys."[32]

The most articulate spokesman of "Solitude Abbeys" was certainly Peter Damian who, while paying homage to the Rule of St Benedict, managed to read into it his own peculiar ideas about mortification. He saw no incompatibility between the monastic concepts of St Benedict and his predecessors, for he urged his followers to abide by "whatever is found in the Rule of St Benedict or in the Institutes or Collations of the Fathers."[33] Encountering the manifest moderation of St Benedict, he argued that the Rule was written for the guidance of innocent souls, that St Benedict had no intention of supplanting the penitential canons applying to sinners, and that therefore "the Rule did not void the precepts of the

32. The terms are taken from Stephen Hilpisch, "The Benedictine Ideal through the Centuries" in *The American Benedictine Review,* XV (1964), pp. 383–386.

33. Quoted in Lackner, *The Eleventh Century Background of Cîteaux,* p. 253.

Fathers who had gone before."[34] Cardinal Damian, however, was quite willing to void in practice seventy-two chapters of the Rule in order to live up to the full extent of the seventy-third.

It is quite possible that reformers of the younger generation realized the inner contradiction of such approaches and as a reaction drew with greater sincerity closer to the Rule. Thus Vallombrosa was not only "founded on the authority of St Benedict," but John Gualbert "diligently began to discern the meaning of the Rule and intended to observe it with all his strength," while urging his disciples to follow it "in everything."[35] Bernard of Tiron and Vitalis of Mortain (Savigny) adopted similar attitudes while the even more exact observance of the Rule appeared to be the very reason of the foundation of Cîteaux.

I have no intention here to discuss the correctness of Cistercian interpretation of the Rule, but I wish to reiterate that the common denominator of all reforming efforts of the eleventh century was the desire to establish a life of heroic mortification spent in retirement from all worldly entanglements. In this the founders of new monastic institutions were eminently successful. The era when abbeys played the role of cultural centers and individual monks acted as scholars, educators and even as statesmen and leaders of a consolidating society, came to an end. Henceforth monks were taken for unworldly contemplatives. If individuals, such as St Bernard, stepped out of their cloisters they were the rare exceptions who, in their embarrassment, felt compelled to offer excuses for their temporary abandonment of their solitude. Professor Norman F. Cantor demonstrated convincingly in one of his recent studies how "the Gregorian radical felt compelled to apply his puritan ideals to all aspects of social life . . . and was driven with all the reckless zeal of the ascetic saint let loose in an imperfect world," the end result of which was that "the monastic order lost nearly all its social utility" and "while the monastic order became spiritually embalmed within the walls of its comfortable establishments, a new, grasping,

34. Blum, *Saint Peter Damian*, pp. 113–114.
35. Lackner, *The Eleventh Century Background of Cîteaux*, pp. 264–267.

penetrating, secularist spirit came to dominate European political life." Thus he does not hesitate to state that the eleventh-century "crisis of monasticism was the crisis of medieval civilization itself."[36]

Even if we restrict our scope to the field of monastic history we must admit that the very success of the reformers carried the germs of another epoch of relative decline. Peter Damian and his heirs did establish a life of heroic asceticism and raised their new abbeys to never experienced heights of monastic perfection, but such standards could not be maintained indefinitely. While insisting on the meticulous observance of certain passages of the Rule, they overlooked its governing spirit of moderation. St Benedict was willing to offer compromises to human frailty, but the new reformers were not. They refused to recognize that institutions banking on lasting success must take into account the limitations of the average, not the ambitions of saints and heroes. Once again, the wisdom of St Benedict proved to be far more enduring than the zeal of unworldly enthusiasts. Most eremitical or semi-eremitical foundations disintegrated, were absorbed within a few generations, or slipped back to insignificance. Of the new crop of monks and canons, only the Cistercians, Carthusians and Premonstratensians remained in the forefront of religious history. The strictly limited role and membership of the Carthusians enabled them to maintain their initial spiritual standards; but the other two, struggling to preserve their over-extended and overgrown institutions, were forced to take the downward road to compromises.

I realize that up to this point I have said nothing about the significant developments of structural nature that accompanied the just sketched moral and disciplinary renewal. Unfortunately, the limitations of this paper exclude the meaningful discussion of this important subject. However, let me emphasize in conclusion that the early success of Cistercians cannot be explained without proper consideration of their institutional advances which, in turn, rested largely on the achievements of some of their predecessors, particu-

36. "The Crisis of Western Monasticism, 1050–1130" in *The American Historical Review*, LXVI (1960), pp. 64–67.

larly those of the Vallombrosan congregation. The adoption of lay-brotherhood, a limited control exercised by the mother abbey, the idea of annual general chapters, annual visitation of each house and the linear subordination of monasteries, each dependent on its founder—all features of Vallombrosa—were later successfully employed and further developed by Cîteaux.[37]

The present discourse, no matter how brief, should not end without touching upon the intriguing question: "What was the mainspring of the eleventh-century religious revolution?" My previous statement to the effect that the monastic phase of this movement was part and parcel of the whole contributes little toward an answer. The problem, of course, is difficult, not merely because of the complexity of the issues under investigation but also because of the relative paucity of source material. In fact, only the Marxist historians seem to have a ready and infallible explanation. According to them the religious revolution of the eleventh century was in reality a disguised manifestation of class struggle, and therefore under the cloak of moral perfection, salvation, poverty and austerity, forces of social and economic unrest must be identified. The best known representative of this school in the West is Ernst Werner of the University of Leipzig, whose book, *Pauperes Christi* (Berlin, 1956), brings out at least one valid point: even in the case of purely religious matters, the consideration of the social and economic background may lead to a fuller understanding of the subject's nature.

This is exactly the ambition of the non-Marxist sociological school. Thus Professor Hugh Trevor-Roper of Oxford, while admitting that behind such phenomena there was always a "complex chemistry of causes," advances the theory that the eleventh-century events were largely the results of a relative over-population followed by widespread agrarian unrest. Just what was the link between religion and economy, he does not say, but he confesses that "history is

37. Roger Duvernay, "Cîteaux, Vallombreuse et Etienne Harding" in *Analecta S.O.Cist.*, VIII (1952), pp. 379–495. Most recently, Denis Meade, "From Turmoil to Solidarity: The Emergence of the Vallombrosan Monastic Congregation" in *The American Benedictine Review*, XIX (1968), pp. 323–357.

full of marvels . . . and surely the rise of western Europe, after its terrible abasement in the Dark Ages . . . is a miracle."[38]

Christopher Dawson deals with the problem in the last chapter of *The Making of Europe* (originally published in 1932) and returned to the same in a more detailed fashion in his Gifford lectures of 1948–49 (published under *Religion and the Rise of Western Culture*, 1950). In the seventh lecture he emphasized that "this movement was at first purely monastic and ascetic," but was subsequently adopted by Leo IX and grew to revolutionary proportions after the rediscovery and employment of Roman Law. "This marks a new departure in the history of Western culture, for it meant that men had begun to reason about the principles on which Christian society was based, and to use the appeal to these principles as a means of changing the existing order." In a descriptive sense Dawson's line of thinking seems to be cogent enough, but he declined to go further into the problem.

Professor Cantor of Brandeis University, in his article already referred to and in his more recent book (*Medieval History*, 1963), concurs with Dawson in stating that the movement of reform was initiated by monks; but, getting to the heart of the matter, he offers an interesting proposition. According to his view, the hidden power behind the movement was the drive of the clergy to maintain their pre-eminence, which was threatened by a great increase of lay piety. Therefore "to many eleventh-century churchmen it seemed that only a greatly improved morality and heightened religious fervor among the clergy could continue to justify the exclusive powers of the *sacerdotium*. Otherwise the *ecclesia* would be absorbed into the thoroughly Christianized *mundus*, and the clergy would lose their distinctive position in a society."[39]

Professor Gerd Tellenbach of Freiburg (im. Br.) simply admitted that "a more than earthly wisdom would have been necessary to foresee this revolution," and "it will never be quite possible to

38. *The Rise of Christian Europe* (New York: Harcourt, Brace and World, 1965), p. 24.

39. "The Crisis of Western Monasticism," p. 62.

discover what were the real causes of the great eleventh-century crisis in Christian history."[40]

Undeterred, I wish to append a few of my own thoughts.[41] I suspect that what made the revolution possible, or perhaps inevitable, was the rising level of education, first among monks, then among the clergy in general. Thanks to intense studies of the Scriptures and Church Fathers, it became possible to construct an image (some would say: a myth) of the apostolic Church, resplendent in the most appealing colors. The comparison of this idealistic picture with the sad realities of the present generated an intense desire for change. Since there were plenty of abuses to be seen even by the unlettered, it was a simple matter to convert the unhappiness of intellectuals to a mass movement. When the cutting edge of Cardinal Humbert's logic was applied to the living tissues of a society held together by immemorial customs, the revolution began. When Gregory VII quoted the Lord saying: *Ego sum veritas et vita,* he added in explanation: *non dixit Ego sum consuetudo, sed veritas.* By then the revolution had already been far advanced.

Louis J. Lekai s o cist

Our Lady of Dallas,
Irving, Texas 75060

---

40. Tellenbach, *Church, State and Christian Society,* pp. 97, 163.

41. Even this thought has been often expressed or implied by others, e.g. by Professor Ladner of the University of California in his above quoted paper, "Reformatio": "The emergence of a strong and successful urge for general reform in that period was due to increasing awareness of a vast discrepancy which existed between the form of life of the contemporary Church of the eleventh century and that of the Apostles, martyrs and early Church Fathers."—p. 173.

THE INTERPRETATION OF A MONASTIC RULE

THE GENERAL CHAPTER of 1967, during its twenty-sixth session, affirmed that the Rule of St Benedict remains the basis of our Cistercian legislation.[1] The same General Chapter also approved a certain number of experiments or adaptations, some of which constitute a departure from a literal observance of the Rule. This raises the question of fidelity to the Rule, a question which concerns every facet of our monastic life. All its dimensions must be studied.

The attitudes which individuals or groups take with regard to this problem often stem from more fundamental, oftentimes quite vague propensities. These attitudes concern the relationship of the Rule to Scripture, to the monastic tradition as a whole, and to contemporary man. And the fundamental problem in every case is one of hermeneutics.

It is this problem of the hermeneutics, or of the interpretation of the Rule that I wish to deal with in this paper. I do not pretend to offer a solution. I simply wish to state the problem in terms as exact as possible, and indicate what might lead to a solution. Nor am I forgetting that solutions to this sort of problem ought first to be worked out in real life, before they can be conceptualized in a satisfactory manner.

1. *Minutes of the Sessions of the Sixtieth General Chapter: Order of Cistercians of the Strict Observance* (Dubuque, Iowa: Regional Conference, U.S.A., 1967), p. 102.

Preliminary Notions: the Task of Hermeneutics

The empirical method has gradually taken over in all the sciences, theology included. As Fr Bernard Lonergan SJ explained at the Theology Congress at Toronto in August 1967, theology has become empirical in the sense that Scripture and tradition no longer offer it premises from which it may draw conclusions, but rather *data* to interpret.[2] Consequently, the most crucial and fundamental problems which present themselves to man today, in every domain of learning, are problems of *interpretation*, that is, problems of hermeneutics. That is why, in what concerns the sacred sciences, the methods of hermeneutics which have been established for biblical exegesis are being rethought more and more, with a view to using them for the study of tradition.

We can distinguish two forms of interpretation with regard to documents considered as part of tradition: historic and dynamic.[3] Historical interpretation consists in discovering the precise meaning of a text in itself, what the author really wanted to say. The instruments used in this sort of interpretation are textual, historical, and literary criticism. This kind of interpretation, while remaining on the historical level, can become systematic if, over and above the use of these methods of criticism, superior norms of interpretation are introduced which bring to light the doctrinal, philosophical and theological presuppositions underlying the text.

But it is also possible to surpass this level of historical interpretation and arrive at an interpretation which is dynamic. That is to say, one may use the interpreted text as a starting point for arriving at a deeper understanding of the *reality* which the text expresses. This method is extremely important for interpreting texts of the Church's magisterium, especially conciliar documents.

The magisterium texts deal with realities which can not be reduced to formulas, and which are infinitely greater than any

2. B. Lonergan, "Theology in its new context" in *Theology of Renewal*, Vol. I (Montreal, 1968), pp. 37f.

3. Here I have used as my basis M. Löhrer, "Überlegungen zur Interpretation lehramtlicher Aussagen als Frage des ökumenischen Gesprächs" in *Gott in Welt* (Freiburg-Basel-Vienna, 1964), pp. 499–523.

E

conceptual expression that one might give them. Even dogmatic definitions, infallible and irrevocable as they may be, never express perfectly and completely the reality to which they refer. Further, although the living magisterium is the immediate norm for faith, the ultimate and fundamental norm is Holy Scripture. Therefore, even if the task of the magisterium is to interpret Scripture, any given text of tradition or of the Fathers of the Church can only be interpreted correctly if it is viewed in the light of Scripture and the whole of the tradition of the Church: these two constitute its integral context.

Everything which I have explained here about interpretation of *texts* holds good for the *facts* of Church History, for tradition manifests itself through these facts also.

Now if we apply these methodological principles to an interpretation of the Rule, we find ourselves in the following position. In order to understand the Rule, we should first work out an interpretation which is critical and historical; that is to say, by using methods of textual, literary and historical criticism we should be able to determine the exact meaning of each part of the Rule, of each of its phrases. In other words, we should be able to discover what the author of the Rule really wanted to say. At this stage of research, it still is not a question of providing a *commentary* on the Rule. This is rather a scientific explanation on which any ulterior commentary would need to be based. Excellent works have already been produced in this line of critical and historical interpretation of the Rule. This work should be followed up. But the results of this historical interpretation cannot aid us in a direct manner to determine the orientation which monastic renewal should take. They have to be completed by a dynamic interpretation.

What is this dynamic interpretation of the Rule? I hope that this will become clearer as we continue with our study. But for the moment, let me say that such an interpretation will consist of a re-evaluation of the Rule as a whole, and of each of its elements in the light of Holy Scripture and the whole of tradition.

Before speaking specifically of our own attitude toward the Rule, we have to ascertain its relationship with Scripture and tradition—

that is to say, the tradition of the Church in general as well as monastic tradition. The plan of this study then appears as follows:

The Rule and the Gospel
The Rule and Tradition
The Rule and Monastic History
The Rule and Ourselves.

The Rule and the Gospel

The Gospel, the fundamental and irreplaceable norm of the Christian life, remains the first Rule for the monk. Hence it is necessary to point out the relationship between the Rule and Scripture. And this, of course, should be done by starting with a notion of Holy Scripture which is theologically exact.

Thanks to developments in the field of the theology of history, we are now accustomed to viewing revelation as something dynamic rather than static. Revelation is the personal entrance of God into human history, and the Christian life is man's response to this personal and completely gratuitous intervention by God. It is this intervention which is the supreme norm of every type of Christian life. Holy Scripture is precisely the objectification in writing—by the inspiration of the Holy Spirit, but in human language—of the divine fact of revelation. Because it is coextensive with the factual reality, this first written objectification has a primary normative value for the whole life of the People of God in the ages following the Incarnation of Christ.

It is enough to read and meditate on the Rule of St Benedict to appreciate its completely evangelical character. It paints a beautiful picture of the Gospel-life lived in its fullness. Does this mean that it is a "digest of the Gospel" as is sometimes said? Actually, such an expression is extremely ambiguous. People who use it all too easily lead one to believe that the Rule gathers everything together from the Gospel which would be useful for monks, so that they need not bother going directly to Scripture. It would be wrong to say that. The Rule is not meant to replace the Gospel, but to lead the monk to it and help him to understand what the Gospel requires of him.

The Rule is an interpretation of the evangelical doctrine on the perfect Christian life. As such, it helps us to understand the Gospel message. But it should be reinterpreted continually, in the light of Scripture and the tradition of the Church. So we must also situate the Rule in its relationship to tradition.

The Rule and Tradition

Tradition is an extremely important human phenomenon. The philosophers who have studied it have been careful to distinguish it from *history*, and to show its relationship to history. While history is the "becoming" which preserves the past, tradition is precisely that which is durable; it stands firm during all the mutations of this "becoming."[4] From the *ontological* point of view, tradition is that which makes it possible for *being* to be permanent;[5] from the point of view of hermeneutics, it is the element which makes knowledge of the past possible.[6] Actually, I cannot interpret and understand (*verstehen*) a text or a fact of the past unless I have a certain anterior knowledge (*Vorverstandnis*) of the ontological reality of which this fact is the incarnation, or of which this text is the objectification. This pre-intellection is made possible by a type of vital communication with this reality, and this vital communication is assured by tradition.

Now, from the strictly theological point of view, tradition is the objective permanence of revelation, in the historical "becoming" of the Church. Tradition and historicity (which means mutation) are correlative realities. The whole work of interpretation consists in discovering the revealed truth which is veiled by various historical and contingent forms of objectification.

As with every other element in the tradition of the Church, the Rule of St Benedict is the objectification of a transcendent and permanent reality (the evangelical doctrine on the perfect Christian life) in contingent and changing historical forms. The interpretation

4. Cf. G. Krüger, *Freiheit und Weltverantwortung* (Freiburg, 1958).
5. Cf. M. Heidegger, *Sein und Zeit* (Berlin, 1926).
6. Cf. H. G. Gadamer, *Wahrheit und Methode* (Tübingen, 1960).

of the Rule will consist, first of all, in distinguishing what in it is *tradition* and what is *historicity*. This can be accomplished if the method of dynamic interpretation about which we were just speaking is applied.

Before going further, we ought to clarify one point. So far, we have been considering the Rule as a spiritual document which transmits to us the message of the Gospel on the perfect Christian life. From this point of view, it is one of the elements in the tradition of the Church, and has as much importance for Christians in general and for theologians as it has for monks and nuns. But it interprets this Gospel message in a specific manner. It bears witness to a certain type of spiritual attitude which characterizes those persons whom history calls *monks* and *nuns*. Thus it transmits the *monastic tradition*.

Monasticism is, in fact, an historical reality. And so within the confines of this reality we must once again distinguish between tradition and historicity. Christian monasticism is characterized above all by a spiritual attitude before God, before men, and before the reality of the world. It is this spiritual attitude, abiding despite the ebb and flow of evolving monastic observances throughout history, which properly speaking constitutes the monastic tradition.

If we are to distinguish in the Rule of St Benedict what is monastic tradition and what are its historical and contingent modalities of objectification (and that is the task of dynamic interpretation), we will first have to determine at what moment the Rule entered the ebb and flow of monastic history as an historical fact. Then we will have to see how monks interpreted St Benedict's Rule in the centuries which followed.

The Rule in Monastic History

a) *The Rule as an Historical Fact*

The Rule of St Benedict which for many centuries has dominated practically all of western monasticism is, without doubt, a document of great value and one which expresses the "monastic tradition" in a very excellent way. Should we conclude from this, as some people are perhaps a little too quick to do, that it is a "synthesis" of the

whole monastic tradition? This would certainly be an exaggeration
and quite incorrect. First of all, monastic history did not end with
St Benedict, nor did St Benedict draw up his Rule in the manner of
a theoretician. With him, there was no question of studying the
whole tradition which had gone before so that he could select and
retain what was best in it. The Rule of St Benedict is situated at a
certain moment in the historical evolution of monasticism.

The ancient East had known two great monastic traditions: the
cenobitic and the anchoretic. Within each of these traditions,
different currents could be distinguished.[7] The cenobitic tradition
came into being just about everywhere at about the same time,
especially in the Judeo-Christian Churches. It had its origin in those
groups of ascetics who had been living within the local Churches
from the early days of Christianity. We find this cenobitic tradition,
expressed with varying differences, amongst the Sons of the
Covenant in Persia and Syria, in Pachomian monasticism in the
Thebaid and in Basilian monasticism in Cappadocia. Alongside of
this cenobitic tradition, the anchoretic tradition gradually developed. It seems that the influence of the Egyptian anchorites was
largely responsible for the spread of this type of life. It is the semi-
anchoretic tradition of Lower Egypt which St Benedict knew,
receiving it through Cassian and the Master. So Benedict was
situated in a very definite current in the evolution of the great
monastic tradition, and to a great extent, he knew nothing of the
other currents. In his day, he could not possibly have known them
all. The fact that he stresses or fails to stress certain particular
elements of monastic tradition could mean that he had made a
choice after a long personal deliberation, but it could also be
simply the result of accidental historical factors.

Benedict did not receive the monastic tradition in a fully developed form. Rather, he received it wrapped in a contingent form of
objectification. No element of the Rule can be properly evaluated
unless it is examined and weighed in the light of the whole monastic

7. I explained this in detail in my article "The Abbatial Office in Cenobitic
Life" in *Monastic Studies,* no. 6 (1968), pp. 3–45.

tradition. A healthy and honest interpretation ought to be able to recognize both the strength and weakness of the Rule of St Benedict as well as the strength and weakness of the monastic current in which the Rule is situated.

b)   *Interpretation of the Rule in History*

Thus far we have seen that the Rule is, first of all, one of the bearers of Church tradition. It is a witness to the Gospel teaching about the perfect Christian life. Further, it is a link in the chain of monastic tradition, handing down to us this "spiritual attitude"— of openness to the Spirit, of total abandonment to God, and of poverty—which is the essence of the monastic life. This spiritual attitude does not exist in an abstract state. It has to be expressed in an incarnate form, and the Rule incarnates it in customs, observances and in the setting of a daily life which is arranged with great detail. From this point of view, the Rule is also a juridical code which prescribes the organization of a monastic community in a specific historical context, for the purpose of assuring the development of this spiritual attitude.

During the course of monastic history since St Benedict we can distinguish two trends of attitude toward the Rule. One sees it primarily as a *spiritual* document which gives witness to the fundamental values of the monastic life and which ought to *inspire* the monks of the generations to come in their living of the monastic life. The other trend sees it rather as a *juridical* code which describes right down to the last detail what the monastic or Benedictine life ought to be.

This same sort of dialectic had already marked Eastern monasticism to a certain extent. It does not seem that the first groups of ascetics which existed within the local Christian communities knew of any other rules than the canonical ones which applied to all Christians. However, as the communities became more organized and their structures became more complicated, the organization of the common life on the practical level became the object of a number of prescriptions. In Cappadocia problems came up when the "fraternities" of St Basil became more organized, and in his attempts to solve them, he went straight to the Gospel. His answers to these practical questions were put together as a sort of "collection," and thus arose his "Rules" which have nothing at all about them which ressembles a systematically elaborated juridical code.

To respond to the various material and spiritual needs of his monasteries, and also to assure the smooth running of the common life, St Pachomius was obliged to draw up a certain number of prescriptions for his monks which also were assembled as "collections," even during his lifetime. But Pachomius took care to concentrate the ascetical efforts of his monks on "the prescriptions of the Gospel," and to orient their attention towards the fundamental spiritual reality of fraternal communion. After his death, his two successors, Horsiesius and Theodore, in their attempts to maintain unity in the Congregation, put much too much emphasis on fidelity to the precepts which Pachomius had drawn up for the monks. The juridical element replaced the charismatic, and this was the cause of a rapid decline in the Pachomian congregation.

Generally speaking, in the East all the ancient rules are considered as a treasure common to the whole of monasticism. They are spiritual documents which one finds in all the monasteries. By their contact with these various rules, the young monks develop "a monk's heart." They do not look to them for directives about the organization of their monasteries on the level of practical detail. Doing that is rather the role of the *typicon* which, ideally at least, should be proper to each monastery.

Even Cassian, great theorizer about the monastic life though he was, does not seem to have written a Rule. He simply presented to the Western monks, by means of his *Institutions* and *Conferences*, the customs and spiritual teachings of the Eastern monks. But more elaborate rules were drawn up in the West. One of them, the *Rule of the Master* which was probably put together by a Roman cleric, served as base for the Rule of St Benedict. The author of this Rule, the *Benedictus vir* of Monte Cassino, presented to his monks the traditional monastic teaching and he did it with rather unusual wisdom and great discretion. At the same time, he drew up a picture of how they should live this traditional teaching in the concrete circumstances of life in an Italian monastery during the sixth century.

For the next few centuries, the attitude in the West toward monastic rules was similar to that which existed in the East. Little by little, the Rule of St Benedict found its way into almost all the monasteries in the West. This, however, does not mean that the other rules were discarded. Rather, in any given monastery, the monks might have been using several rules simultaneously for their spiritual orientation. No one even thought about conforming the details of daily monastic life to the prescriptions of one or another of these rules.[8]

Charlemagne, who wished to rule the Church as well as serve it, imposed the Rule of St Benedict on all the monasteries of his realm. It would seem that, in the circumstances in which monasticism found itself at that time, the only way of reestablishing a certain "rectitude of life" (precisely that *honestas morum* about which St Benedict speaks in Chapter Seventy-three of the Rule) was to impose a uniform Rule on the monasteries. Benedict of Aniane, supported by Louis the Pious, put himself to this task with great energy. A *Capitulare monasticum*—which constituted actually an *adaptation* of the Rule of St Benedict—was established at Aix-la-Chapelle in 817, and the emperor designated *inspectors* who were responsible for putting the new decrees into effect. One abbey, Inde, was even set up as a "model" monastery. This organization was an ephemeral thing and did not last far beyond Benedict of Aniane's lifetime. During the ninth century, monasticism again fell into a period of decadence. It became evident that a mere reform of institutions, even one based on an excellent Rule, would never be enough if the Spirit was lacking.

But the Spirit was going to inspire a great spiritual renewal about a century after the Synod of Aix-la-Chapelle: the reform of Cluny. Working within the juridical framework established by Benedict of Aniane, this reform was to be a return to the funda-

8. See J. Hourlier, "La Règle de St Benoît, source du droit monastique" in *Etudes d'Histoire du Droit Canonique* (Paris: Aubier, 1967), pp. 157–168.

mental monastic observances: silence, work, stability, prayer. It is true that Cluny developed a liturgical cult which was exaggerated, but the criticisms directed at Cluny on this score are often exaggerated, too. The monasteries of the Cluny Federation were real centers of prayer and union with God existing in the midst of a world marked more than ever by violence, immorality, and injustice. And they remained centers of intense prayer for a very long time.

Obviously, the Rule of St Benedict was the basis of the Cluniac reform, for it was the basis of all western monasticism at that time. But it was interpreted with discretion and wisdom by the Abbot of Cluny who was the superior of all the monks of the "Congregation." Cluny's centralization had drawbacks, of course, as any kind of centralization does. It also had advantages. Besides freeing the individual monasteries from feudal domination, it permitted the first abbots of Cluny (who were great spiritual masters and nearly all of whom were abbots for a very long time) to exercise a direct spiritual influence on thousands of monks, and thus to maintain a very high degree of spiritual life in several hundred monasteries (more than a thousand, when Hugh died in 1109).

The wave of reform which manifested itself in monasticism toward the middle of the eleventh century cannot be taken as an indication that Cluny was in a state of decadence. On the contrary, it bears witness to the success of the Cluniac reform and to the vitality of a type of monasticism which had attained a sufficient degree of maturity to give rise within itself to a new need for something better, for a reform which would be more profound and more radical. Just about everywhere, and at the same time, there appeared a strong desire and movement toward a monastic life which would be poorer, more simple and more solitary than the life in the huge Cluniac monasteries, although these abbeys had played an admirable role during their period of history. From this current which, as a whole, wanted to be faithful to the Rule of St Benedict (that is to be authentically monastic), there arose the foundations of Camaldoli, Vallombrosa, Grandmont, Fontevrault, Chartreuse, Molesme, Cîteaux. They all drew their life from the same movement of the

Spirit. They did not look for a new interpretation of the Rule of St Benedict. They simply wanted to live, in an authentic way, each one according to his own manner and with great spontaneity, what everyone recognized as the life intended by St Benedict: a life that was simple and poor, a life of solitude.

The original attitude of the founders of Cîteaux was marked by this spontaneity and this simplicity. Soon, however, the needs of self-justification brought on by their polemics with the Benedictine monks obliged them to explain why they had abandoned the *traditional* customs which for so long had been taken to be an official interpretation of the Rule in the West. They had opted for a stricter observance of the Rule, a *literal* observance even. It is important to make a clear distinction between the charism and initial spiritual aspirations of the founders of Cîteaux, and their self-justifying rationalizations.

As long as the first founders were alive, and even during the next generation, the vitality of the initial charism was strong enough to counterbalance any excessive rigidity or strictness occasioned by the principle of literal observance of all the prescriptions of the Rule to the exclusion of all the monastic *customs* which had developed after the Rule was written. St Bernard, even though he inclined to absolute principles such as those he puts forth in the *De praecepto et dispensatione*, also knew how to exercise common sense, reasoning and charity on the practical level. Unfortunately, it is more difficult to transmit the charism of discretion than it is to transmit absolute principles.

The growth of Cîteaux was rapid and prolific. We have a right to be proud of it. But the historian who is going to be honest cannot conceal the fact that this Golden Age was very brief (much shorter than that of Cluny, for example). Very soon we see that a number of practices directly opposed to the original intentions of the founders were introduced. The Cistercian monasteries became just as rich as those of Cluny. After having rejected the *Customs* of Cluny as so many unjustifiable additions to the Rule, the Cistercians found that their *Customs* were more numerous and complex than those of Cluny! They so forgot about the simplicity of their predecessors and the sharp criticisms of St Bernard, that the Cistercian Abbots, a few centuries later, sought to obtain, and in fact did obtain, the pontifical insignia. The lay brothers were often exploited, and the monks, counting on them for their material subsistence, often fell into an idleness which was not at all akin to mystical *otium*.

What were the causes of this rapid diminution of the primitive ideal? The principal reason usually given is that the growth, both in the number of monks and of monasteries, was too rapid. But we must look for a deeper reason, and I am inclined to believe that it is rather the legalism which resulted from pushing the principle of literal fidelity to the Rule too far. The fundamental obligations of the monastic life: poverty, solitude, prayer, make demands on the monk which are almost unlimited. When the monk applies himself to listening for the promptings of the Holy Spirit, he is led by him into an ever-deepening understanding of these demands, and also to a more authentic monastic life on the practical level. But when he establishes himself in a static position by a literal observance of a text that has been written once and for all, he is no longer sensitive to the dynamic action of the Holy Spirit. He no longer obeys the law which is "written in his heart," but is satisfied with conforming his actions to some exterior law. And God knows how fertile the human imagination is when it comes to devising a harmony between the text of a rule and certain things which are most opposed to its spiritual dynamism.

This legalism was a great hindrance to the flowering of charisms. The great Cistercian authors such as William of St Thierry, Guerric of Igny, Amadeus of Lausanne, Aelred of Rievaulx, Isaac of Stella and Adam of Perseigne, practically all belonged to the same generation. Most of them had received their formation before they came to a Cistercian monastery. Even though their spiritual works are very often of great value, only a relatively small number of these works have a character which is specifically monastic.

The Charter of Charity, which had as its goal the union of monasteries in the bond of charity, had seen uniformity of observances as a means of maintaining this union of charity. But as the

Order spread throughout Europe, the General Chapters were continually harassed by this question of *observances*. They continually had to be giving reminders about them, or modifying them, or mitigating them. The Rule itself is very rarely mentioned in the Acts of the General Chapters. ·

By the fifteenth century, the Order had become a vast organism without sufficient life-breath to permit a reform which would have revived the whole. At that moment God raised up certain charismatic men who reformed their own monasteries, and around their own monasteries grouped other houses of monks. This was how several of the Congregations began. The duration of their prosperity depended on whether they clung to and kept alive the original charism of the founder, or whether they simply went about observing the rules he had established. This was the criterion that determined whether they lasted for a longer or shorter time.

A charism, of course, because of its very nature can not be "institutionalized." But all the same, adequate institutions are needed to maintain life in the dynamism which has been set in motion. This passage from charism to institution is always an extremely delicate matter. Unfortunately it is often a passage to legalism. That is clearly what happened in the case of the Pachomian congregation, under Horsiesius and Theodore. I feel that at Cîteaux, also, a too-literal attachment to the customs established by the founders led—after a marvelous but brief period of development—to a certain drying-up of Cistercian spirituality.

This phenomenon is common enough. We can find it outside of monasticism, outside of Christianity even, in Islam for example. And it appears with a strange sort of similarity. With regard to Islam, Jacques Jomier has written: "At Medina, during the lifetime of Mohammed, Islam was a veritable theocracy. At any moment, new oracles might announce new orders from above to the people. It was God, the faithful believed, who guided his people, shepherded by their leader. After the death of Mohammed it is difficult to speak of pure and simple theocracy. The Koran became the supreme law, and numerous points which had been passed over in silence were gradually made the object of legislation. Thus a whole body of legislation came into being. At the time the Arabic empire broke up, Islam had become, according to the expression of Louis Gardet, a 'Nomocracy'."[9]

The following remark by the same author with reference to Islam, might be applied to more than one phase of monastic history: "As a religion of law, Islam permits the majority of her faithful to settle down with a good conscience once they have accomplished all the prescribed observances. This results in a state of satisfaction and serenity, except in the case of certain mystics who thirst for the absolute."[10]

Conclusion: the Rule and Ourselves

The fundamental obligation of contemporary monasticism, and that of each individual monk, is to hearken to the life-giving Spirit, in an attitude of openness and docility. The Spirit speaks in a million ways, and one of the special channels through which he reaches us is, of course, the Rule. But to discover the message of the Spirit in the Rule, we must know how to interpret it. In order to do this, we must consider it from three different points of view.

As a document of the great *Church tradition*, the Rule transmits to us the evangelical doctrine on the perfect Christian life. From this point of view, it has just as much value for the Christian in general as it has for the monk himself. It is one of many documents in which and by which the Church has objectified, during the course of the ages, its understanding of the Gospel. Obviously, it is not meant to replace the Gospel—a misunderstanding which might result from clumsy usage of the expression: "The Rule: digest of the Gospel." Rather, its goal is to help us better understand the requirements of the Gospel.

As a document of the *monastic tradition*, the Rule teaches monks of all eras and all persuasions the fundamental spiritual attitude which *makes* the monk. The first obligation of the monk with respect to the Rule is, therefore, to meditate on it unceasingly, to let himself

9. J. Jomier, *Introduction à l'Islam actuel* (Paris, 1964), pp. 29f.
10. *Ibid.*, p. 194.

be penetrated with it, and to let it create in him the spiritual attitude which will make him a real monk. And it is through his personal and vital experience, much more than through abstract formulas, that he will arrive at expressing what this state of soul is—this attitude toward God, toward man, toward created things, which characterizes the monk. One might describe this attitude in general terms this way: the monk is a man who has abandoned, as far as is humanly possible, everything which men are wont to consider helpful for organizing their life on this earth. He has put himself in an impossible situation; that is to say, in a situation where he must count on God for everything, where he can no longer count on anyone or anything but him. That is the significance of his solitude, his poverty, and his celibacy.

The Rule presents this spiritual attitude to him, not in an abstract form, but incarnated in customs and practices, in a type of daily life intimately linked to a specific historical context. Thus it takes the form of a *juridical code*.

As a document of Church tradition, the Rule of St Benedict has an unquestionable value for all Christians and its interpretation is subject to the same rules as any other document of the Church. As a witness of the monastic tradition, it has a value for all monks, but particularly for those who belong to the great cenobitic tradition which the Rule has handed down to our day. As a juridical code describing the concrete realization of this spiritual attitude in a detailed way and in a setting of daily life, the Rule had an immediate value as norm only for the monks for whom it was first written, those living in the time of St Benedict, although even from this secondary point of view it continues to give inspiration to monks through the centuries.

The task of the monastic orders, and the task of each individual monk, then, is to try earnestly to arrive at a comprehension ever new and ever deeper of what the Gospel requires of man, and to continue the renewal of their spiritual orientation and the dynamism which characterizes monastic life. Under the guidance of the Spirit they must unceasingly seek for the most authentic and true concrete realization of this spiritual attitude, in forms of life adapted to our living contemporary context. Take an example: evangelical poverty. The Rule, drawn up in a sociological context completely different from ours, cannot teach us how we should practice poverty today. But it should create in our hearts a spirit of poverty. And if we are really poor in spirit, we will certainly practice a poverty which is authentic. If, on the other hand, we are just concerned with observing the Rule's precepts telling us what we should do with our earthly goods, we may easily justify, in the name of fidelity to the Rule, all sorts of situations which, in our contemporary context, are frowned upon by the *consensus Ecclesiae* as being contrary to evangelical poverty.

Another example: prayer. The exigencies of the Gospel with regard to prayer are, quite clearly, the same for all Christians. The Rule simply reminds us of them. But it is normal that the monk, who lives in the presence of God and for him alone, should consecrate a greater part of his time to prayer, and especially if he is a cenobite to a public expression of his prayer in union with his brethren. The Rule teaches him how to establish an organic unity between private and communal prayer. It also teaches him how to integrate times of communal prayer into the general framework of community life. This is the fundamental cenobitic attitude which the Rule teaches us, and we will never be able fully to sound its depths.

In addition to all this, St Benedict describes the structure which these times of communal prayer should have, and he does this by means of a detailed juridical code. What he prescribed was based on the Roman liturgical customs of his day, and, obviously, he took into consideration the spiritual needs of his monks, their cultural level, and the rhythm of daily life in the Italian countryside during the sixth century. We can see that fidelity to the Rule of St Benedict cannot consist in slavishly copying these structures which are so closely bound to an historical context of the past. It consists, rather, in *taking its spirit* so that we can, in our turn, express our common experience of the Mystery of Christ through our worship, taking into consideration the theological mentality and the liturgical tradition of our twentieth-century Church. It will mean also taking into consideration our own particular spiritual needs as influenced by our sociological and psychological context, and thus arrive at the rhythm of life of an authentic contemporary monasticism.

The task of reinterpretation of the Rule and of monastic renewal which has the contours I have just described cannot be the work of theorists. It ought to spring from the spiritual experience of the monastic orders and communities themselves. And to pursue such a work what we need above all is persons of spiritual greatness, charismatic men and women who know how to breathe a new dynamism into the monastic orders. Structural reforms are often necessary, sometimes to favor the flowering of charisms, sometimes for preserving the fruits of these charisms. But the monastic history shows us that a juridical reform remains fruitless unless it receives its life-breath from the Holy Spirit.

Armand Veilleux ocso

Abbey of Mistassini,
Village-des-Pères, P.Q., Canada

F

THE DEVELOPMENTAL DYNAMICS OF THE CISTERCIAN REFORM

THIS BRIEF STUDY in Cistercian history is meant to deepen our appreciation for, and investigate the nature of something mentioned already in this Symposium but which no other paper treats *ex professo*: the evolution within the Cistercian reform itself, the dynamic nature of this reform and the change, if there was any, or at least the possibility of change, within the spirit and aims of the founders and the members of the Cistercian Order.

If we are going to follow the suggestions of Bernard Lonergan on the different methodological functions in theology, such a study as this could be called *dialectics*. This presupposes investigation of the historical facts, their interpretation and knowledge of their historical context. Dialectics consists in comparing the various interpretations which different people have given to these facts, with a view to obtaining a true vision of reality and committing oneself to it through personal conversion. It is an encounter of persons and their doctrine. That is really what we are involved in here. We are going to see how this fact, the Cistercian fact, evolved, if it did, through the encounters of different persons in relation to this one movement.

To see the basic dynamics of the Cistercian movement, we can take as an example a more modern event, the Apollo project, the man on the moon. The modern movement started some time ago and its development has been subject to various influences in the course of its short history. Some of these influences come from outside the project itself and some come from within it. As we know it was galvanized by the fact that the Russians started before the Americans. This is an external fact which has caused changes in plans on the part of the Americans. It has accelerated the movement and changed methods. Time is another of the external facts that influence such development, to know the right timing. Then there are the internal factors of the project, the persons involved, plans modified through dialogue, the delay of the whole project because of the death of three astronauts.

We can thus see that, though it had a very specific and explicit purpose, an aim, a spirit, nevertheless the Apollo project was subject to development on the part of both external and internal factors. Something similar happened with the first Cistercians. We shall here look briefly at how the developmental dynamics of the Cistercian movement were affected by the influence of external factors. Then we shall consider internal factors and what is commonly spoken of as the difference between the "first generation" of Cistercians and the second.

The Influence of External Factors

With regard to the external factors, the most important point to realize is that the Cistercian reform took place within a general reform movement. We who live in the years following Vatican II have some idea of what this implies. Since another paper in this Symposium[1] treats of this precise point, it need not be developed here. We should just realize that the Cistercian movement was really the crown, the result and the fruit of a whole century of monastic reform movements.

In general, what characterized the Cistercian reform was the search for *authenticity*. This is frequently asserted, but it is more difficult to specify what authenticity means. Some would say that it is related to "authority," a more juridical concept. Others prefer to see it as derived from "author," implying a return to the sources. This is more of an historical definition. Let us attempt a dynamic definition, a more theological interpretation of the historical facts, a

---

1. Cf. above, Louis Lekai, pp. 27ff.

deeper penetration into this authenticity which certainly was one of the chief criteria for the reform movement of which the Cistercians were the best representatives. In this sense authenticity is the *correspondence of structures to charisms*. It springs from the inner necessity on the part of human nature, and all the more on the part of the Church of the Word Incarnate, to sacramentalize the impulse of the Spirit which is the heart and soul of the Church and of any movement within the Church. Authenticity is simply the capacity to express exteriorly in some poor way, not perfectly but at least adequately, the interior thrust of the Spirit: express exteriorly the interior dynamism within the structure. In other words, there is a correspondence of structures to charism. This is really the basic force in the reform movement.

Now, historically, the structures of the Cistercian reform were influenced by Cluny. In those days Cluny was the "big brother," the one who was always watching. Its influence in the eleventh-century and early twelfth-century monastic world was not exclusive but it certainly was dominant. Molesme, despite the reform movement of which it was an expression, adopted the structures of Cluny.[2] Thus Cîteaux in a true sense was a reform movement not only in relation to Molesme but beyond Molesme in relation to Cluny,[3] and the later controversy between St Bernard and Peter the Venerable was simply a development of the basic reaction on the part of the Cistercians against Cluniac structures. What characterized these structures was a highly centralized form of government. The abbot of Cluny was the abbot of all its foundations and small priories, and responsible also for hundreds of monasteries of varying size and importance. A common conception of Cluniac monasticism is that it consisted in very large monasteries. This is not really true. Cluny itself was big, but the majority of Cluniac monasteries

2. Jean-Baptist Van Damme, *Les Trois Fondateurs de Cîteaux* (pro manuscripto, Chambarand, 1967), pp. 31–35. An English translation of this will appear as No. IX in the Cistercian Studies Series.

3. For further development of this and the following paragraphs, see Comunidad de Azul, *La comunidad monastica en los movimientos de Cluny y de Cister*, in *Cistercium*, XXI (1969), pp. 3–40, with the references indicated there.

were more like granges, highway houses on the side of the road. They were small chapels with communities probably averaging between six to ten members. The superior of these communities was a Prior named and removed at the discretion of the abbot of Cluny. The novices had to go to Cluny to make their profession. The income of these little houses also went to Cluny. This was not because of greed on the part of Cluny, but rather a defense mechanism to protect these little houses from the greed of the nobles and the feudal lords. The vast authority and prestige of the abbot of Cluny protected these monasteries from a hostile environment where greed, force of arms and untamed passions dominated the secular scene. The highly centralized structures of Cluny were a necessary defense against this milieu.

The spirituality of Cluny would inevitably express this centralized defense mechanism. The world was viewed in a somewhat dualistic fashion. The world outside the monastery was looked upon rather negatively. At the same time, the Cluniac attitude toward material goods was really very Christian: the monk is a priest of creation, whose vocation is to glorify God by using the material goods of the world and dedicate them to art and to liturgy in order to give glory to God and establish the kingdom of God on earth. Almsgiving was another expression of this same world view. The asceticism of Cluny was based on this outlook. At its heart was fidelity in body, mind and heart to the Divine Office. It was a liturgical asceticism with surprising flexibility in the day to day monastic life. The structures and the spirituality of Cluny enjoyed a great success, especially in the last part of the tenth century, through the eleventh and up to 1109, when Hugh, the last of the four great abbots of Cluny, died. This was more than ten years after the foundation of Cîteaux.

Cîteaux was an attempt at what we may call a humanizing of the Cluniac structures. One of the points which was at the forefront from the very beginning of Cîteaux was the desire to have autonomous abbeys and abbots. The lack of this was one of the weakest points of the Cluniac system. Perhaps the first Cistercians did not realize it entirely, but nowadays we can see that it was not merely a going back to the Rule of St Benedict, which prescribes an abbot in charge of the monastic family. It was really a human necessity. If monastic life is to be an evangelical life and to sanctify men, to lead men to a God of love, then it should provide a milieu in which basic human necessities are met, and to have a more or less independent family environment is one of these human necessities. Psychologically we need to feel that our family can stand by itself. This is one of the arguments for the autonomy of a monastery. Thus we can understand the feelings and intuitions of the first Cistercians in this regard.

Actually, even before the founding of Cîteaux, in the foundation of Aulps by Molesme in 1097, this necessity of having a local abbot was stressed.[4] The tendency toward local autonomy is thus at the very root of the reform of Cîteaux. The other salient features, solitude, poverty, a balanced life in which a total gift of self can most perfectly be reached, all these presupposed local autonomy.

Another of the basic factors behind the success of Cîteaux over the other previous reforms which were in many ways similar to it was that the secular culture of the time had reached a more purified grade of humanistic values. It had become a truly fertile bed for a new type of spirituality, where greater emphasis is given to the human person and to his interior dignity above all the material world. Thus we see in the eleventh and twelfth centuries the development of schools, trade guilds, the capacity to travel more from town to town without fear of being waylaid by bandits. Especially important was the development of courtly love. Human romantic love was one of the preoccupations of that day: what it was and how it should be expressed.[5] This resulted from the increased sensitivity on the part of society to human values, of which love is the greatest, and explains how St Bernard can enter Cîteaux and express the value of the monastic life which he embraces there in terms of love.

---

4. See *Documenta pro Cisterciensis ordinis . . . studio,* ed. J.-B. Van Damme (Westmalle, 1959), p. 3.

5. Cf. Etienne Gilson, *The Mystical Theology of St Bernard* (London, 1940), pp. 200–202.

Summing up briefly the role of external forces upon the development of the Cistercian reform, we can say that the first Cistercians were searching for authenticity of external structures in correspondence to the interior dynamism of the monastic life. In the process, they were reacting somewhat to an inauthentic structure as represented in the Cluniac monasticism. The amazing growth of the Order was made possible by the favorable milieu of the society of that period in European history.

Internal Dynamics of the Cistercian Movement
a)   *The First Founders*

Now let us take a look at the internal factors which influenced the development of the Cistercian phenomenon. These are both more interesting and more delicate than the external factors. First of all, is there any development among the three first founding Fathers, Robert, Alberic and Stephen, in regard to general spirit and specific aims? Does St Stephen show any development over the intuitions and purposes of St Robert? This requires considerable study. A necessary preliminary step is to arrive at a critical text of the basic documents of this period.

We can, however, observe certain signs of evolution. In general, there seems to have been a very natural and healthy shift of emphasis from a more negative attitude to a more positive purpose. We see this in secular movements, for instance in the founding of a country. There is first a strong, somewhat negative reaction, a war of independence, a declaration of affirmation of liberty. It is usually expressed in a negative way: "We don't want to pay tea taxes." "No one can tell us what to do," or "No taxation without representation." All these are claims for liberty, but in a negative sense. However, they are enough to set the ball rolling. Then the revolutionaries ask themselves, "Well, here we are, free; now what do we do with our freedom?" That is the way by which structures begin, such as the Constitutional Congress which met eleven years after the Declaration of Independence. This type of development occurred not only in America but in other countries as well. It corresponds to the nature of any institutional movement. The dynamism is basically one, but the first expressions of it tend to be negative. Something more positive follows later.

We can see this duality at work in the founders of Cîteaux. There was from the beginning a driving thrust toward authenticity of structures and simplicity of life, but the Little Exordium shows the inevitable reaction against Molesme:

> You pledged yourselves to follow from now on more strictly and more perfectly the Rule of St Benedict, which so far in that monastery you have observed poorly and neglectfully. Since it has been proven that because of many hindering circumstances you could not accomplish your aim in the aforementioned place, we . . . consider that it would be expedient for you to retire to another place.[6]

The result of this affirmation of authenticity was the founding of the New Monastery. It would seem that the emphasis placed on their debt of conscience to live according to the Rule of St Benedict came more as a justification of their action, which at that time had to be found in a written document. This explains the great emphasis placed on the Rule in the primitive documents, especially the Little Exordium.[7] The Rule of St Benedict was the obvious choice to justify juridically, but not artificially, the interior dynamism of the reform which had sprung from a quest for authenticity inspired by the Holy Spirit.[8] This reference to the Holy Rule was the springboard for a more positive affirmation of the reform's purpose which reaches its zenith in the mystical doctrine of St Bernard.

Other more specific developments in the first years of the New Monastery were the introduction of the lay-brothers by St Alberic

6. Little Exordium, trans. Robert E. Larkin, in Louis Lekai, *The White Monks* (Okauchee, Wis., 1953), p. 252.

7. Cf. J.-B. Van Damme, *The Essential Factors of the Cistercian Reform,* (pro manuscripto, Westmalle, 1967), pp. 4–5.

8. Cf. *Note from the Psalter of St Robert,* trans. M. B. Pennington, in "Three Early Documents" in *Cistercian Studies,* IV (1969), p. 143 and Little Exordium, *loc. cit.,* p. 253: "These men, while still living in Molesme and inspired by divine grace . . . ."

and the approbation by the Pope of the autonomy of Cîteaux. This latter is expressed in a letter found in the Little Exordium, which includes the very meaningful phrase, "We forbid anyone change your way of life."[9] This marks the beginning of a secondary dynamism which will make itself felt more strongly in later years: unity of observance. From the statement of Pope Paschal II it is just one logical step to the decision that, when monasteries are founded from Cîteaux, they will follow the same observance as the Mother House.[10]

A further development is St Stephen's greater stress on true physical separation from the world. Thus he bans the nobles from holding court at the New Monastery.[11] We see then even among the first founders a certain evolution.

b)   *The Generation Gap*

We come now to the arrival of St Bernard. There certainly is a development, or at least a contrast, between some elements of the Cistercian reform which the first founders established at Cîteaux and the attitudes of the second generation, especially as they are expressed by the abbot of Clairvaux. In general we can reduce the contrasting elements to five:

i) The first difference we note is that of *spirituality*. Perhaps a better word would be spiritual tonality. It is what strikes us in the sermons of St Bernard, especially in those on the Canticle of Canticles. The tone here is different from that in the Charter of Charity or in other early writings such as the Little Exordium. The question is, is there inconsistency between the abbot of Cîteaux and the abbot of Clairvaux?

The very fact that St Bernard influenced the composition of both the Charter and the Exordium[12] will make us hesitate in giving an

---

9. Little Exordium, *op. cit.*, p. 261.

10. *The Charter of Charity*, trans. Denis Murphy sj, in Louis Lekai, *op. cit.*

11. Little Exordium, *loc. cit.*, pp. 264–265.

12. Cf. J.-B. Van Damme, *Les Trois Fondateurs*, p. 168.

affirmative reply to the question. Perhaps it can best be answered by saying that Stephen is a realist and Bernard an allegorist.[13] The abbot of Cîteaux has the realism of a legislator, St Bernard has the imagination, the intuition of someone who has experienced the depths of the Christian mystery which is beyond words. Therefore the allegory. The basic fact is that Bernard first of all gave himself over to the reform of Cîteaux in soul and body. Under the tutelage and watchful eye of St Stephen he experienced in the New Monastery what can be called the mystery of Cistercian life.[14] With his intellectual training and genius he was able to penetrate and analyze this experience in a way we cannot demand from St Stephen, nor from any other Cistercian Father.

St Bernard was a religious genius who analyzed a profound experience and expressed it. But what he expressed was the same Cistercian experience which the first generation of founders had sought for and lived. He was entirely in line with them. What he added was an analysis of this spiritual experience, his own experience, which he made with the help of his great personal capacities of analysis, synthesis and expression. But as regards spirit and aim, Bernard's orientation is a very consistent expression of the fundamental aim and spirit of the founding Fathers. The spirituality of the second generation was like the fruit which bursts forth from the tree, or like a mighty river which is such because of what it has received from the streams which are its source.

Actually, in looking back upon the first generation, we can see that St Stephen and the other founders also gave expression to a religious experience. Although the Little Exordium was probably written by a disciple of St Bernard at Clairvaux, nevertheless it represents a tonality more akin to the foundation at Cîteaux. In it we have the phrase, "discarding the old man they enjoyed putting

---

13. Commission d'Histoire de l'Ordre de Cîteaux, *Bernard de Clairvaux* (Paris, 1953), pp. 170–180. These pages are the most thorough treatment in print on the thorny question of the relations between the first two Cistercian generations.

14. Gilson, *op. cit.*, pp. 4–18.

on the new one."[15] This putting on of the new man was simply the putting on of Christ, and St Bernard's experience was nothing else but this. He experienced it and expressed it in an especially profound way, but it is specifically the same experience as the putting on of Christ by the founders of Cîteaux.

Another example of this basic unity of spirituality: love is given as the motive for the union of the monasteries described in the Charter of Charity[16] and the letter of St Stephen accompanying the first Cistercian Hymnal also underlines the motive of love.[17] St Bernard comes, experiences this same love of Christ and expresses it as only he can. There is a difference, but it is merely a difference of intensity and expression.

A final basis of unity of spirit between the generations is found in the Rule of St Benedict. The first generation centered their way of life on fidelity to the Rule. Now the center of the Rule, as we see it in the finale of the steps of humility, is simply the victory of love over fear and pride. It is this victory of love, at the very heart of the Rule, which St Bernard and the other Fathers of the second generation were able to express.

ii) A second point of development between the two generations, the one which has probably caused the most comment in recent years, is the question of *monastic simplicity and poverty*. The facts here are obvious, e.g. the explicitly different attitudes concerning the embellishment of manuscripts. In the first years of Cîteaux, under the direction of Alberic and Stephen, the manuscripts copied in the monastery's modest scriptorium were embellished with colored miniatures, according to the custom of the time. Also, sculpturing and music were encouraged. Then St Bernard appears, with his more ascetic and austere norms. It is significant that the exchange of criticisms between Peter the Venerable of Cluny and the Cistercians did not occur with Stephen, whose position as abbot of Cîteaux corresponded with that of Peter, but rather with Bernard who at

15. Little Exordium, *loc. cit.,* p. 262.
16. Charter of Charity, Preface, *loc. cit.,* p. 267.
17. In "Three Early Documents," *op. cit.,* pp. 144f.

that time was only thirty-two years old. Besides this, the enactment of the General Chapter against colored miniatures and ornate sculpturing occurred immediately after the resignation of Stephen as abbot of Cîteaux. All this seems to indicate the extensive influence of St Bernard and a marked difference of opinion between the second generation and the first. In fact it has been suggested that this was one of the major causes for St Stephen's resignation.

Against such an hypothesis of conflict between the two first generations, more recent studies[18] indicate that it would be more logical to attribute these differences to other factors. The fact that Peter the Venerable writes to Bernard and not Stephen should be attributed to the letter which the former had written to his nephew, Robert, who had left Clairvaux for Cluny.[19] Peter's letter was simply a rebuttal of Bernard's. Besides, Bernard had an uncle who was a monk of Cluny; he came from a well-known family of that region and his own personal genius was undoubtedly beginning to assert itself by that time. For all these reasons it would not be out of place if Peter the Venerable directed himself to Bernard instead of to St Stephen.

In general, there are two ways of interpreting the emphasis placed by the second generation Cistercians on external simplicity. One way is to attribute it to a real difference of spirit and a clash of personalities between St Bernard and his spiritual father, Stephen. However, this clash of personalities is not confirmed by any evidence or witness. It can only be admitted by presuming a very successful deletion of references to it in all existing documents of the period. On the other hand, the change of emphasis is easily explained as a normal evolution due chiefly to the polemics against the Cluniacs. St Bernard replied to Peter the Venerable by writing his *Apologia* to William of St Thierry. It is an accusation against both the Cistercians and the Cluniacs. Bernard admits that the Cistercians may be lacking in charity, discretion and humility. Then he points

18. Cf. Commission d'Histoire, *op. cit.,* and Van Damme, *Les Trois Fundateurs.*

19. Letter I in *The Letters of St Bernard of Clairvaux,* trans. B. James (London: Burns Oates, 1953), pp. 1ff.

to the failings of the Cluniacs: fine foods, furs, large ornate churches, costly paintings and statues, departures from the faithful observance to the Holy Rule.[20]

Bernard, with a rhetorical exaggeration typical of him and of the epoch, traces in the *Apologia* the outline of a program of Cistercian simplicity and poverty which was accepted by the Order, including St Stephen, as a norm for future regulations. It is even highly probable that Bernard consulted with Stephen before answering the charges of the abbot of Cluny. A recent study of St Stephen Harding describes the situation:

> We do not have to wait until the diatribe of St Bernard against the frivolities of sculpture and painting of his time in order to recognize the firm decision of the founders of Cîteaux to seek a spiritual beauty characterized above all by a stripping away of all that could distract a monk from prayer. . . . This manifests the true unity of spirit and of heart between father and son, between St Stephen and St Bernard. For, contrary to what is commonly thought, these two abbots do not differ in the least in their conception of the sobriety and simplicity which characterized the Cistercian reform. Everything that St Bernard says in the *Apologia* can be found in the form of laws among the legislative texts in force in 1119 and even since the beginnings of Cîteaux. Bernard had a great esteem and a profound veneration for him whom he called "The Lord of Cîteaux." These sentiments were reciprocated on the part of the abbot of Cîteaux who loved to recognize and to foster the manifold gifts of his spiritual sons.[21]

There were undoubted differences of temperament, of character and of religious feeling between Stephen and Bernard, but until some truly valid evidence of a sharp split between them is produced, it would be more historically correct to explain the added stress on

20. Cf. especially *Apologia ad Guillermo*, nos. 16ff., *S. Bernardi Opera*, ed. Leclercq and Rochais, Vol. 3 (Rome: Editiones Cistercienses, 1963), pp. 95ff.; trans. M. Casey, *Cistercians and Cluniacs: St Bernard's Apologia to Abbot William, The Works of Bernard of Clairvaux*, Vol. 1, Cistercian Fathers Series, I.

21. Van Damme, *Les Trois Fundateurs*, pp. 115, 150–151. See Little Exordium, c. 17, p. 265.

external poverty and simplicity as a legitimate development in expressing a single principle of monastic asceticism which the first two Cistercian generations held in common.

iii) A third area in which there is evident a difference between the Cistercians of the first and second generations is in the *policy of expansion*, the establishment of foundations. The basis of this difference is the extremely rapid expansion of the Order, especially after 1134, that is to say after the resignation of St Stephen as abbot of Cîteaux. It is here especially that we meet St Bernard as a unique personality. We know how young men and old from all walks of life were drawn into the wake left by Bernard in his trips through Europe. His own personal experience of the Cistercian vocation as the only means by which he himself could fully correspond to God's call, and his realization of the power of the love of Christ to turn human weakness into a meeting place with the Spouse persuaded him that all men received an equal call. The result was a prodigious rate of expansion for the whole Order and, above all, for Clairvaux and its foundations.

It has been well said that, given the fact that the Cistercian way of life was called upon to develop, expand and multiply, "it was better that this be done under the aegis of one inspired, a great spiritual theologian,"[22] even though such a spiritual leader should cast into the balance, as was humanly inevitable, his extraordinary personality and his own personal charisms. These personal charisms of the abbot of Clairvaux, it hardly needs to be stated, did not coincide at every point with the most authentic expressions of the intentions of the first founders of Cîteaux. The resultant crisis of growth reached its climax with the incorporation into the Order in 1147 of the Congregations of Savigny and Obazine. Bernard heartily approved of the incorporation of these monasteries despite the fact that they continued to have, and were permitted by the General Chapter to have features which went against the Cistercian ideals of poverty and separation from the world: serfs, tithes and a certain apostolate.

22. Cf. *infra*, J. Leclercq, "The Intentions of the Founders of the Order of Cîteaux," p. 115.

It seems that he was unconcerned with these uncistercian elements and the consequences which they imply.

At the same time, it must be admitted that St Stephen himself never opposed the Order's expansion. The incorporation of Savigny and Obazine occurred over ten years after his death. There is no evidence that during his lifetime he opposed Bernard's charism of drawing men to the reform. Actually, Bernard himself frequently discouraged other monks from becoming Cistercians.[23] He thought it better for them to remain in their own houses and improve the observance of their own monasteries. Nevertheless, it is safe to say that Bernard's policy in favoring the incorporation of Savigny and Obazine in 1147 is the largest single witness to a difference of spirit between him and St Stephen, and between the second generation and the first.

If we should ask of the Cistercians, as Fr Basil Pennington has indicated,[24] what they chose and why they chose it, it is especially necessary here that we ask why the second generation permitted the incorporation of elements which were obviously contrary to fundamental principles of the first founders of the Order. The reason is probably that they did not think of the consequences. A lessening of standards concerning poverty and separation from the world was certainly not in the minds of the Cistercians of 1147. Clairvaux, in particular, until the year of St Bernard's death, resolutely refused to accept donations of property with serfs.[25] It is thus not so much a difference of aims and intentions, as of means used and permitted. There seems to have been in St Bernard a certain naive enthusiasm, perhaps a fruit of his own religious experience, which went beyond the more cautious and more

---

23. Cf. St Bernard, *De Precepto et Dispensatione*, no. 46, *S. Bernardi Opera*, ed. Leclercq and Rochais, Vol. 3, p. 285; trans. C. Greenia, *Monastic Obligations and Abbatial Authority: St Bernard's Book On Precept and Dispensation*, *The Works of Bernard of Clairvaux*, Vol. 1 (Cistercian Fathers VI.); Letters 3, 32ff., 65ff., 253, 382, 396; trans. James, Letters 3, 33ff., 68ff., 328, 419, 428.

24. Cf. *supra*, p. 1.

25. Leclercq, *infra*, p. 126.

humanly prudent spirit of Stephen Harding. Bernard had experienced in himself and in others the overpowering force of God's grace, which had overcome such obstacles to Christ's kingdom that he knew that God could perform miracles. As often happens with the saints, one could say that he was over-idealistic or unrealistic. He was over-optimistic. He did not see, perhaps, all the human elements which would jeopardize his own ideals. He did not fully realize that other people had not had the same experiences which he had had.

At any rate, this is certainly what happened in 1147. It was only five years after the incorporation of the Congregations of Savigny and Obazine into the Order that the General Chapter decided not to establish any more foundations.[26] On the level of quantitative expansion, the Order had over-developed, and the second generation saw very quickly, even before the death of St Bernard, that the policy of multiplying foundations was doing harm to the spirit according to which it had been founded and through which it had developed.

iv) The fourth element which might seem to show a development between the first and second generations is that of *apostolic activity outside the Order*. It might be thought that St Bernard, by his many travels on behalf of the Church, introduced an extraneous element into the Cistercian spirit. It has been pointed out that a third of St Bernard's monastic life was spent in long trips through Europe, while another third was spent in shorter trips and absences because of sickness. Thus only a third of his monastic career was spent in the monastery of which he was abbot.

We have to say, however, that Bernard made up in quality what he was unable to give in temporal quantity. Moreover, he himself was the first to say that he was not the ideal on this point. Several times he made strong resolutions never to go out of the monastery again, except under obedience and, in fact, his departures were imposed from without and cannot be taken to represent his aim or intentions. Nevertheless, they do bear witness to a tension inherent

26. Statutes of the General Chapter of 1152, no. 1, ed. J. Canivez, *Statuta Capitulorum Generalium Ordinis Cisterciensis ab anno* 1116 *ad annum* 1786 (Louvain: Bureaux de la Revue, 1933), vol. I, p. 45.

in the developmental dynamics of the Cistercian reform. The tension experienced by Bernard is felt also with the growth of the Order. Society and the Church will inevitably demand help from any generation of Cistercian monks, who in turn have the burden of both serving the Church and defending their charism from extraneous elements. Ordinarily they will not have the apostolic charisms of the abbot of Clairvaux, which of themselves are extraneous to the Cistercian charism.

v) A final contrasting element between the first Cistercians and their successors consists in the marked growth of the *power of the General Chapter*, with a corresponding decline in the role of the abbot of Cîteaux. This has been made especially clear by the recent studies of Fr Jean-Baptiste Van Damme.[27] We can here only present the conclusions of his papers which are based on careful analyses of the primitive documents and of the living context from which they grew.

The undeniable fact is that both the Little Exordium and the Charter of Charity were subject to important internal changes, additions and precisions throughout the first 70 years of the Order's existence. Especially important was the development experienced by the Charter of Charity. The document, whose first draft was made necessary by the foundation of Cîteaux's initial daughter house, La Ferté, in 1113, was presented to Pope Callixtus II for his approval, which was duly given in 1119. At this time there were less than fifteen monasteries in the federation of abbeys. The first granddaughter house of Cîteaux, Trois-Fontaines, was founded by Clairvaux in 1118 and seems not to have influenced the document presented to the Pope.[28] At this time Stephen, the abbot of Cîteaux,

---

27. See his major studies on the development of Cistercian law: "Genèse des Instituta Generalis Capituli" in *Cîteaux*, 12 (1961), pp. 28–60; "Autour des Origines Cisterciennes" in *Collectanea OCR*, 20 (1958), pp. 156–168; "Formation de la Constitution Cistercienne" in *Studia Monastica*, 4 (1962), pp. 111–137; "Les pouvoirs de l'Abbé de Cîteaux aux XII et XIII siècle" in *Analecta Cisterciense*, 24 (1968), pp. 47–85.

28. Charter of Charity, *loc. cit.,* p. 270; and Van Damme, "Les pouvoirs", pp. 48–49.

G

with the Conventual Chapter of that house, was the supreme authority within the Order. The abbots of the dozen-odd daughter houses belonged to the Chapter, and met annually at the mother house. They were all subject to Stephen as to their Father Immediate, as the following passage of the Charter of Charity, written in the person of "Father Stephen and his brethren," indicates:

> We wish henceforward and command them (i.e., the other abbots and brethren) to observe the rule of St Benedict in everything, as it is observed in the New Monastery, and to understand it in no other sense than that which our pious forefathers of Cîteaux have given to it and maintained, and which we ourselves now understand and hold after their example.[29]

Other passages, however, show clearly that at a later date, with the vast multiplication of filiations, the abbots themselves, united in General Chapter, constituted the supreme authority of the Order:

> In the General Chapter, the abbots shall consult upon matters that appertain to the salvation of souls, and shall ordain what is to be corrected, or what carried out in the observance of the rule and the institutions of the Order. They shall likewise mutually confirm each other in the bond of peace and charity.[30]

The change of authority is especially obvious in the final statute of the Charter of Charity treating of the deposition of the abbot of Cîteaux.[31]

This important evolution in the government of the new Order began immediately after 1120, when it became clear that the daughter houses of Cîteaux were in their turn to found many new abbeys. It found expression in the decisions of the General Chapter of 1134, probably due in part to the resignation of St Stephen as abbot, and was codified in the final redaction of the Charter of Charity made in 1165.[32] The supreme authority of the Order,

29. Charter of Charity, *loc. cit.,* pp. 267–268.
30. *Ibid.,* p. 270.   31. *Ibid.,* p. 273.
32. For details, see Van Damme, "Les Pouvoirs," pp. 50–59.

which at first was oligarchical in nature, becomes collegial. Until 1120, the abbot of Cîteaux directed the new Order in spiritual and disciplinary matters, as an abbot presiding over his conventual chapter. The other abbots were responsible in the administration of their abbeys to him and the rest of the community of Cîteaux. After 1120, however, the practical details of an expanding union of autonomous abbeys necessitated a development in the juridical structure of the reform. The General Chapter became independent of the conventual chapter of Cîteaux and subjected to itself the abbot of the Order's first house, together with all other Fathers Immediate. Because of his house's importance in the history of the Order, the abbot of Cîteaux enjoys certain prerogatives at the General Chapter, the more important of which is his influence in forming commissions and in bringing long debates to a necessary conclusion.

Was this dynamic evolution in the power of the General Chapter a perversion or a consequence of the spirit and aims of the first Cistercian generation? Without hesitation we can say that, far from being a perversion, it was in full harmony with the tendency that, as we have seen, was at the center of the Cistercian reform: the movement toward autonomous houses with their own abbot, living according to the Rule of St Benedict. Although we can well believe that St Stephen Harding experienced great tensions in guiding his daughter houses and their respective filiations to a happy balance of autonomy and unity, there is no evidence that he himself opposed this evolution, which he must have seen as a practical and logical necessity. The overcentralized system of Cluny served as a warning to both first and second generation Cistercians of the dangers to be avoided. The basic thrust of the Order's governmental evolution, however, sprang from inner necessity rather than from a reaction against Cluniac paternalism.

Conclusions and Contemporary Applications

We have seen that the developmental dynamics of primitive Cîteaux was in the direction of authenticity of structures, their more perfect correspondence with the monastic charism. This dynamism was first expressed negatively in relation to the Cluniac structures followed at Molesme. It achieved a more positive formulation in the Little Exordium and the Charter of Charity. Its spiritual content found expression in the words and writings of St Bernard and the other Cistercian Fathers of the second generation.

In this process of self-development and expression a certain evolution was both necessary and healthy. We have seen signs of such evolution among the first founders of Cîteaux and have indicated five general areas of development in the years which constitute the Golden Age of the Order, the years of the second generation, from 1113 to 1153. These areas are spirituality, monastic simplicity, expansion of the Order, apostolic activity and the authority of the General Chapter. What do these elements of growth within the Cistercian event imply for an evaluation of the Cistercian charism both in the twelfth century and now?

First of all, there is possible, within the Cistercian Order, a generation gap, a difference of opinions or of emphasis due to age, social structures, and the like. Our study shows that this is normal and is far from being a sign of sickness or of lack of authenticity. It is really a sign of dynamic life and growth, highly compatible with fidelity to the Cistercian charism. We have seen this especially in comparing the second Cistercian generation with the first.

Yet we have seen that the generation gap was not as great as has been frequently stated. It would be fruitful for further research to show how the differences between the two generations were influenced by the changed social environments from which their respective members came into the monastery. We should also advert to the important fact that there is a more fundamental difference of spirit between the third Cistercian generation and the second than there is between the first two generations. In other words, the time after the death of St Bernard was a time of more essential modification within the Order than that which occurred in the passage from the first generation to the second. It was a time of codification rather than of growth. The death of Bernard in 1153 thus marks a point at which the less favorable consequences of policies adopted or permitted in previous years became increasingly evident, without the personal dynamism of the abbot of Clairvaux to hold them in check.

A second conclusion arising from reflection on the development of the Cistercian reform is that the Cistercian spirit allows for a legitimate plurality of expression within the one vocation. How wide can this plurality be? As regards the first two Cistercian generations, we can say that the plurality of expression is almost exclusively a matter of emphasizing certain aspects of the spirit and aims more than others (poverty and simplicity), and drawing out the fruit of the founders' basic intuitions (spirituality and authority of the General Chapter).

We say "almost exclusively a matter of emphasis" because the incorporation of the Congregations of Savigny and Obazine into the Order represents less fidelity to the aims and spirit of the founders and a certain imprudent lack of foresight and authenticity. Far from being a dynamic development, it was one of the contributing factors to a paralyzing stagnation which becomes more evident as the thirteenth century approaches. Plurality, then, should not compromise values such as poverty, separation from the world, or the integrally contemplative life which are at the heart of the Cistercian reform.

The plurality in the expression of spiritual values is especially significant. We have seen that a body of mystical theology was developed which was not contrary by any means to the intentions of the first founders of Cîteaux, but gave a tonality to Cistercian spirituality which was not so in evidence at the beginning. The charity of Christ was the heart and foundation of the Cistercian life for both generations. Stephen Harding crystallized juridically this charity as the binding force of a new type of monastic confederation, based essentially on love rather than on a feudal type of hierarchal paternalism. St Bernard and the other Cistercian Fathers expressed the same charity as an internal force which overcomes the infinite distance between God and man in order to achieve the aim of all monastic structures—the union of spirit between creature and Creator.

This difference in emphasis reveals a tension or dialectic at the heart of the Cistercian charism. It is the dialectic between juridic structures and spiritual liberty, between the monastic institution and the personal experience of God. A lesson which we can learn from the first years of the Cistercian Order is that both elements are necessary. Structures are ambivalent. They both hide the spiritual and lead to it. They are only a means, but without a balanced juridic structure the spirit soon weakens and vanishes. It is the task for each generation to recognize the necessity for *both* elements, to pay special attention to the needs of the Order in each concrete set of historical circumstances, and to see that the structures of the Cistercian life do truly serve their spiritual purpose. This tension is one of the primary factors in the developmental dynamics of the Cistercian reform.

The basic criteria for judging plurality within the Cistercian charism is, it seems to me, the fundamental intuition of both the first and the second Cistercian generations. It could be called the *eschatological orientation* to accomplish in one's own life, body and soul, the reign of God; to experience the permanent interior dimension of the Kingdom of God and to make this dimension available to other men on the institutional level, in so far as this is possible.[33] In this context we can understand how secondary elements such as art, music or literature, could find different modes of expression among the first two generations, whereas the incorporation of Savigny and Obazine, with their compromising elements, represents an aberration from this fundamental orientation.

A final lesson we can learn from our brief study is the primacy of love in both the spirit of the founders and in the developmental dynamics of the Cistercian reform. We have seen in different ways how the expression of the love of Christ poured forth by the Holy Spirit was subject to development as the first generation gave place to the second, and as the second ceded to the third. The first founders expressed their love in the establishment of a way of life,

---

33. This orientation is implicit in the statutes of the Little Exordium restricting involvement in worldly affairs, *loc. cit.*, pp. 263ff., and explicit in the writings of the Cistercian Fathers. See especially, St Bernard, *Sermons on the Song of Songs, passim.* Cf. Comunidad de Azul, *art. cit.*, p. 95.

an institution, an Order. The second generation took this way of life and found through it the experience of the Lover. The third generation could only attempt to maintain this institution and this experience from excessive contamination by extraneous elements.

The basic dynamic of the Cistercian movement is thus the expression of the love of Christ in a union of cenobitic abbeys dedicated, above all, to the permanent interior dimension of the Kingdom of God. This was the driving force witnessed to in sacrificial silence by the founders of the New Monastery, institutionalized through the prudence of St Stephen and proclaimed by Bernard of Clairvaux as the pearl of great price.

Augustine Roberts ocso

Nuestra Señora de los Angelos,
Azul, Argentina

THE INTENTIONS OF THE FOUNDERS
OF THE CISTERCIAN ORDER

ACCORDING TO VATICAN II, the norm for the renewal of religious orders should first of all be founded in the Gospel. Secondly, it should be based upon the proper spirit and aims of the founders: *fundatorum spiritus propriaque proposita,*[1] and then also upon the "sound traditions which form part of the patrimony of each institute." This third element is worded in such a manner as to give the impression that traditions might have been introduced which are not, or are no longer, signs of health, but of age or illness. Practices recorded in texts such as constitutions, customaries, prayer books, should be subject to re-examination.[2] Between the unalterable factor which is the Gospel and these changing data of history, the permanent point of reference remains "the spirit of the founders"—and this includes a certain inspiration. It is, then, precisely a question of discerning "what purposes, what intentions" the founders, under the Spirit of God, sought to realize in the Church and within an institute which would come to their followers as a heritage, living and efficacious for salvation.

Whoever wishes to seek the answer to this question in regard to the Cistercian Order should reread the primitive texts as objectively as possible, adhering very closely to their content and paying special attention to their vocabulary. They are the sources that bear

---

1. *Perfectae caritatis,* no. 2.   2. *Ibid.,* no. 3.

witness of the origins. Moreover, he must consider their literary genres, taking into account their rhetoric, their exaggeration, their themes and their common background.[3]

Research material pertaining to the origin of the Cistercian Order is of three kinds, and these must be examined: documents of a historical nature relating to the beginnings, the writings of the privileged witness—St Bernard—and, finally, the comments of those who fell heir to this tradition during the first generations of the Order and who testify to the contemporary thought concerning the origins.

THE FACT AND THE INSTITUTIONS

To know the facts and the institutions it is necessary to read consecutively each of the documents which tell of them.[4] Through such a procedure one comes to know the circumstances of the foundation of Cîteaux, the intentions of its founders and the first statutes they enacted.

Before examining the documents it is good to point out the difficult problem of method which they raise. Indeed, there can be no question here of anticipating the results of the vast and delicate research work which remains to be undertaken. A critical edition of the earliest monuments of Cistercian history is still lacking.[5] One of the first tasks of the investigator will be to disclose as well as possible what lies beneath what might be called the maze of successive editorial layers, the stages of elaboration of each of these texts. On one and the same page can be found, for example, elements dating back to 1119 and others which belong to the year 1151. As is normal, legislation followed life and developed with progressing experience.

3. For the sake of convenience the texts here are cited according to the edition of J.-B. Van Damme OCSO, *Documenta pro Cisterciensis Ordinis historiae ac juris studio* (Westmalle: Typis Ordinis Cist., 1959). (Hereafter Doc.) Where possible an English translation will be indicated.

4. The texts are used according to the chronological order given by Van Damme, *op. cit.*

5. This fact is pointed out by P. Zakar, "Réponse aux 'Quelques à-propos' . . ." in *Analecta Cisterciensia*, 21 (1965), p. 166.

Thus, for example, it was only little by little that the Cistercian concept of ownership was clearly defined. The minute examination of numerous charters, in part unedited, and of Papal bulls, will some day permit a glimpse of how this came about.[6] Literary analysis and diplomatic inquiry will enable the reader to discern in the documents, which tradition goes back to the first generation— that of the founders—and which dates from the second generation. The latter, under the influence of St Bernard, and under pressure of various circumstances, in particular the conflict with the Cluniacs, has, so to speak, produced a theory of what was first lived—a process which inevitably involves an interpretation of the facts, a reinterpretation of the first documents and an elucidation of the intentions of the founders. It is, therefore, evident what care must be taken in the study of the texts as we have them today and what prudence is required in reaching conclusions.

Events and Circumstances

There are two documents purported to be contemporaneous with the beginnings of Cîteaux and anterior to the appearance of all the literature concerning it. The first is the Foundation Charter of the Abbey of Aulps of 1097. This document states clearly the intention of the founders. It employs the word *arctius*, which reappears later many times in the Cistercian documents. It is used to express the determination "to adhere to the precepts of St Benedict more strictly." The same document returns to the question of this distinctive strictness more than once.[7]

6. Two studies of J. Dubois OSB illustrate the kind of research that must yet be done: under the title of "L'institution des convers au XIIe siècle, forme de vie monastique propre aux laics" in *I Laici nella "societas christiana" dei secoli XI e XII* (Milan: Ed. Vita e Pensiero, 1968), pp. 183–261, in particular pp. 186–199 and 210–212, consecrated to the Cistercian lay-brothers, he gives interesting and new insights on the Cistercian origins; and in an article on "Les ordres religieux au XIIe siècle selon la curie romaine," *Revue Bénédictine*, 78 (1968), pp. 87ff. he points out again other facts and problems. The end of the present article is not to enter into the controversy, nor to bring new matter to it, but to propose a synthetic view which comes out of an impartial and, so to speak, ingenuous reading of the texts which we actually have.

7. Doc, p. 3.

The second document is of the concord of Molesme of 1110 signed by the three abbeys of Aulps, Balerne and Molesme. In it, we find a concern lest they fail to have sufficient respect for the Holy Rule. In both these documents the communal structure established in the Rule is taken for granted. It is a matter of communities governed by an abbot. However, in the second, one can detect a marked insistence on the conventual—today we would say "collegial"—character of the decisions: "the judgment of all the rest of the brethren . . . the whole community of the brethren taking part . . . by common consent . . . indeed the whole community, the little and the great, the seniors with the juniors."[8]

The two important documents attributed to the year 1119 have a character at once doctrinal and legislative, but they differ in kind— and this difference is important to note. The Little Exordium recounts an experience, and by means of it describes the round of daily life such as they loved to represent it to themselves. The Charter of Charity establishes the organization of the Order.

From the prologue of the Exordium one sees that what specifies the foundation is the intention of observing the Holy Rule, of entering upon the narrow way which it points out, *in arta et angusta via quam regula demonstrat*. Now this it would seem was undertaken by the founders of Cîteaux as if it had never before been done.[9] They insist on this point in the first chapters, where they reproduced letters of Church authorities approving the foundation and granting it privileges. They live "beneath the shelter of the Holy Rule," *sub custodia sancte regule*.[10] Until then "it had been kept negligently and with tepidity," *tepide ac negligenter*; but now they want "to adhere to it more strictly and more perfectly," *arctius deinceps atque perfectius*.[11] They had been guilty of transgressions, *de transgressione regule*

---

8. ". . . *ceterorumque fratrum iuditio . . . assistente etiam toto conventu fratrum . . . communi consensu . . . immo totus conventus, pusilli cum magnis, senes cum iunioribus. . . .*"—*ibid.*, pp. 4–5.

9. *Ibid.*

10. C. 1, Doc, p. 6, trans. R. Larkin in *The White Monks*, L. Lekai s o cist (Okauchee, Wis.: Cistercian Fathers, 1953), p. 252.

11. C. 2, *ibid.*

beati patris Benedicti; they now want to live in observance of the Rule, *observantis sancte regule.* It does not say precisely how they intended to do this but the whole context suggests that it is simply a matter of more fervor and generosity.

One point is stressed from the very beginning: where and in what type of locality they will devote themselves to this observance of the Rule. In a place characterized by a real separation—actual, local, geographic—from men, from "seculars," that is to say, those who lead an ordinary life in society. Like Molesme, Cîteaux is a monastery,[12] a community (*congregatio*),[13] a church (*ecclesia*);[14] but as far as its site is concerned, it is a "desert," *heremus.* Many times it is so designated[15] and so described,[16] and, as such, it is distinguished from Molesme, for the latter is a monastery, a *cenobium*, a *claustrum*,[17] and nothing more; it is not a "desert."[18] It is here for the first time—and in a sense made clear by the context—that the expression "new monastery" appears. Molesme and Cîteaux are two abbeys (*abbatie*),[19] but the latter is new in relation to the other: *abbatia illa . . . quae novum monasterium dicitur.*[20] Save for a really isolated location, it is not a question at this juncture of innovation, but simply of the fact that one of the two monasteries is more recent than the other. To the word *Cisterciensis*, at first rare, is preferred the expression "new monastery," which appears as many as six times on a single page;[21] farther on in the text the expression the "new cenobium" is also used.[22]

---

12. C. 3, *ibid.,* p. 7; trans. Larkin, p. 253.

13. C. 14, *ibid.,* p. 12; Larkin, p. 261.

14. C. 4, *ibid.,* p. 7; Larkin, p. 254 (translated as "monastery"); c. 9, Doc, p. 10; Larkin, p. 257 (translated as "community").

15. C. 3, Doc, p. 7; Larkin, p. 253; c. 5, Doc, p. 8; Larkin, p. 254; c. 6, Doc, p. 8; Larkin, p. 255.

16. C. 3, Doc, p. 7; Larkin, p. 253.

17. C. 14, Doc, p. 12; Larkin, p. 261.

18. C. 6–7, Doc, pp. 8f.; Larkin, pp. 254ff.

19. C. 7, Doc, p. 9; Larkin, p. 257.

20. C. 8, *ibid.*   21. C. 7–8. *ibid.*

22. C. 14, Doc, p. 12; Larkin, p. 261.

There is a logical development in this series of documents. After the question of the location comes the purpose of the foundation—to establish a *religio*, and even a *vera religio*.[23] What does this expression mean? Is it only a matter of the religious and monastic life? The monks who came from Molesme were already living such a life. It is a question of something more, of a religious spirit which really animates the life with a sincere desire for monastic fervor, for a "stricter and holier way of life in keeping with the Rule of St Benedict."[24] Actually, in what will this stricter conformity with the Rule consist? In abandoning the customs of certain monasteries. These customs were mitigations in so far as forsaking them will make the life more difficult. Renewal and fervor then implied this: a return to the Rule without mitigation.[25] The Molesmians and other monks of the traditional type perceived quite clearly that this was something new, and they reproached these innovators who were making themselves singular in their midst, *quasi singulares et novi monachi inter eos*. This situation of contempt, of inferiority, helps to place the Cistercians among the "poor of Christ." And so up to this point there is no question of innovations in the domain of institutions, that is, of laws or of customs, but simply a rejection of certain established customs—relaxations which rendered monastic discipline broader, less austere: *seculares latitudines . . . etiam monasterii laxioris minus austeras angustias reliquistis*.[26]

The Purpose

Following this series of documents emanating from those in authority and confirming the purpose of the founders, the founders themselves formulated their aims in a significant page of capital importance, every word of which is telling. It is the one entitled

---

23. C. 11, Doc, p. 10; Larkin, p. 259, "true religious life."

24. C. 12, Doc, p. 11; Larkin, p. 259. In place of the expression "holier" (*sacratiorem* or *sanctiorem*), a part of the manuscript tradition has "more hidden" (*secretiorem*).

25. C. 12, Doc, p. 11; Larkin, p. 259.

26. C. 14, Doc, p. 12; Larkin, p. 261.

Instituta. It was unanimously drawn up—*unanimiter statuerunt*—by the founding community itself.[27] What do we find there? First, the determination to choose the Rule of St Benedict as the norm and to hold to it. In what practical way? By rejecting everything that is opposed to it. Some examples follow immediately. They concern clothing, bedding and nourishment. Now on these points, due to a lack of austerity and poverty, there have been infractions of the "purity" of the Rule and of its "rectitude": *puritas regule, rectitudo regule.* Yet the Rule must be adhered to in the matter of regular observance and ecclesiastical precepts, *tam in ecclesiasticis quam in ceteris observationibus regule.* (The word "ecclesiastical" was, it would seem, applied to a section of canonical legislation for the liturgy which passed into the Rule.) The result is to be a spiritual interior renewal. As St Paul said, they will then put on "the new man."[28]

Once the general intention has been stated, the document proceeds to specify what is to be rejected and what is to be retained. Everything contrary to real poverty and to a real separation from the world is to be rejected. Goods reserved to ecclesiastics, such as churches and altars, from which come tithes, and other revenues are to be renounced, as well as goods pertaining to laymen, such as ovens, mills and farms worked by peasants, because all these bring the monks into contact with those who live in the world. The Cistercians took separation from the world very seriously. Consequently they would seek to do their own work. We discern in these statements what might be called a very clear determination to declericalize monasticism. Tithes and other fees belonging to the priestly ministry and the rights and privileges of clerics were for monks an usurpation contrary to the established law and tradition of the Church: *hoc veluti aliorum jus injuste sibi usurpare detractabant.* From this point of view, even ecclesiastical property belonged to the riches of this world and must therefore also be renounced: *Ecce huius saeculi divitiis spretis.*

What will they substitute for these sources of revenue? What will

27. C. 14, Doc, p. 13; Larkin, p. 262.
28. Eph 4:24.

characterize these "new soldiers of Christ"? Their poverty: *ceperunt novi milites Christi cum paupere Christo pauperes inter se tractare . . .* This poverty should not exclude the exercise of hospitality toward all, rich and poor, in conformity with the Rule and the continual practice of tradition: *hospites divites et pauperes . . . quos ut Christum suscipere praecipit regula.* How they are to find the means for this? By an innovation for which the Rule does not provide, but which will enable the monks to observe the Rule better. They will work but they will be helped by "lay brothers." These men while not monks will be treated as if they were. Workmen will also be hired for wages, but they will not belong to the monastic community. Thus, the desired objective can be achieved; a complete and continuous practice of the Rule. *Plenarie die ac nocte praecepta regule . . . servare.*

To the concern of poverty is added the preoccupation for remaining in solitude. The land they plan to develop will be "remote from the habitations of men."[29] They will have only "the vineyards, meadows, forests and mills" necessary for the monastery itself, *ad propies tamen usus,* in order that they will not have to mingle or mix with others. The lay brothers will live on *curtes,* land under cultivation that does not adjoin the monastery; the monks themselves will remain "in the cloister, according to the Rule." And in accordance with the will of St Benedict, they shall not establish themselves either in towns or villages, or even near them. Finally, and again in conformity with what St Benedict did at Subiaco, a foundation will be composed of twelve monks and an abbot. Are we to see in this last prescription a precaution against that form of prosperity which resides in large numbers, a desire to have only small communities so as not to be engaged in vast enterprises which necessarily put the monks in contact with seculars? What is here said concerning the foundation of a monastery would not seem to be prejudicial to possible future growth.

To this page, essential because so full of indications of the explicit purpose of the founders, the three last chapters of the Exordium add a few more directives. Thus, it was decided to forbid the duke from

29. ". . . *ab habitatione hominum remotas.* . . ."

holding court in the monastery and to reject everything that might be contrary to "poverty, the guardian of virtue," everything that might suggest the superfluous, or would be "super" in the twin meaning of this word: magnificence and pride. There follow some examples of simplicity in construction and furnishings. Always present is the deliberate desire for a solitude and a poverty that are real, in order to be able, as one of the final formulae reiterates, "to keep the Rule" by "loving the hard and bitter precepts."[30]

Legislation

The growing community and the possibility of new foundations in different dioceses, *in diversis episcopatibus*,[31] and in different regions, *in diversis partibus*,[32] necessitated legislation. To organize this growing federation, while taking care at the same time to ensure that it continued to be animated by the same spirit, they made a "pact" in which they had in view, "only charity and the good of souls."[33] The resulting document is known as the Charter of Charity. It has come down to us in two forms, both of which must be studied.

The formulation attributed to the year 1119 has nine chapters. From it we ascertain the intention to realize three principal ideas: poverty, observance of the Rule and identity in customs. Poverty is at first simply mentioned in opposition to its contrary, avarice resulting from accumulation of revenue.[34] It is on fidelity to the Rule that they insist most of all; it must be followed in everything,

---

30. C. 16, Doc, pp. 14f.; Larkin, p. 266.   31. C. 17, *ibid.*

32. *Carta caritatis,* Preface, Doc, p. 15; trans. D. Murphy sj, "The Charter of Charity," in L. Lekai, *The White Monks,* p. 267. (The expression *mundi partes* does not signify here, as it would by literal translation, "parts of the world." In medieval Latin, the word *mundus* was used like its English equivalent in such expressions as "the whole world." Cf. Blatt, *Novum glossarium mediae latinitatis* [Copenhagen, 1965], s.v. *Mundus,* col. 943. It is important to realize that the term means "country" or "region"; for nothing indicates that the founders of Cîteaux had any "world-wide" vision. The identity in customs which was later imposed on all parts of the world does not respond to an intention of the Fathers.)

33. *Ibid.*   34. C. 1, Doc, p. 16; Murphy, p. 268.

per omnia, and its interpretation must be that of the Fathers, the founders of Cîteaux, as well as in accord with subsequent interpretations.[35] Finally, it affirms that all should use the same liturgical books. The motif of this fundamental identity of life is clearly enunciated: it is charity which is to be manifested in action: "in our daily actions let there be no discord, but let us live together . . . in charity."[36] They affirm the principle of unity, but they are careful not to specify the details of its application, except where it is a matter of ecclesiastical texts and chants.

These three demands, poverty, fidelity to the Rule, and unity, suffice to determine a way of life, an "order" in the sense not of an organization but of an "order of life"[37] which is identified with the observance of the Rule: "precepts of the Rule or our order."[38] This identification is made several times.[39] But the word *ordo* is also found in contexts where it has both the meaning of "observance,"as was just indicated (and this is in more traditional usage) and the meaning of "order" in the later sense of a "religious order."[40]

The first danger which threatened an abbot and, consequently, the point which the visitor should examine above all in his administration is that of granting too much importance to temporal interests: "anxious beyond measure for the things of the world."[41] Here, again, there is found the two-fold concern for separation from the world and poverty,[42] but care is to be taken that the poverty will

---

35. C. 2, *ibid.*   36. C. 3, Doc, p. 17; Murphy, *ibid.*

37. *"ordo vitae."*   38. *"precepta regule vel ordinis nostri"*—C. 4, *ibid.*

39. C. 7, Doc, p. 17; c. 8, p. 18; c. 9, pp. 18f.; Murphy, c. 6, p. 270.

40. C. 10f., Doc, p. 20; Murphy, c. 11f., pp. 272f. The gradual evolution of the terminology situates itself between the two terminals which are characterized by J. Hourlier OSB: "Originally the word 'order' did not at all indicate what we understand by religious order. It meant a way of life, a discipline. This meaning is fully evident in the title of a ninth-century customary: *Ordo in monasterio qualiter . . . Deo militari opportet. . . .* Similarly, *Regularis ordo, Ordo monasticus. . . .* The evolution from one meaning to the other was slow. It would be useful to establish from the texts when it was fully accomplished, perhaps not until the XIIIth century."—"Cluny et la notion d'ordre religieux" in *A Cluny: Congrès scientifique* (Dijon, 1950), pp. 219f.

41. *"secularibus rebus nimis intentus."*

42. C. 7, Doc, p. 17; Murphy, c. 6, p. 270.

H

not go to the point of "penury."[43] Finally, importance is attached to insertion in the local Church; it will fall "to the bishop, the canons and the clergy" of the diocese "to remedy the situation created by an abbot who transgresses the Rule."[44] Once again, this conforms to the text of the Rule.[45]

The second formulation of the Charter of Charity attributed to 1123–1124, is incorporated in the Exordium. In this text, developed and reworked, we find again the same data but with some significant modifications.

From the start, in a phrase charged with biblical allusions, it speaks of the impossibility of combining the practice of virtue with the possession of great property.[46] Here, the first intention of the founders is one of poverty: up to now, they have failed to live up to the Rule because they have failed in poverty; their proposal to live a strict life, *artum propositum*,[47] should put an end to this situation. To realize their design they seek to live in a solitary place, in a true desert, *heremus*.[48] Thus, it is this way of observing the Rule, by living poorly, which leads them to greater austerity and to a real and effective separation from the world.

The second chapter insists anew, and forcefully, on poverty. Abbot Stephen Harding distinguished himself by his fervor and his religious sense, *religio*, his poverty, his ardent love of the discipline of the Rule. In this formulation, poverty is named before observance and, immediately afterwards, it is again mentioned first—"poor of Christ, heirs of poverty"—in conjunction with "austerity."[49]

In Chapter Three the expressions "Cistercian Order" and "our

43. C. 7, Doc, p. 18.

44. C. 8, Doc, pp. 18f.; Murphy, p. 271; already in the Little Exordium, c. 3, Doc, p. 7; Larkin, p. 253.

45. *Rule of Saint Benedict,* 64:4.

46. *Exordium Cistercii,* c. 1, Doc, p. 21: "Ceterum quia possessionibus virtutibusque diuturna non solet esse societas . . . , elegerunt pocius studiis celestibus occupari, quam terrenis implicari negociis." "Moreover, because possessions and power do not usually give a community long life . . . , they chose rather to occupy themselves with heavenly things rather than get involved in earthly affairs."

47. C. 1, Doc, p. 22.   48. C. 2, *ibid.*   49. *Ibid.*

Order" make their first appearance, the latter still identified with the Rule, *regule vel ordini*.[50] This holds true for the two following chapters;[51] the Cistercian manner of life consists in observing the Rule. Here, too, is mentioned the intervention of the bishop and the clergy of the diocese in case of a transgression on the part of the abbot. Further on, the prescription aimed at preserving identity in prayer and conduct is expressed, no longer in a practical and concrete manner, but by means of an abstract term: *unitas*. The word "charity" is no longer employed. It is no longer merely a matter of understanding and observing the Rule in the same way, *regula beati Benedicti uno modo intelligatur, uno modo teneatur*. It is a question of identity. The word *idem* is to be found four times in reference to books, nourishment, clothing, manners and customs.[52] This term appears here for the first time in Cistercian legislation, in a context where uniformity seems to take precedence over charity. Actually, all the rest of the document goes on to specify just what these practices are, these applications of the Rule, these customs and herein we have the beginning of a tendency toward codification which, hereafter, will be more and more accentuated.

In Chapter Fifteen, after a reference to the fact that they "shall live by the labor of their hands," it is stated that they may possess what they need for this, including animals—excepting those which serve vanity or curiosity—and they may have granges. Here again one notices in relation to the first edition of the text, a lowering of standards. They are no longer at the level of life according to the Spirit of Christ, but at that of psychology, even including such petty things as having pets. This is doubtless a consequence of the growth in the number of monks, a fact verified at the very beginning of the document.[53] All these decrees are to curb abuses which have crept in. Toward the end of the document the exigencies of monachism pure and simple, of *monastica puritas* are set forth. There all revenue which does not come from work is excluded.[54] In the

50. C. 3, *ibid.*, p. 23.   51. C. 4f., Doc, p. 24.

52. C. 9, Doc, p. 26.   53. C. 2, Doc, p. 23.

54. C. 23, Doc, p. 28.

last two chapters the desire of poverty is applied to all the liturgical accouterments.

To the documents that have just been analyzed, two others can be added in which we also find expressed the intention that governed the beginnings of Cîteaux. The first is the *Monitum* of Abbot Stephen Harding on the subject of the chant. In it it is affirmed that they have "decided to observe, in this place, the integrity of the Rule of St Benedict with the most assiduous attention," *Benedictus in sua regula quam in hoc loco maximo studio decrevimus observandum.*[55]

The second text is the charter drawn up at Cîteaux in order to relate the foundation of the abbey. In it, too, is set forth the purpose of following "the Rule of St Benedict more closely and more faithfully," *Regulam S Benedicti arctius atque fidelius.*[56]

The Traditional Character and the Originality of Cîteaux

From a perusal of the documents relative to the origins of the Cistercian Order it is evident that it was not the reform of an already existing institution, but the beginning of a new institution differing from the prevailing expression of monasticism. This was judged in the light of the Rule of St Benedict and found to be wanting because it adopted customs dispensing from real collective poverty and separation from the world. Finding monks too closely linked to the world, too similar to it, the founders of Cîteaux wanted to remedy the situation by freeing themselves from the prevailing customs—and in this sense they were innovating—in order to return to the sole practice of the Rule of St Benedict. It is never said that they intend to observe it "to the letter," but rather to observe it in all its purport, in accordance with all its requirements. Such is the meaning of the expressions: "strictly, perfectly, faithfully, fully, day and night, most zealously, through everything the purity and rectitude of the Rule."[57] They expected to realize this purpose by

---

55. Ed. J. Marilier, *Chartres et documents concernant l'abbaye de Cîteaux* (Rome: Editiones Cistercienses, 1961), p. 55; trans. M. B. Pennington in *Cistercian Studies*, 4 (1969).   56. *Ibid.*, p. 50, no. I.

57. "*arctius, perfectius, fidelius, plenarie die ac nocte, maximo studio, per omnia, puritas et rectitudo regulae.*"

locating on sites which were truly solitary, and by adopting a form of poverty which included living by their own labor and that of their lay brothers. Both as a sign and as a cause of charity, they likewise decided to maintain uniformity with respect to their manner of interpreting the Rule, and their way of celebrating the Divine Office, and then gradually with respect to other usages.

Finally, there are two other aspects characteristic of the founding of Cîteaux. In the first place, it is not the work of one man, saint though he may be, but of a group of monks in the bosom of a community, that of Molesme. They had the consent, of course, of the Abbot, Robert, who, moreover, joined the group, though shortly afterwards he would have to leave them. But the charism of founder was given to this fervent, dissenting group. It was a work carried out from below or, as one would say today, on the horizontal level.

In the second place the vertical aspect is not to be neglected. It is represented by the abbot of Molesme who approves of the project and even assumes the leadership of the group, by his two successors, Alberic and Stephen Harding, by popes, cardinals and the legate. Finally it is represented by the bishop of the place who intervenes at Rome in favor of the group,[58] who grants permission for the establishment of lay brothers,[59] and who, along with his canons and clergy, will exercise a certain control over every foundation made in his diocese.[60]

ST BERNARD, THEOLOGIAN OF THE CISTERCIAN LIFE

This foundation of Cîteaux, whose purpose and principal characteristics the historical documents have revealed to us, had been interpreted by St Bernard with all the intensity and penetration, as well as the originality that lay within his literary talent, his genius as

---

58. *Exordium parvum*, c. 3, Doc, p. 11; Larkin, *op. cit.*, pp. 252f.
59. C. 14, Doc, p. 12; Larkin, p. 253.
60. *Carta caritatis*, c. 8, 11, Doc, pp. 18ff.; cf. note 44 *supra*.

a theologian, and his experience as a man of God. His testimony is worthy of special record for three reasons: first of all, because the Saint had a part in the events after 1111, secondly because of the doctrinal interest of his writings, and finally, because of the profound influence he exercised on the evolution of the Order.

Although St Bernard had a synthetic mind he did not leave a systematic exposition of the Cistercian life. However, throughout his work there are scattered pages, sentences, and simple allusions which pertain to it. His statements, therefore, cannot be analyzed in any chronological order as was the case with the historical documents. They must be grouped according to the principal themes which stand out amid all that he has to say. These would seem to be three in number: renewal, purity and poverty.

The Cistercian Renewal

Bernard was fully aware of the newness which the Cistercian observance represented in relation to that of the older, more traditional type of monasticism. When Drogon wanted to transfer to Pontigny, he spoke of his wanting to submit himself "to the observance of a new discipline", *novae observantiis disciplinae.*[61] What constitutes this newness St Bernard is unable to reduce to a few innovations of the practical order. Preoccupied with the spiritual life, he regards it as a reality far more significant. It is essentially a question of interior renewal, of a reform of the whole man. To Suger, who reestablished a stricter observance at St Denis, Bernard wrote that he was establishing the austerity of a new way of life, *novae conversationis austeritas,*[62] "something beautifully new," *novitatis decus,*[63] in relation to the past, to the former state of affairs.[64] To Warren of Aulps who reformed his monastery Bernard sends congratulations because he had become a "new soldier in Christ,"—*novus in Christo miles* inaugurating "new combats,"

---

61. *Ep.* 34, 2, PL 182:140; trans. B. James, *The Letters of St Bernard of Clairvaux* (London: Burns Oates, 1953), Letter 35, p. 69.

62. *Ep.* 78, 4, PL 182:193; James, Letter 80, p. 113.

63. *Ibid.*   64. *Ibid.,* no. 5.

nova bella, contrary to "the traditions received from his predecessors," *tuorum praedecessorum traditiones.*[65] Thus to renew, counter to traditions, is well within the line traced by the Fathers of Cîteaux whose purpose was to seek new fervor. For there is no exterior renewal unless the interior man changes first: "and though the exterior man is undergoing corruption, yet the interior is being renewed from day to day. And whence such ardor in renewing observances if not from the renewal of the inner man?"[66] This interior renewal is the fruit of "purity of heart."[67] It will be necessary to speak of this later. Suffice it here to note that for Bernard everything is integrated: observance and interior freedom, the renewal of discipline and charity.

To pass over to the Cistercian life was nothing else than to renew oneself in this sense and to do so entirely. It is to change oneself through a total conversion, by returning to the purity of the Rule. Bernard affirms this with vigorous insistence in a letter to Abbot Richard and the monks who with him had left the Abbey of St Mary of York in order to begin a new monastic life at Fountains, just as the Fathers of Cîteaux had done not so long before: "newly, in holy newness renewing, changing, the purity of the Rule."[68]

Thus Bernard, theologian of the spiritual life, explicates what was implicit in the intention of the Cistercian founders. He is so persuaded that the new observance of the Rule suffices to assure the interior renewal of every monk who adheres to it, that he tends to attribute to Cîteaux and its institutions a monopoly of all true monastic renewal. This is evident in a case in which an abbot with a few of his monks left their Cistercian community in order to realize, apart from it, that which they believed to be favorable to their sanctification. He reproaches Arnold of Morimond with having "the presumption to undertake something new" and to "lead the young with him," *rem tam novam praesumis, iuvenes tecum*

---

65. *Ep.* 254, 1, PL 182:459; James, Letter 329, p. 408.

66. "*Et si homo exterior corrumpitur, sed interior renovatur de die in diem, Unde etenim tantus ardor innovandi ordinis, nisi ex renovatione mentis?*"

67. *Ep.* 254, 6, PL 182:462; James, Letter 329, p. 411.

68. *Ep.* 96, PL 182:229; James, Letter 171, p. 241.

ducis.[69] He insists very much on the order, *ordo noster,*[70] in the double sense of a way of life and an institution. For a Cistercian there is no longer any place for anything "new." In the case of a conflict between the interior aspirations of conscience and the *ordo,* it is the latter which must prevail. It is less a matter of customs than of juridical structure and hierarchy. He who searches for a new way is a "transgressor of his profession"; he "prefers his private good to the common right."[71] A charism of renewal such as that of the Fathers of Cîteaux is henceforth no longer possible. To free oneself from the institution is to act against the Order and that in a disorderly fashion—*inordinate,*[72] *inordinatus homo.*[73] Thus, not only does Bernard identify interior renewal, for a Cistercian monk, with fidelity to the institution according to which he has made profession, but, on account of the authoritarianism which is the disadvantage of his strong personality, this great man of the spirit comes to the point of enclosing the charism within a structure which limits its possibilities of realization.

Cistercian Purity

The Cistercian renewal consisted, as we have seen, in a return to the "rectitude" and the "purity" of the Rule. Bernard adopts these forms of expression, especially the second, but to it, he gives a fuller meaning by showing that this "purity of the Rule" is a particular realization of the gift of "purity of heart."

The Purity of the Rule

He affirms first of all that to live according to the purity of the Rule is to take seriously one's profession. To the founders of Fountains who have just adopted the observance of Cîteaux he says: "As to whether those who have made profession of the Holy Rule

69. *Ep.* 4, 3, PL 182:91; James, Letter 4, p. 22.
70. *Ep.* 4, 2, PL 182:90, James, p. 22; *Ep.* 6, 1, PL 182:90, James, Letter 7, p. 25.
71. *Ep.* 7, 16, PL 182:102; James, Letter 8, p. 35.
72. *Ep.* 6, 1, PL 182:92; James, Letter 7, p. 25.
73. *Ep.* 6, 2, PL 182:93; James, *ibid.*

can, with a tranquil conscience, fall short of its purity, you your-selves have found the answer."[74] Writing to the abbot of St Mary's of York, the monastery they had left, he gives to their departure, the same interpretation: they were fearful of not living up to their profession, *citra professionis suae propter conscientiam remanere*; they wanted more fully to enter into the graces of the religious life, *religionis proposito ad altiorem gradum transire*.[75] Two among them, by leaving the group, did not remain in the same degree of purity to which they had risen, *intra puritatis gradum cum ascenderant*; but they can still return to it "if they wish to return to that purity from which they rashly fell away."[76]

In what, precisely, does this purity of the Rule consist? St Bernard explains this as clearly as possible in a text which echoes the historical documents which we have seen. In the treatise *On Precept and Dispensation*, in reference to one who desires to pass "from the Cluniac institutions to the strict poverty of the Cistercians," he says that he "prefers the purity of the Rule to these customs," *eligens prae illis nimirum consuetudinibus magis Regulae puritatem*.[77] It is, then, a matter of observing the Rule itself, purely and simply, "to live purely according to the Rule, to observe the Rule purely."[78] Actually, one can live "in accordance with the Rule" in two ways. One can follow "usages which are good and not opposed to the Rule," *boni usus a Regula non discordant*.[79] In this case the Rule is not followed with absolute exactness, *non ad unguem*,[80] but with the addition of customs which are good, *cum bonis consuetudinibus*.[81] Or, one follows the Rule in the "strict and literal manner of the Cister-

---

74. *Ep.* 96, PL 182:229; James, Letter 171, p. 241.

75. *Ep.* 313, 2, PL 182:519; James, Letter 169, p. 238.

76. ". . . *si velint resumere puritatis gradum a quo temere corruerunt.*"—*Ibid.*

77. *De praecepto et dispensatione*, 46, in *S. Bernardi Opera*, ed. Leclercq and Rochais, vol. III (Rome: Editiones Cistercienses, 1963), p. 285; trans. C. Greenia, *Works of Bernard of Clairvaux*, vol. I, Cistercian Fathers Series, I.

78. ". . . *pure iuxta Regulam conversari, ad purum Regulam observare. . . .*"—*Ibid.*, no. 47.

79. *Ibid.*, p. 286.   80. *Ibid.*, no. 48.

81. *Ibid.*, no. 49.

cians," *Cisterciensium districtionem litteratoriam,*[82] "entirely, purely
and to the letter," *ex integro pure ad litteram.*[83] Thus to act is to prefer
that which is "stricter and higher," *altiora seu artiora,* to that which
is "inferior, more relaxed," *inferiora vel remissiora.*[84]

This is the first time that the text mentions the phrase *ad litteram*
in relation to the practice of the Rule. The expression taken in
context calls for entering into the aims dictated by the Rule. St
Bernard accumulates formulas all of which say the same thing; *ad
litteram* means nothing other than the three words which precede it:
ex integro, pure. Also, in the *Apologia,* after stating that among the
Cluniacs there are practices prohibited by the Rule, for example
details pertaining to food and clothing,[85] Bernard says to the
Cistercian that neither does he observe the Rule literally in all its
details: "But if you think that all who profess the Rule should
observe it literally so that you would grant not the slightest deviation from it, then I can surely tell you that neither you nor he (the
Cluniac) is keeping it."[86] Indicating that the Rule is composed of
"spiritual precepts," *spiritualia instituta,* which are more important
than the "corporal observances,"[87] Bernard says that one must hold
to that which is "better," *meliora,* more than to particular points,
minima.[88]

Purity of Heart

What is there better than the spiritual gifts, *charismata meliora,*
humility and, above all, charity?[89] This last word, "charity,"
completes the answer to the question of ascertaining what it means
"to live according to the purity of the Rule." It means a total
generosity, without compromise; and in this sense "purity" is
nothing other than an integral religious life, particularly as it was

---

82. *Ibid.,* no. 48.   83. *Ibid.,* no. 49.   84. *Ibid.,* no. 45, p. 284.

85. *Apologia,* 12, *ibid.,* pp. 91f.; trans. M. Casey OCSO, in *The Works of
Bernard of Clairvaux,* vol. 1, Cistercian Fathers Series, I.

86. "*Quod si Regulam ab omnibus, qui eam professi sunt, sic ad litteram tenedam
censes, ut nullam omnino dispensationem admitti patiaris, audacter dico, nec tu eam,
nec ille (Cluniacensis) tenetis.*"—*Ibid.,* no. 14, p. 93.

87. *Ibid.,* no. 12, p. 91.   88. *Ibid.,* no. 13, p. 93.   89. *Ibid.*

understood at Cîteaux. Speaking of mitigations in this regard, Bernard expresses himself in various synonymous ways such as, "unbecoming to religion, contrary to purity, particularly inconsistent both with the decency and simplicity of our Order."[90] Purity applied to the monastic life is, then, according to St Bernard, a fidelity to the Rule which admits no concession to self-love; it is the monastic ideal accepted in all its essentials and after the manner of the Cistercian Order. Bernard sums it up in these words:

> Our life is abjection, humility, voluntary poverty, obedience, peace and joy in the Holy Spirit. It is submission to a master, to an abbot, to a rule and to a discipline. It is application to silence, the practice of fasting and vigils. It is to be exercised in prayer and manual labor. Above all, it consists in following that most excellent of ways which is charity.[91]

Practices such as these constitute the fundamental observance of the Rule. There is no aim but charity and this is nothing other than purity of heart.[92] After pointing out to Abbot Warren of Aulps that the reform of his monastery is the effect of his interior renewal, Bernard asks him from where he received these "very pure fruits." What tree could have borne them if not that of "purity of heart"? "For when has a soul that lacked this purity sought out and chosen with so much zeal the purity of the Rule?"[93]

Thus to seek the purity of the Rule is an indication of purity of heart and this is charity: It consists in two things: to seek the glory of God and the good of one's neighbor. "*Porro puritatis cordis in duobus consistit: in quaerenda gloria Dei et utilitate proximi.*"[94] The

---

90. *Ep.* 345, 2, PL 182:551; James, Letter 388, p. 459.

91. *Ep.* 142, 1, PL 182:297; James, Letter 151, p. 220.

92. This notion of purity of heart is that which Cassian proposed and which the Rule of St Benedict supposes, as W. Tunyk OSB, has shown: *Vision of Peace: The Wisdom of St Benedict and his Rule* (New York: Farrar Straus, 1963), *passim.*

93. *Ep.* 254, 6, PL 182:462; James, Letter 329, p. 411.

94. *De moribus et officio episcoporum,* 10, PL 182:817.

Bernardine—and Cistercian—notion of the purity of the monastic life according to the Rule is not understandable unless it is situated in a general theology of charity conceived as purity of heart. Charity is a right intention, *intentio pura*, proceeding from an undivided heart. So says St Paul: *Caritas de corde puro*.[95] It is exempt from egoism and completely disinterested, seeking only that which is of Christ: "For I am not aware of having sought anything for myself but only the things of Jesus Christ."[96] Thus understood, purity has a broader signification than that moral cleanliness, that *munditia*, which, in a restricted sense, is sometimes called "purity." Both the one and the other are the conditions of contemplation according to these words of the Lord: "Happy are the pure of heart: they shall see God."[97] To this same beatitude is opposed not only sin which sullies the heart and the memory, but all self-seeking: "The heavenly Father calls pure of heart those who seek, not their own interests but those of Jesus Christ and that which is useful, not for themselves but for the many."[98] It is, then, a matter of asceticism leading by the path of charity to contemplation,[99] to the exercise of the virtues—chastity, charity, patience, humility—and to the other fruits of a "pure conscience," which "make one loveable to God, acceptable to men and capable of being imitated by them."[100] Thus understood, purity has a very broad significance: "As the natural state of the body is health so that of the heart is purity. The anxious heart will not see God. Now the human heart was made to see its Creator. Here we understand purity simply in the sense that in everything we do, we confess to God humbly and simply in prayer, and that we

---

95. 1 Tim 1:5. *De diversis*, 35, 6, PL 183:636f.

96. *Ibid.*, 7, PL 183:637.

97. *In festo omnium sanctorum*, 1, 13, *S. Bernardi opera*, vol. V (Rome, 1968)

98. *De conversione*, 32, *S. Bernardi opera*, vol. IV (Rome, 1966), p. 109; trans. W. Williams, *On Conversion* (London: Burns, Oates & Washbourne, 1938), c. 19, p. 50.

99. *De gradibus humilitatis*, 10, *S. Bernardi opera*, vol. III, pp. 30f.; trans. G. Webb and A. Walker, *The Steps of Humility* (London: Mowbrays, 1957) p.63.

100. *De diversis*, 16, 1, PL 183:579.

also confess to a man."[101] Thus, purity gives rise to confident self-accusation, to thanksgiving for pardon received, to prayer, in short, to "confession" in all the biblical and traditional meaning of this word.[102]

Does this mean that we shall see God here below? Contemplation is bound up with the inchoate eschatological state in which we are in this life. It is the beginning of likeness to God. But to see God fully, as he is, we must be in a state of purity equal to his own, *pari puritatis*. This is reserved to the completion in glory[103]—there where this promise "they shall see God" will be fully realized. "In order that a pure face may look upon the naked truth, *cum pura intueri potuerit veritatem*, it must be transformed into his glory.[104] We must tend toward it, prepare for it, in such a way that we may know God better by means of interior experience. We must become capable of speaking to him, just as one lives for him, without any turning back on oneself. Once again, Bernard concludes an admirable development on purity of heart by identifying it with charity: "Light is purity, light is charity, which seeks not its own."[105]

Charity, Principle of Evolution

We must rise to this height in order to know what Bernard thinks of the evolution of institutions. For him such evolution forms a part of an incipient eschatology, always in progress. It must lead to the summit, to the end which is total purity, face to face contemplation. Everything else is relative and susceptible to change. Interior renewal and renewal of observance can be realized thanks

101. *Ibid.*, n. 2, col. 580. Concerning the word "confession," I have gathered together texts under the title, "La confession, louange de Dieu," in *La vie spirituelle*, 118 (1968), pp. 253–265.

102. Cf. "Confession et louange de Dieu chez S. Bernard," in *La vie spirituelle*, 119 (1968).

103. *Super Cantica*, 31, 2, *S. Bernardi opera*, vol. I (Rome, 1957), p. 220; trans. A. Luddy, *St Bernard's Sermons on the Canticle of Canticles* (Dublin: Browne & Nolan, 1920), vol. 1, p. 366.

104. *Ibid.*, 62, 7, *S. Bernardi opera*, vol. II (Rome, 1958), p. 160; Luddy, vol. 2, p. 215.

105. *Ibid.*

to a capacity for innovation which enables one to discern in the present, received from the past, that which must be conserved, transformed or recreated. We must know how to apply to monasticism the program of that reforming bishop, St Malachy: "In the councils, the ancient traditions are revived, at least those whose values have been confirmed. . . . But we do not content ourselves with restoring the past, we create the new." *Nec modo nova instaurantur: cuduntur et nova.*[106]

What is there then in monasticism that is absolute, fundamental? The "Rule of God." The Rule of St Benedict is just a manifestation of it. "Listen to the Rule of God to which the Rule of St Benedict is in no way contrary."[107] But in the Rule we must distinguish between, on the one hand, particular practices having value for a certain time and milieu and, on the other hand, major points, those which determine spiritual attitudes: "those which are of major importance in the Rule, that is the spiritual directives."[108] The first are subject to evolution, to *dispensatio*, in the traditional canonical meaning of this word, that is modification rather than "dispensation."[109] It is never, then, a question of observing the Rule "to the letter" in all matters without any change.[110]

On this point Bernard could not have expressed himself more clearly than he did in the treatise which he entitled *De praecepto et dispensatione*. Among the prescriptions of the Rule there are those which are immutable, responding to spiritual exigencies—charity, humility, gentleness. They come not from Benedict, but from God himself. As for the others, they are indispensable in the sense that they are "necessary" to those who voluntarily assume them, but not

106. *Vita S. Malachiae*, 42. *S. Bernardi opera*, vol. III, p. 348; trans. H. Lawlor, *Life of St Malachy of Armagh* (New York: Macmillan, 1920), c. 6, n. 23, p. 81.

107. ". . . *attendite in regulam Dei, cui utique non dissonat institutio sancti Benedicti. . . .*"—*Apologia*, 12, *op. cit.*, p. 91.

108. ". . . *quae maiora sunt Regulae, spiritualia scilicet instituta. . . .*"—*Ibid.*

109. Under the title, "S. Bernard dans l'histoire de l'obéissance" in *Recueil d'études sur S. Bernard et ses écrits*, III, (Rome: Ed. Storia e letteratura, 1968), pp. 299f., I have indicated texts and references.

110. *Apologia*, 14, *op. cit.*, p. 93, cited above in note 25.

by a necessity that does not admit of change, of *dispensatio* for reasonable motives: "I would call them necessary, but without pretending that a dispensation cannot be granted when reason and necessity require it."[111]

Becoming more precise, Bernard considers some prescriptions of a permanent character, such as are found in the great rules of monastic and canonical life, or in the canons sanctioned by authority. Normally these remain in force until the authority which decreed them decides they should be changed. The vocabulary he uses indicates the different areas and degrees of permanence— *sancita stabiliter perserverant*—and the times or the motives for modification: "it is permitted to modify or to change . . . to dispense by reason of person, place and time." The change, the *mutatio*, is in reality a *dispensatio*, which can be made only by competent authority.[112]

Now what is to be the criterion by which one will judge if a change, a *dispensatio*, is legitimate? It will be charity, which, as we have seen, is nothing other than purity of heart: "As long as they promote charity these precepts remain fixed and immutable and cannot be changed, not even by superiors. However should they ever be found contrary to charity . . . is it not clearly just and fitting that they should be omitted, suspended or altered for the sake of the charity which conceived them? It would certainly be blameworthy to hold in opposition to charity that which was ordained solely for charity. So then let those prescriptions which we have classified as 'stable' be respected even by superiors, so long as they serve the interests of charity."[113]

If that is true of the Rule of St Benedict it is also true of Cistercian institutions.

Cistercian Poverty

In regard to Cistercian renewal, along with the purity of the Rule, Bernard speaks most often of voluntary poverty. He does so with

---

111. "*Ita sane necessaria dixerim, ut ex eis minime praeiudicetur necessariis rationabilibusque dispensationibus.*"—*De praecepto*, 2, *op. cit.*, pp. 255f.

112. *Ibid.*, no. 4, pp. 256f.   113. *Ibid.*, no. 5, p. 257.

almost obsessing insistence—a clear sign of the importance he accords to it. Actually it is or should be a part of every monastic life just as much as work or a hidden life in solitude. Bernard sums it up in a letter to the Archbishop of Sens: "Work, the hidden life and the poverty of the monastery—these are the characteristics of monks, their titles to nobility."[114] Poverty goes hand in hand with humility. Thus Bernard reproaches the ostentation of Cluniac abbots as being contrary to both virtues.[115] He demands of all the monks a poverty which is real; they are to be poor men: "What is this to paupers, to monks, to spiritual men?"[116]

At least he would have it so in the case of the Cistercians. To pass over to Cîteaux as we have seen, is to adhere to a strict poverty: "to embrace Cistercian poverty."[117] Writing to his nephew Robert, Bernard says that to leave Cîteaux is to abandon poverty,[118] that "voluntary poverty" which is inseparable from the other major observances—fasts, vigils and silence.[119] Learning that Thomas of Beverley has decided to embrace the Cistercian life, Bernard congratulates him on his "love of holy poverty."[120] In the description he gives of his order, he allots to "voluntary poverty" a primary place.[121]

It is, then, a fact: poverty constitutes one of the important, essential components of the Cistercian life. It is qualified as "voluntary" because the Cistercians can, like other monks, be legitimately rich. In his affirmations Bernard goes beyond the immediate and practical to protest against the affluency of some monasteries outside

114. *De moribus et off. episc.*, 37, PL 182:833.

115. *Apologia*, 27, *op. cit.*, pp. 103f.

116. "*Quid haec ad pauperes, ad monachos, ad spirituales viros?*"—*Ibid.*, 28, p. 106.

117. "*Cisterciensium sese stringere paupertatem.*"—*De praecepto*, 46, *op. cit.*, p. 285.

118. *Ep.* 1, 3, PL 182:72; James, Letter 1, p. 4.

119. *Ep.* 1, 4, PL 182:73; James, Letter 1, p. 4.

120. *Ep.* 411, 1, PL 182:619; James, Letter 108, p. 157.

121. *Ep.* 142, 1, PL 182:297; cited above in note 30; James, Letter 151, p. 220.

of Cîteaux, and against the theoretical justifications for such a state of affairs. In this he is in conformity with the intentions of the Fathers of Cîteaux as they are found in the documents. Voluntary poverty is a prerequisite of the contemplative life as well as of the active life.[122] Bernard is not only a reformer and a moralist; he is also a theologian and each time he denounces a deviation, he shows by contrast the right way: "He, Christ, did not act so," *Non ita Christi*.[123] We should not be surprised to see him situate monastic and Cistercian poverty in a Christological synthesis.

Poverty, like the purity of which it is a form, has an eschatological dimension. It is a beginning and an anticipation. It is leading to a completion. In it are to be found the two aspects of the Paschal mystery: renunciation and transcendence, death and glorification. If monks "follow the poor Christ"—"they have followed him in his poverty"—it is to win him, to possess him, to overtake him in his glory.[124] The Fathers of the Church have magnificently elucidated this mystery of redemptive poverty inaugurated by the Incarnation, by the annihilation, by the voluntary *kenosis* of the Son of God, which was transformed by his glorification into eternal riches.[125] In his brilliant, traditional and personal way Bernard has developed the same theme many times basing himself on the verses of St Paul which inspired the great theologians of the fourth and fifth centuries, and which Vatican II has brought into relief.[126] "Being rich he became poor for your sakes. . . ."[127] "Now, how can anyone who together with him has gone so far seek the riches of the world?"[128]

122. *De diversis*, 48, PL 183:671.

123. *De moribus*, 33, PL 182:830.   124. *Apologia*, 3, *op. cit.*, p. 83.

125. Under the title, "Il s'est fait pauvre. Le Christ modèle de la pauverté volontaire d'après les Pères de l'Eglise," in *Aspects du monachisme hier et aujourd'hui* (Paris: Ed. de la Source, 1968), pp. 51–67, I have cited some texts. A trans. of this vol. will appear as No. VII in the Cistercian Studies Series.

126. *Perfectae caritatis*, no. 13.   127. 2 Cor 8:9.

128. *In Resurrectione*, 3, 1, S. *Bernardi opera*, V, p. 104; trans. A. Luddy, *St Bernard's Sermons for the Seasons and Principal Festivals of the Year* (Dublin: Browne & Nolan, 1921–1925), vol. II, Third Sermon for Easter, p. 200.

I

If ever there was a "voluntary" poverty, it was certainly that of Jesus Christ. Equal to the Father and universal Master of the creation, he freely renounced every privilege in order to enter upon the role, far more, to take the very nature, the "form," of the slave. His poverty led him to obedience and renunciation in order to fulfill the Father's will, even to death, even to death on the cross, as St Paul says to the Phillippians.[129] With the Father, with the glory which was his since the beginning of the world, he had everything except this poverty, for the sake of which he became flesh and lived among us.[130] It behooves us now to imitate him by a voluntary poverty, but which, for us, becomes necessary because promised—*paupertatis voluntariae scilicet, et ex volutate necessariae*. It is a poverty which must be interior (that is humility): "Hasten therefore to become poor in spirit." Yet it must be real as regards exterior things: "materially needy," *in opes rebus*; based on the confidence that God will take care of us temporally and spiritually—"and may the Lord be solicitous of you."[131] Provisional, "momentary," it leads to the sublimity of that eternal glory where we attain to true riches, to the contemplation which is the goal of Cistercian monastic purity.[132]

The principle enunciated by Bernard on the subject of material goods should be understood in this wise: the less one has of them, the better, *quanto strictius, tanto melius*.[133]

The Influence and the Limits of St Bernard

The interpretation that St Bernard gave to the Cistercian life certainly had great influence and forms a part of the history of the

---

129. *Ep.* 462, 2f., PL 182:663f. (Not in James.) Cf. Phil 2, 5.

130. *In vigilia Nativitatis*, 1, 5, *S. Bernardi opera*, vol. IV, p. 201; trans. Luddy, *Sermons for the Seasons*, vol. 1, First Sermon for Christmas Eve, p. 315.

131. ". . . *ut Dominus sit sollicitus vestri.*"—*Ep.* 462, 7, PL 182:665f. (Not in James.)

132. *Ibid.*, n. 8, col. 667.

133. *In Ps. Qui Habitat*, 5, 2, *S. Bernardi opera*, vol. IV, p. 403; trans. Sr Penelope CSMV, *Lent with Saint Bernard* (London: Mowbrays, 1953), p. 32.

beginnings of Cîteaux. In a measure it determined it. Did it modify it? In other words, was it authentic, did it conform to the intentions of those who had been the first "authors," the fathers of the institution; or was it something wholly new, marked by his personality? It seems that the first hypothesis of this alternative has been verified: as regards the essentials, Bernard simply discerned with deftness the major orientations which had determined the origins of the Order and keenly analyzed the whole content of the Cistercian fact.[134] But he accomplished this with his own genius, with his own character and temperament. This calls for a twofold comment.

First, he contributed greatly to the prosperity of the Order. Was it not he who caused the growth in numbers? But these resulted, on the one hand, in a certain lowering of standards as regards the purity of the ideal, and, on the other hand, in a need for legislating to remedy the abuses which inevitably accompany growing numbers. In spite of the exaggerations of hagiographers who attribute the influx of recruits wholly to him, we know that prosperity, both as to the number of vocations and the extent of possessions, began before him and developed also apart from his line of Clairvaux, especially in that of Morimond which seems to have been somewhat the rival of Clairvaux. In fact all the "new" orders of the period were winning recruits, because the Gregorian Reform was bearing fruit and because, in such a situation, everything that is new or renewed, everything that is born or reborn, attracts, increases, looks to the future with assurance. The brilliant personality of Bernard only favored this tendency. The Cistercian Order was called upon to develop, to expand, and it was inevitable that there, as elsewhere, the rudimentary legislative system of the origins would have to be strengthened. All in all, it was better that this was done under the aegis of one inspired, a great spiritual theologian.

134. The resemblance between certain texts of St Bernard and some of those in the *Exordium Cistercii* and the *Summa Cartae caritatis* is such that one can attribute these two texts to him; in reality, as I have shown in the article "L'Exordium Cistercii et la Summa Cartae caritatis sont-ils de S. Bernard?" in *Recueil d'études sur S. Bernard*, vol. II (Rome: Ed. Storia e Letteratura, 1966), pp. 169–181, they seem rather to come from his milieu.

There is little doubt that at times, Bernard cast into the balance the weight of his extraordinary personality, but this was in special, exceptional cases, marginal with respect to the Cistercian life. For example, a case such as that of Arnold of Morimond had not been foreseen by the legislative.[135] It was resolved by Bernard in an authoritative and restrictive manner. It could have been otherwise, had Providence not caused these two men to belong to the same institute. Similarly, in the problems of *transitus* from one order to another, Bernard was sometimes one-sided.[136] However, it is the doctrinal principle which he advances, that of "liberty of spirit," which, on this point, brought about the relaxation of the canon law of the Church.

But, if beyond such outbreaks of partiality, of even human passion, one seeks to discern the monastic message of St Bernard, one sees that he prolongs the aspirations of the Fathers of Citeaux.

EXCURSUS

St Bernard and the Roman Curia

In respect to the relations of the Order with Rome there is a fact that deserves mention. St Bernard, who enjoined abbots to obey their bishops, also did very much and, doubtless, more than any one else in his time to set forth, defend and justify the authority of the Apostolic See. This is borne out by his treatise, *On Considera-tion*, no less that by the intervention he sought of the Pope at the time of the Abelard proceedings at the Council of Sens. However, he maintained complete liberty in the judgments he made regard-

---

135. In regard to this case, cf. L. Grill, "Morimond, soeur jumelle de Clairvaux" in *Bernard de Clairvaux* (Paris, 1953), pp. 117ff., and "Der hl. Bernhard von Clairvaux und Morimond, die Mutterabtei der österreichischen Cistercienserklöster" in *Festschrift zum 800-Jahrgedachtnis des Todes Bernhards von Clairvaux* (Vienna–Munich, 1953), pp. 31-116; see also the precisions brought to the matter by J.-B. Van Damme, "Genèse des Instituta generalis capituli" in *Cîteaux*, 12 (1961), pp. 43ff.

136. Cf. A. Dimier, "S. Bernard et le droit en matière de transitus," in *Revue Mabillon*, 43 (1953), pp. 48–82.

ing the justice of certain interventions on the part of Rome, in cases where fair procedure had not been respected.

The action taken in the affair of his young nephew, Robert, who passed from Clairvaux to Cluny, was efficacious but unlawful, and it is described with all the exactness that could be desired: representations are made at Rome, "the apostolic authority is forced," "suggestions" are made to the Pope of motives the truth of which are questionable and, at Rome, there is no attempt to understand the other party who is judged *in absentia. Mittitur interea pro eo Romam, Apostolica compellatur auctoritas, et, ut Papa non neget assensum, suggeritur ei . . . Non fuit qui refelleret (nec enim contradictor est exspectatus), judicatum est de parte, abjudicatum absentibus.*[137] Bernard protests. He calls upon a higher authority, that of Jesus Christ: *Tuum, Domine Jesu, tribunal appello. . . .*[138]

When the departure of Arnold of Morimond is made the object of a similar maneuver, Bernard denounces it; in an incredible manner the Pope has been "circumvented" by liars, or overcome by the insistence of plaintiffs. "I will by no means believe that the Pope did this unless you got around him by lying or overcame him by importunity." Among other objections was that of not taking the bishop of the place into account: "and, moreover, the contempt of their own bishop."[139] Bernard uses the same word *"circumvenire,"* to characterize the manner in which the Pope was informed of and influenced in the settling of another affair, that of the Abbot of Lagny: "not just anyone, but to get around the very prince of the Apostles." But that is human and can slip in surreptitiously: "I do not impute to my Lord, nor to any man, that which can slip in surreptitiously." Still, there is the duty of informing the Pope of all the aspects of the problem so that he may reestablish justice once he knows the truth, *ut veritatem agnoverit.*[140]

---

137. *Ep.* 1, 6, PL 182:73; James, Letter 1, p. 4.

138. *Ep.* 1, 7, PL 182:74; James, Letter 1, p. 5.

139. *"Propriumque insuper contemnendi episcopum"*—*Ep.* 7, 9, PL 182:99; James, Letter 8, p. 31.

140. *Ep.* 231, 3, PL 182:419; James, Letter 310, p. 381.

Also the letter to Haimeric, "Chancellor of the Holy Roman See," concludes with a point blank rejection of all the denunciations that are not made the object of an inquiry in due form. He hopes that this past method of deciding will come to an end: "that the Roman Curia cease from passing judgments in favor of those present and prejudicial to those absent."[141]

THE WITNESSES

After listening to those who created the Cistercian life and then to him who was its greatest prophetic voice, it is now time to attend to those innumerable witnesses—*nubes testium*—who, whether from within the new institution or from outside, have said what they thought of it, of its evolution and of its fidelity to its origins. Only a few instances can be noted here, yet they are sufficiently varied to give an idea of the reactions of the "public opinion" of the period (if the modern term may be applied to those distant times).

Fervent Disciples

First might be cited the disciples of the founding Fathers and of St Bernard himself. The biographers of Christian of Aumone gathered up the recollections that were in circulation at Cîteaux and elsewhere during the first half of the twelfth century. Now what they set forth as the characteristic of the Order, and this is the reason the hermit wanted to join it, was its poverty: "He had heard of the fame of the Cistercian Order and with burning heart desired their poverty."[142]

Eugene III had been a novice at Clairvaux in the time of St Bernard. When he became Pope he addressed to the General Chapter of the Order a message, in which, after a long preamble,

141. ". . . *cesset Romana curia pro voluntate assistentium facere praeiudicium in absentes.*"—*Ep.* 48, 3, PL 182:157; James, Letter 51, p. 81.

142. Under the title, "Le texte complet de la Vie de Christian de l'Aumône," in *Analecta Bollandiana*, 71 (1955), p. 33, I have edited this text. We find the same thing à propos of the Abbey of Barzella; *ibid.*, c. 24, p. 41.

and with all the rhetoric of the Curia, he says something quite specific: the goal of the founding Fathers was contemplative solitude: "they flew to solitude; . . . with Mary they sat at the feet of Jesus."[143] He was not unaware of the temptation to which the Cistercians of that time, now become numerous and prosperous, were exposed,—the temptation to exercise an influence other than that of the repose of contemplation and the silence of the desert: "Several times they have wanted to call you away from your occupations and your business." Resist, he says, and keep your eyes always turned toward the state of humility which your Fathers wanted for you: "choose rather to be an outcast in the house of God." In short, he warns the General Chapter that the life or death of the Cistercian Order depends upon its fidelity to the contemplative ideal. The importance of this authentic interpretation of the Cistercian event on the part of a pope must not be minimized. In terms reminiscent of those of recent popes and of Vatican II, he shows that the norm must remain the goal of the founders which had, moreover, the value of a prophetic sign: "bring before the mind's eye the instructions of your Fathers and regard them as prophetic examples."[144]

Let us now turn to some former novices of Bernard. One of them, Geoffroy of Auxerre, was destined to succeed him. He, too, writes of the origins of his Order, "since the pristine holiness of our Cistercian Order is to be found in its foundation. . . ." What was the purpose of the founders in making this new foundation? To revivify the observance of the Rule of St Benedict: *Ad redivivam observandae regulae beati Benedicti professionem.*[145] How? By "voluntary poverty" and "claustral solitude."[146]

---

143. "*ad solitudinem volaverunt . . . , ad pedes Jesu cum Maria sederunt.*"—*Inter Ep. S. Bernardi,* 272 bis, 2, PL 182:477.

144. "*ad mentis oculum patrum vestrorum instituta reducite, et propheticum habentes exemplum . . .*"—*Ibid.,* no. 3, PL 182:428.

145. Under the title, "Le témoignage de Geoffroy d'Auxerre sur la vie cistercienne," in *Analecta monastica,* II, Studia Anselmiana 31 (Rome, 1953), p. 193, I have published this text.

146. *Ibid.,* p. 180.

Another witness of the fervor that prevailed during the time of St Bernard is Peter of Roye who, in an enthusiastic letter, addresses himself to the provost of the Canons of Noyon. What stands out in it from amidst all the flowery rhetoric is the insistence on the renewal of the interior man, thanks above all to that form of humility which is poverty[147] and to contemplative solitude.[148] Both are to be found in the humble work of the monks[149] and in the simplicity of their way of life.[150] All that was new with respect to the forms of monastic life known up to that time. It was carrying through the new ways that had marked the origins of Cîteaux, "the New Monastery of the new Father," to use the expression of the Chronicle of Mortemer (an abbey of the Clairvaux line).[151]

Finally, Fastrede, who was the third successor of Bernard, having first been one of his novices, reminds one of his confrères of the obligation he is under of remaining "the disciple and imitator of evangelical poverty," *paupertatis evangelicae discipulus et imitator.*[152]

The Witnesses from Outside

Not all the outside witnesses are admirers. Neither are they detractors. But some do defend the status quo and in doing this they sometimes declare, with a precision that we cannot afford to neglect, exactly in what way Cîteaux seemed to them to be original. Now the strongest reproach levelled at Cîteaux is that of having innovated: "the newness of a separate institution," writes an anonymous author responding to the criticisms of St Bernard.[153]

---

147. *Inter Ep.S. Bernardi,* 492, 7, PL 182:710.   148. *Ibid.,* no. 8.

149. *Ibid.,* no. 9, col. 711.   150. *Ibid.,* no. 10, col. 712.

151. *"novum monasterium novi patris"*—PL 160:392.

152. *Inter Ep. S. Bernardi,* 491, PL 182:705. If nearly all the witnesses cited here are disciples of St Bernard, it is because it is they who above all thought of expressing themselves on the problem studied here; they clearly do not represent the whole of the Cistercian tradition. In *La spiritualité au moyen âge* (Paris, 1961), I have given a full list of "non-claravallian Cistercians," pp. 266–270.

153. Under the title, "Nouvelle réponse de l'ancien monachisme aux critiques des cisterciens," in *Recueil d'études sur S. Bernard,* II, p. 80, lines 185f. I have published this text.

"Founders of a new religious life . . .,[154] another order, you hold another way of life . . . ;" these are some of the statements of a famous *Riposte*.[155] "Emulators of a new institution," says Orderic Vital, who attributed to certain Cistercians the pretension of observing the Rule to the letter: "Like the Jews in regard to the Law of Moses, they decree that the Rule of St Benedict is to be kept to the letter."[156] There is too much irony in this sentence for it to be taken seriously.[157] More balanced in his judgment, Peter the Venerable tried to show that the ideal or program of poverty was common to both the Cluniacs and the Cistercians, but each realized it in a different way.[158]

Among the admirers, the first, chronologically, of those who expressed themselves at length, is Thurstan, Archbishop of York. He had to defend the monks of St Mary's who founded Fountains. He did so in 1132 in the form of a letter addressed to Archbishop William of Canterbury. His testimony, Clairvallian in its inspiration, is highly interesting. From the very beginning he admits that what the monks were undertaking was an "unusual thing," something truly "new": *res insolita, novitas res*. It consisted—and it will be remembered that such had been the case with the Fathers of Cîteaux—in desiring to lead a better life, *melior vita*, "following the Rule of St Benedict," *juxta Regulam beati Benedicti*, in conformity with their profession.[159] The abbot of the monastery abandoned by these monks is horrified by such an astonishing

---

154. Ed. A. Wilmart, "Une riposte de l'ancien monachisme au manifeste de S. Bernard," in *Revue Bénédictine*, 46 (1934), p. 326, line 642.

155. *"alium ordinem, aliam tenetis religionem"*—*Ibid.*, p. 335, line 991.

156. *"Decreverunt Regulam Benedicti, sicut Judaei legem Moysii ad litteram servare penitus."*—*Hist. eccles.*, 3, 8, 25, PL 188:637.

157. A little further on (*Hist. eccles.*, 3, 8, 26, PL 188:644) Oderic, alluding to the Cistercians without naming them, says that he has little esteem for austere monks who make innovations, *novas traditiones*.

158. *Inter Ep. S. Bernardi*, 299, 7, PL 182:402; ed. G. Constable, *The Letters of Peter the Venerable* (Cambridge, Mass.: Harvard University, 1967) I, p. 278.

159. *Inter Ep. S. Bernardi*, 490, 1, PL 182:697f.; trans. M. B. Pennington, "Three Early Documents," in *Cistercian Studies*, 4 (1969), The Epistle of Thurstan of York on the Founding of Fountains Abbey, no. 3, p. 149.

novelty, *novi rumoris miraculum exhorruit*, because he knows the inability of an aged institution to renew itself: "He has denied . . . that ancient rites and ingrained customs . . . can be . . . changed." To which the prior, the leader of the dissenting group, replies that there is nothing really new, but only a determination to return to the authentic and ancient religious life instituted by St Benedict: "We do not attempt to do anything new. We ought to take up . . . the ancient and authentic religious life of our Blessed Father Benedict . . . and observe it gladly with all our strength." The "new" is merely a return to the sources, a going beyond "our customs," *nostrae consuetudines* (to use the prevailing monastic expression). Thus, during the period after collation which we moderns would call "recreation," they refused to allow certain ones to indulge in nonsense and insignificant chit-chat: *alii recedunt vicissim ad nugas et inutiles garrulasque confabulationes.*[160]

The Cistercians were carrying out a return to "the purity of the Gospel," to "what Christ taught." This evangelical spirit was clearly manifest among the monks of Clairvaux—"the Gospel shines forth clearly in them . . .; it is as if the Gospel has come alive in them. . . ." Its first manifestation was a poverty that was real, which made them "content with a little land and some cattle," *modica cultura terrae et usu pecorum contenti sunt.* God is enough for them: "their portion is God alone." They seek only humility, love of God and neighbor, union with God. Does not all this savor of the Gospel?—*sapit Evangelium?*[161] Further on, there is renewed insistence on the same two characteristics: "to follow the poor Christ in voluntary poverty," *pauperem Christum in voluntaria paupertate sequi*; and "to observe fully Evangelical peace and the Rule of St Benedict," *evangelicum pacem regulamque beati patris Benedicti plene observare*;[162] "totally to fulfill the Rule, one's profession and the Gospel," *plena observatio Regulae ac professionis suae et Evangelii*;[163]

160. *Ibid.*, n. 2, col. 698f.; Pennington, no. 4, p. 150.
161. *Ibid.*, n. 3, col. 699f.; Pennington, no. 6, p. 151.
162. *Ibid.*, n. 7, col. 701; Pennington, no. 14, p. 154.
163. *Ibid.*, n. 10, col. 702; Pennington, no. 19, p. 155.

"to observe the Gospel and the Rule of St Benedict in truth,"
Christi Evangelio et Regulae beati Benedicti in veritate cupiunt oboedire.[164]
These are the characteristics of the Cistercian life: "the sense
of purity," *puritatis ingenium* and "the return to the entire
observance of the Rule," *sanctae Regulae renovationem et probatissimam
integritatem.*[165]

Just before his death in 1148, William, the former abbot of St
Thierry, writing the first book of the *Life of St Bernard*, recalled
that St Stephen Harding had left "holy poverty" as a heritage to his
posterity and that his "austerity" had stemmed from this poverty
and had consisted principally in it.[166] From the very start, Clairvaux
had lived in "poverty of spirit," *in paupertate spiritus.*[167] It was a
real poverty which could be seen, of which one could be aware,
"an awareness of voluntary poverty for the sake of Christ." This
was the goal of the renouncements of these "poor of Christ," who
were monks—not only to be poor, but to feel it, to experience it.
From this sprang "the simplicity and unpretentiousness of the
buildings and their inhabitants" as well as their silent work, inter-
rupted solely by prayer. Another characteristic was the solitude
which the community enjoyed and which everyone in it enjoyed.
The result was "solitude of heart,"[168] and union with God.
William then goes on to indulge in another description of their
poverty.[169]

One Hundred Years Later

As in everything else, time did its work: usage, if not decadence.
But those who did not resign themselves to this made a return to

164. *Ibid.*, n. 11, col. 703; Pennington, no. 20, p. 156.

165. *Ibid.*, n. 13, col. 704; Pennington, no. 22, p. 157.

166. *Vita prima S. Bernardi*, I, 18; PL 185:237; trans., G. Webb and A.
Walker, *St Bernard of Clairvaux* (Westminster, Maryland: Newman Press,
1960), p. 34.

167. *Ibid.*, n. 25, col. 241; Webb and Walker, p. 44.

168. *Ibid.*, n. 35, col. 247f.: "*Ad aliquam conscientiam voluntariae pro Christo,
paupertatis . . . solitudo cordis. . . .*"; trans. Webb and Walker, pp. 59f.

169. *Ibid.*, n. 36, col. 248; trans. Webb and Walker, pp. 60f.

their origins. About a century later, Helinand of Froidmont, in his *Chronicle*, summed up the Charter of Charity by recalling the major points: "purity of the Rule," solitude, poverty and work.[170] The author of the *Life of St Robert of Molesmes* stressed the newness of Cîteaux: "the observance of new institutions."[171] He recalled their aim: "that they might observe the Rule of St Benedict more fervently."[172] At the beginning of his *Exordium Magnum or An Account of the Beginning of the Cistercian Order*, Conrad of Eberbach placed the founders in the midst of a long story: "the unction" of the Holy Spirit had inspired St Benedict to give to all the West the observances found in his Rule: fasting, vigils, work and other precepts. The whole had been approved by Pope St Gregory in order that monks "might order their life according to this norm and abandon other customs," *reiectis ceterarum institutionum consuetudinibus ad eius normam cunctam suae vitae ordinem informarent.*[173] The Council of Aix of 817 had made this Rule obligatory and sufficient for the life of the monks "in all their conduct."[174] It had been circulated throughout Gaul by St Maur.[175] Following a period of decline it had been "restored" at Cluny under Odo,[176] and then under St Hugh.[177] But in spite of the latter's efforts, the general decadence of the monastic order required a renewal, a return to truth, "corrected and renewed, in line with truth."[178] The criticisms Bernard addressed to the Cluniacs in his *Apologia* were only too well deserved.[179] From where did the veil come? From conforming to "strange and false customs, *peregrinis et adulterinis consuetudinibus?* Whence the pride that the Cistercian feels at the thought that his Order has been renewed and brought back to the way of truth:

170. PL 212:1004.

171. Ed. K. Spahr, *Das Leben des hl. Robert von Molesmes* (Fribourg, 1944), c. 13, p. 17.

172. *Ibid.,* p. 16.

173. D. 1, c. 4, ed. B. Griesser (Rome, 1961), p. 52. An English trans. will appear as Vol. 30 in the Cistercian Fathers Series.

174. *Ibid.,* p. 53.   175. *Ibid.,* c. 5, p. 53.

176. *Ibid.,* c. 6–8, pp. 54ff.   177. *Ibid.,* c. 9, pp. 57f.

178. *Ibid.,* p. 59.   179. *Ibid.,* p. 60.

in renovato et ad tramitem veritatis per Cistercienses patres correcto monastico ordine?[180]

When he starts the account of the beginnings of Cîteaux, Conrad singles out the characteristics very clearly: "voluntary poverty for the sake of Christ,"[181] preference of the Rule to "the customs,"[182] because the latter depart from the former: *consuetudines ordinis a regula, quam professi erant, nimium discrepare,*[183] and the decision to observe the Rule "perfectly,"[184] and "entirely,"[185] He insists on the novelty of this: "a new religious life,"[186] "newly established,"[187] "a new order."[188] The principal point on which the "customs" are opposed to the Rule is that by dispensing with, or preventing manual labor, they are doing away with true poverty, *veram paupertatem.*[189] Thus, they prefer holy poverty to customs: *sanctam paupertatem magis redolentibus consuetudinibus commutantes.*[190] The first marvelous facts, *miracula*, in the Cistercian Order, reported by Conrad, are a reward for the practice of poverty.[191] Further on, he reverts to the principal characteristic of this renewal: it is a return to the Rule, "a renewal of the order in accordance with the Rule."[192]

Conrad is, therefore, a faithful witness and an authentic interpreter of the intentions of the Fathers of Cîteaux. For him, as for them, everything consists in a renewal that was a return to the Rule, in preference to customs, and which manifested itself principally by an effective poverty.

CONCLUSIONS

Intentions and Realities

The texts just analyzed attest, with an insistence that is monotonous, that the intentions of the founders of Cîteaux and of those who inherited their work were clear. They knew very well what they

180. *Ibid.*

181. *Ibid.*, c. 10, p. 61.

182. *Ibid.*, p. 62.

183. *Ibid.*, c. 11, p. 63.

184. *Ibid.*, p. 62.

185. *Ibid.*, p. 63.

186. *Ibid.*, c. 21, p. 77.

187. *Ibid.*

188. *Ibid.*, p. 78.

189. *Ibid.*, p. 77.

190. *Ibid.*, p. 78.

191. *Ibid.*, c. 24–25, pp. 83f., c. 28.

192. *Ibid.*, c. 29, p. 86.

wanted. Does this mean that they realized them in every particular, steadfastly, without any deviation? Other documents show that the facts sometimes stood in contradiction to the objective. It will suffice here to cite a few examples.

It has been remarked that in the realm of poverty and solitude there is an infraction of the Charter of Charity in the very foundation document of Cîteaux: an alodium of Raynard of Beaune is allowed to remain, along with its serfs, on the property which he has donated.[193] A historian has noted that "soon, the burden of donations would cause the entire Order to deviate from its route." What happened in this regard at Clairvaux? "The authority of St Bernard seems to have been strong enough that, up until 1153, only insignificant lapses can be noted due doubtless to the excessive zeal of a donor. . . . Now it is in 1153, the very year of the death of St Bernard, that we find the first serious infraction of the principles."[194] Sixteen years later the deviation was to become so great that Alexander III would be able to denounce a total transformation of the institution: "the entire way of life has undergone injury and change, a decline from the established customs, a leaving behind of the original manner of life of the institution."[195] The General Chapter reacted energetically to remedy the abuses, yet it cannot be said that it was totally successful.[196]

What about customs? They simply multiplied and became more and more precise until they developed into collections of "usages" more voluminous than those of many monasteries of the more ancient type. As for the relations with the local Church, there is a

193. Ed. Marilier, *op. cit.*, p. 50, III. This fact and other similar cases, dating from the time of the foundation, have been pointed out by J. Dubois OSB, in a review of Marilier in *Revue d'Histoire de l'Eglise de France*, 48 (1962), pp. 125f.

194. R. Fossier, "L'essor économique de Clairvaux" in *Bernard de Clairvaux* (Paris, 1953), p. 190.

195. Apostolic Letter, *Inter innumeras*, 1169, in the text which I published under the title, "Passage supprimé dans une épître d'Alexandre III" in *Revue Bénédictine*, 62 (1952), pp. 149–151.

196. See the texts I have published under the title, "Epîtres d'Alexandre III sur les cisterciens" in *Revue Bénédictine*, 64 (1954), pp. 70–82.

noticeable concern in the historical documents and in St Bernard, that they remain close, without prejudice to a recourse to Rome in case of conflict with the diocesan bishops. We know how energetically St Bernard opposed the abbots in his Order who should withdraw themselves from the authority of their bishops: "they themselves scorning to obey their bishops."[197] This attitude was not inspired by God, "because, should an abbot . . . say: 'I refuse to obey the bishop,' this is not from heaven."[198] Was it not undoubtedly true that some abbots in the Cistercian Order deserved the invectives he addressed to others: "With great effort and at a great price they have obtained apostolic privileges which permit them to lay claim to pontifical insignia for themselves so that, like the bishops, they can wear the miter, ring and sandals."[199] After the death of Bernard, exemption spread throughout the Order, where the use of *pontificalia* became so general that at a recent period it was presented as the sign of exemption. Other areas, too, could be cited in which the facts stand in contradiction to the intentions of the founders.

However, these intentions remained quite clear, showing what ought to have been and what ought to be in spite of the pressure of circumstances, common practice and the weakness of men. Contemporary historians of the Cistercian movement have not ceased to place the primitive objective in the forefront. Actually, it surpasses its realizations, it is what is best in early Cîteaux, that by which its Fathers proposed an ideal and sought to give an example. The intentions remain the norm and it is for history to discern them.

Criteria for a Renewal

If, during a period of renewal, monks wish to act as did the founders, and conformably with their intentions, it seems that the

197. *De moribus et officio episcoporum*, 33, PL 182:830.

198. *De consideratione*, 3, 18, *S. Bernardi Opera*, III, p. 445; trans., A. Luddy, *St Bernard's Treatise on Consideration* (Dublin: Browne & Nolan, 1921), p. 102. Cf. B. Jacqueline, "A propos de l'exemption monastique" in *Bernard de Clairvaux*, pp. 339–343; *Papauté et épiscopat selon S. Bernard de Clairvaux* (Saint Lo, 1967), pp. 113f.

199. *De moribus . . .* , 36, PL 182:832.

norms can be summarized in the key words which constantly recur in the texts that speak of the Fathers of Cîteaux.

Renovatio

Besides the interior renewal of fervor in the Holy Spirit, this term implied for them, and should therefore mean to their heirs, the capacity to make changes in established practices. One of the strong points of the Cistercians at the beginning of the Order and throughout the entire twelfth century, was that they adapted to the conditions of their times and that their legislation did not cease to evolve and profoundly so. They exemplify this great law of the history of societies and of the Church; periods of evolution of law are the most fruitful from every point of view, for evolution is a requirement of life. Just as the Cistercian Fathers knew how to adapt themselves, their heirs should be able to do likewise, and not look upon former solutions adopted under certain given circumstances for a time which is not theirs, as definitive and the only ones possible. Monks today must know how to break with the past, how to return to the intentions through all the realizations, how to rediscover the spiritual tradition beyond the historical traditions. And it must be done, as was the case at the beginning of the twelfth century, by taking into account the socio-economic context which is changing today as it was changing then.

Paupertas

This has to be real collective poverty with as few commitments of an economic nature as possible, assuring first of all to the abbots and then to the monks, the greatest amount of spiritual liberty with regard to the demands of temporal administration.

The subsistence of the monks and their influence by means of hospitality should be assured by work which, in the Middle Ages, was "manual labor," agrarian in type, but which can take on other forms in other times and yet remain real work.

The solution that consisted in the institution of the lay brothers and of utilizing hired help constituted, at the beginning of the twelfth century, a compromise between a true poverty founded on work and the prevailing social structures including serfdom. It resulted in creating, alongside the communities, or within them, a category of religious which, in the course of history, sometimes assumed characteristics and was subject to consequences contrary to what was intended. On the one hand, they very soon formed a sort of religious proletariat. From its very first redaction, the lay brothers' *Usages* attests to an exploitation of the brothers, and this fact doubtless motivated some of the rather numerous revolts which occurred among them.[200] On the other hand, while the Cistercians had the intention, in the way noted above, to abandon clerical structures, the existence of these lay coadjutors to whom they confided the cultivation of the granges and temporal affairs actually reinforced the clerical character of their life. Many lay brothers were of noble origin and remained important personages to whom the temporal administration was entrusted. This had the advantage of freeing the abbots from such tasks and, on this point, there was a return to the Rule of St Benedict. But, at the same time, it reduced the monks, so to speak, to "doing the liturgy" and *lectio divina*, and to doing only that without fulfilling either the duties of the pastoral ministry inherent in the life of clerics, or any work which was real, demanding, efficacious, and remunerating. In this sense, they were going contrary both to the Rule and to their own original intention.

Solitudo

There must be a real and effective separation with respect to the ordinary society of men, with a view to favoring the contemplative life, assiduous prayer and penance joyfully undertaken. The "remembrance of God" and the "pleasing devotion" of St Bernard

---

200. Under the title, "Comment vivaient les frères convers" in *Analecta Cisterciensia* 11 (1955), pp. 239–258, and in *I Laici nella "Societas Christiana"* (Milan, 1968), pp. 152–173, I have given some indications. In fact, many of the revolts of the lay brothers came about when the monasteries turned from the old type of economic structure, relegating to a secondary and seemingly unimportant position those important lay "leaders" who were often the lay brothers. There is a somewhat similar situation today as automation leaves skilled laborers unhappy as the significance of their skills is lost.

K

and others are equivalent to the "constant prayer" and "ready penance" of *Perfectae caritatis*, no. 7.[201]

This separation from the world was conceived by the Fathers of Cîteaux as a geographical solitude, that is, a withdrawal into the plains and the forests, away from urban and other settled areas. It can take on other forms in an urban-type civilization or in one that is in the process of urbanization, but it does not remain Cistercian unless it is real, that is, guaranteed by the observance of enclosure and filled by a contemplative life lived by monks fraternally grouped together in a community, whatever be their number.

Puritas Regulae

If the Rule of St Benedict remains the fundamental law of the cenobitic life, it is only, as the Fathers of Cîteaux understood it, in the sense that it should be preferred to the usages subsequently introduced. Monks today must know how to go back, beyond "the observances" of a period that has passed, to "the observance" of the Rule. In regard to the Cistercian "usages" one must have the same courage that the Fathers of the twelfth century showed toward the "customs" of ancient monasteries, and devise observances which, while responding to the requirements previously set forth, are equally conformed to the capacities and needs of contemporary man and to the socio-economic conditions of our times.

All literalism then, be it in the interpretation of the Rule or in the application of the "usages" introduced after the twelfth century, is contrary to the intention of the Fathers of Cîteaux. Like them their followers in the light of experiments taking place, even those outside the Order,[202] must know how to choose from among observances, Cistercian and others, and also from among the prescriptions of the Rule,[203] only those which are still truly useful. This last point

201. *"memoria Dei; iucunda devotio; assidua prece; alacris paenitentia."*

202. Cf. B. Schneider, "Cîteaux und die benediktinische Tradition" in *Analecta S.O. Cist.*, 16 (1960), pp. 165–254; 17 (1961), pp. 73–114. I have written on the results of this study in "Une thèse sur Cîteaux dans la tradition monastique" in *Collectanea O. Cist. Ref.*, 24 (1962), pp. 358–362.

203. Under the title, "Le monachisme et S. Benoît" in *Aux sources de la spiritualité occidentale* (Paris, 1964), pp. 15–33, I have brought out these values.

does not fail to pose a delicate problem, but one that present-day monks should not fear to tackle.

The spiritual program set up by the Rule, thanks to an admirable balance of values which must mark all monastic life, is not an element of the Rule which is passé because linked to an age no longer ours.[204] The elements which are outmoded are practical details of observance and some moral considerations which are conditioned by a reading of Holy Scripture which can no longer be ours or by an anthropology which belongs to the past.

For example, to justify common ownership by a recourse to what is said of the primitive community of Jerusalem in the Acts of the Apostles, is not in conformity with the true meaning of these texts.[205] Nor does it indicate the only possible form of monastic poverty, or even necessarily the best form for today.[206]

Likewise, although the Rule contains an excellent doctrine on obedience,[207] it nevertheless describes practices which make one think that its form of obedience is for docile and ignorant children, perpetual minors, something apt to favor infantilism rather than the maturity and the sense of responsibility demanded by *Perfectae Caritatis* (no. 14). The exercise of authority and of submission foreseen in the Rule is, on certain points, fit for monks whom it would be considered normal to chastise by beatings. Such an idea would not even occur to us today. We must free ourselves from what was written for men of this sort.

204. A. Wathen, "Relevance of the Rule Today" in *American Benedictine Review*, 19 (1968), pp. 234–253, has shown that, "seemingly irrelevant prescriptions of the Rule may have some relevance today" (p. 246), not so much in themselves as in regard to the whole, to the "balance" (p. 250) which they suppose and favor.

205. Cf. J. Dupont, *Etudes sur les Actes des Apôtres* (Paris, 1967) pp. 503–512.

206. Cf. J. Winandy, "Le sens originel des conseils évangéliques" in *Collectanea Ord. Cist. Ref.*, 22 (1960), pp. 109–111. The whole of this excellent study has been reproduced in *Etudes sur les Instituts séculiers*, I (Paris, Desclée de Brouwer, 1963), pp. 299–317.

207. Under the title, "L'obedienza religiosa secondo la Regola de S. Benedetto" in *Vita Monastica*, 14 (1960), pp. 51–63 and "Religious Obedience according to the Rule of St Benedict" in *American Benedictine Review*, 16 (1965), pp. 58–85, I have developed this doctrine.

What remains of value in the Rule of St Benedict is that which in it is evangelical. And that by itself will suffice to create forms of poverty, obedience, designation of the superiors, participation in government, silence, enclosure, asceticism and prayer that will allow today's monks to realize St Benedict's project—to seek God.

The authentic, fundamental law to which the Rule itself refers us is in the last analysis the Gospel. We should re-read the Rule seeking to discern what in it conforms to the current approach to the Gospels and to present-day anthropology: the spirituality, the asceticism, the psychology, the economy, the legal structures, the hygiene, etc. And if finally there remain but a few of the observances fixed by the Rule that are still viable we should not be frightened. Why should we not have the right—indeed, more—the duty to re-cast in a century so profoundly different from that of St Benedict, what he had fashioned for his day?[208] In so far as they could, the Cistercian Fathers accomplished this for their age, but they were conditioned by a Rule considered as sacred and inspired, and, consequently, in a certain sense, untouchable. St Benedict, himself, had no such anterior rule to respect, not even that of St Basil for which, however, he shows marked veneration. A man of God, or a group like that of the founders of Cîteaux, could, in our days, act in like manner: preserve a veneration for the Rule of St Benedict but create anew without concerning oneself with any sacred antecedents other than those of the Gospel.

Caritas

The intention of the Rule and that of the Fathers of Cîteaux is to lead to purity of heart which is that charity toward God and man

208. J. Hourlier OSB, "La Règle de S. Benoît source de droit canonique" in *Etudes d'Histoire du Droit canonique Dédiées à Gabriel Le Bras* (Paris, 1965), I, pp. 157–168. The author brings out the real value, although relative and limited, of the Rule and he considers the Cistercian effort to return to the Rule, which "perhaps deformed the spirit of the Rule, very certainly the monastic tradition." (p. 163) He concludes with these words: "Its fortune (the Rule's) through the centuries has not given it a character which it did not possess in itself, an absolute value. To remind oneself of this through historical studies will offset mistakes. We don't have to guess as to the opportuneness of looking back in order to create the future."

of which Jesus Christ, in the Gospels, has given the example and the doctrine. The norm of renewal in every field—poverty, solitude, observances—should, then, be charity. In particular, identity in customs and in liturgical books was conceived, at the beginning of the twelfth century and within a very limited geographical area, as a means of favoring and expressing charity, union of hearts, a "unanimity" which was not "uniformity."[209] Today, in a pluralistic epoch, wherein charity expresses itself in a respect for diversity and in giving to men of all civilizations the means of developing the God-given characteristics proper to them, uniformity in ways of praying and acting would run counter to the intentions of the Fathers of Cîteaux.

Finally, just as they wished to renew the monastic life in the spirit of the great movements in the Church of that time, marked as it was by the effects of the Gregorian Reform, so, too, their heirs should enter joyfully into the movement of the post-Council Church. The return of the local Church to the forefront and a new style of relations with the Roman Curia form a part of the reform inaugurated by Vatican II. We have seen that these two traits are also in accord with the conduct of the first Cistercians.[210]

Jean Leclercq OSB

Clervaux Abbey,
Luxembourg

209. Under the title, "Une ancienne rédaction des coutumes cisterciennes" in *Revue d'Histoire Ecclésiastique*, 47 (1952), p. 175, n. 1, I have pointed out the change from *unitas* (unity) in the ancient edition of the *Brothers' Regulations* to *uniformitas* (uniformity) in a later edition.

210. As I complete this I am bound to thank those specialists in the fields of history and the monastic institutions of the twelfth century to whom this study owes some useful suggestions: Fathers J. Dubois OSB, Remi Gosselin O CIST, J. Hourlier OSB, N. Huyghebaert OSB, H. de Sainte Marie OSB, J.-B. Van Damme OCSO.

A SOCIOLOGICAL APPROACH TO THE HISTORY
OF A RELIGIOUS ORDER

W E ARE HERE today for the purpose of discovering the intentions and aims of the founders of Cîteaux with a view to finding an answer to the present "crisis" of monasticism, and thus passing judgment on it. This implies two types of operation: the one concerned with the past—the establishment of facts, their interpretation in the light of historical context and theological implications,— the other more directly concerned with the present —the discernment of those facts inherited from the past which are still valid in this second half of the twentieth century.

With regard to the past, research can be carried out by two of several possible methods: the one, analytic, consists in tracing the evolution of facts as it is revealed by chronology, philology and the other disciplines of history; the other, synthetic, looks at this evolutionary process as a whole, that is, it considers it as a socio-logical factor of unification. And as we read through the documents relating to Cistercian origins, we do in fact come across many a word closely connected with the sphere studied by the sociologist whose discipline deals, among other things, with groups and regul-ations. He uses words like status, classes, structures, function: whereas Cistercian sources refer to groups of men and to institu-tions, making frequent use of terms such as: *congregatio, ecclesia, coenobium, claustrum, abbatia, monasterium, unanimiter, transgressio, rectitudo, consuetudines, observantia, regula, custodia;* and others which evoke a process of evolution: *inchoata, coeperunt, novitas, renovatio.*

Thus it would seem legitimate to interpret the facts offered by the sources we are considering here in the light of the historical sociology of religious orders. This has already been done in a masterly way by Fr Tufari sj, professor of the Faculty of Social Sciences in the Gregorian University, and all that follows in these pages is entirely dependent on his teaching. I am most grateful to him for the insights he has given on this problem, and I very much doubt whether I shall be able to do justice to them here.

Hitherto, the history of religious orders has been connected more with the history of spirituality, the ascetic life, and man's personal encounter with God, or even the history of legislation, rather than with the evolutionary development of groups within the Church. The aim of the interdisciplinary method of historical sociology is to bring into evidence any elements of a given situation which are of such general nature that they are applicable in other circumstances. Let us consider, for example, the main processes and elements of the history of a religious order; birth and origin; growth and evolution; fatherhood, leadership, founder and foundation; charism and identification with the order; the part played by the rule; identity crisis and growth within the order; affiliation and achievement in the religious life. No specific application will be made at this stage to the Cistercian origins. That will be matter for further reflection.

Origins

A distinction may be made between the birth *of* the order, a fact which depends on the leader and his leadership, and birth *in* the order, which is a process of socialization brought about when a new member joins the order and is integrated into it.

We may also distinguish between the birth of and in a "movement," and the birth of and in an "association." A movement—be it religious, social, political, ideological—concerns a large number of people; it appears as being called for by the life of this particular group of people, and not merely as an organization of the externals of their existence. An association, on the other hand, is restricted to a smaller number of persons; it has a well-defined organisation and structure; it may have grown out of a movement, or be the expression of it. In the case of religious orders, and of the Cistercian Order in particular, we may ask ourselves whether it is in any way comparable to what is today called a movement.

Growth

When we speak of growth in connection with an order as part of the Church, we are dealing with a process of evolution which has two aspects: growth *in* the Church, and growth *of* the Church. The first may give rise to deviations, it may be accompanied by disease on account of the presence from birth of some corruptive virus. In this case the Church has to control, and, when necessary, intervene with a remedy. It is her business to watch over the good use in an order of both initiative and flexibility.

On the other hand, the structural change of an order may result from the growth of the Church herself, leading to changes in her structure and thought in one or more domains. We may wonder how the internal evolution of an order can be accomplished within an evolving Church. Does the order necessarily have to undergo change in precisely those same structural and conceptual domains as does the evolving Church? Has the Cistercian Order ever been faced by such a problem in the past? Is it so in the present?

Further growth, that is evolution, may be provoked by a period of crisis: a situation where it is impossible to continue in the same state of affairs. Under such conditions, there are two possible solutions: reform, implying return to the original spirit within the order and/or outside it, but within the Church; or, a new foundation.

How are these phenomena and growth to be explained? Do they occur simply in virtue of social determinism, or are they dependent on the "great man theory"? It is probable that both factors come into play, especially when there is a group charism, as there was with the first Cistercian fathers, the first Carmelites, or the seven founders of the Servites. This gives great importance to the concept which will be evoked next.

Fatherhood

The founder is always the one who takes the initiative to start something new; this newness may be a rebirth, so to speak, of the order, in which case the founder is also a reformer. Whatever the intention of the founder, birth or rebirth, it is manifested in the resulting foundation. This is dependent on other factors, both external and internal; it gives a concrete form to legislation, and makes use of a certain formalization of behavior which in its turn implies a unity of law, a universality of rule, which yet leaves room for adaptation to local conditions.

This process of birth, or rebirth, is one in which the original personal experience of an individual becomes the experience of a group of individuals, of a community. The experience no longer belongs to the sphere of the psychologist of religion, but to that of the sociologist of religion.

What are the personal and specific elements evoked by the term "founder"? This is not entirely equivalent to the sociological category "leader," but knowledge of the concept content of this last word can shed light on that implied by "leader."

A leader is an organizer, a person gifted with certain qualities which enable him, in a given situation, to stimulate a group of which he becomes head, chief, superior by reason of his human ability and intelligence, or else his spiritual charism, very often because of both. And he is accepted because he says things which are relevant and meaningful for a movement or group. He responds to imperious needs with new solutions. He has become aware of these imperious needs by his personal experience and life, and he expresses them and the solutions he proposes in a way which is meaningful for others, either in writing or by his example, often by both. This aspect of leadership is frequently that which is at the origin of a religious order. The leader is not necessarily a man out of the ordinary; practically each new situation reveals new leaders. This is a fact which is verified in society—in politics, for example— and in the Church which, in the nineteenth century, had many founders of religious orders not all of whom were either first-class saints or geniuses.

Not every great religious personality is a leader: some are saints, they have a deep personal encounter with God; some are doctors, they supply new ideas, new solutions, of the speculative order; some, again, are leaders, they propose new solutions in the practical order. In other words, there are some who see and cannot do, others who neither see nor do, and a few who see and do.

The leader or founder draws up a chart, a rule, a written manifesto of his intention, born of his personal experience; this will always be the basic foundation, the blue-print, upon which his future disciples will build and often modify. This process of modification and change often leads to what may be termed the "third superior" theory. There are many possible examples to support this view, but fundamentally it may be summarized as follows.

The leader-founder is usually a strong personality: a genius and a saint; he has an intuition of what must be done within the Church in order to reply to new needs and situations. After him comes his successor, who is a sort of sub-leader; he usually has a less strong personality than the founder whom he has known, to whom he is personally and deeply attached and whose work he wishes to continue. Then comes the "third superior" who, chronologically speaking, may be the fourth or fifth; he has not known personally the first leader and thus is sentimentally free, he admires him and now feels himself to be responsible for maintaining his foundation. Thus, he sets about stabilizing, organizing facts which had so far been nothing more than empirical and historical solutions to a given situation which, though it existed in the founder's time, is now long past. In some cases the "third superior" may come to be considered as the real founder of the order under the form it took in the second generation after the founder's death. And it is here that we witness the shift of importance from the psychology of the founder to the sociology of the foundation—a process of gradual change, of evolution, brought about by the medium of the first companions and those who interpret the message of the deceased founder. It sometimes happens that some of the companions of the founder leave the foundation when this has passed into his successor's hands. Frequently, also, it is in the third generation—

always psychologically speaking—that some powerful mind elaborates the theology of the order, some gifted biographer sets down the legend of the founder, and a great legislator drafts the constitutions.

Thus it is not sufficient to have a simple change from the founder's charism to a consecutive administration which is nothing more than a meaningless bureaucracy; the two are complementary. The charism must be incorporated in a rule, a law, an organization, an administration; and these in their turn must be animated, inspired by a charism, an enthusiasm.

Charism and Identification

The problem here is to know just how far the personal inspiration, the gift of grace—let us say, of Saint Ignatius—may be communicated to the thirty thousand Jesuits of the actual generation, and be common to each one as well to the many others in past and future generations? How can many religious identify themselves with the charism of their founder? This is the problem of the relationship between his charism and the process of identification with the founder, the foundation and the order.

To be able to solve this problem, we must have some general notion of what is meant by identification: this consists in the "internalization" of self with a role or a group. It should be recalled at this point that Jung introduced a distinction between person and personage as did Gabriel Marcel between person and function. I am not what I do, and I must not identify myself entirely with it; I should, rather, identify it with what I am. I must integrate my activity into my personality.

Now, what is meant by "charism of the founder?" It is not necessarily that which has made him personally a saint, but that which makes him *act* as a *founder* for a *group*. Generally, a person has a certain line of conduct and, to a certain extent, his future action is predictable. In the case of a founder, the charism consists precisely in the inspiration which leads him to take a certain line of action resulting in the foundation of a religious order. The founder's charism is limited to the foundation.

Thus, not everything which the saint said or did is to be considered as holy with regard to the order, even though it may have
been holy with regard to his person. His charism exists, but it is
not evidenced by every one of the different manifestations of his
sanctity.

Furthermore, in the event of an order evolving, one cannot say
that it has degenerated, even if it is far removed from the founder's
original intention. This evolution may be a betterment, a progress
which he himself might well have brought about and approved
in a situation different from that existing in his day. No order has
remained statically and totally identical with its original self,
neither is it dynamically and totally different.

It now remains to be seen how a number of persons can be made
to identify with the structural and organic fixation of the founder's
charism.

The Rule

Let us first distinguish between the end and the way. Members of
an order have to identify with certain spiritual values constituting a
common end, and with certain norms constituting a common way.
The rule is the expression of these values and norms, this common
end and way. The rule is the mediator in the dilemma which might
arise from the confrontation of personal experience and common
institution, for it makes an attempt at respecting each member's
personal religious experience which can never be sacrificed to the
institution nor absorbed by it. It is thus that all rules which have any
lasting value are impregnated with a personalist character such as is
found in the Rule of St Benedict. It is thus, too, that the "Constitutions" may well be a menace to the rule, which they absorb, or they
may become so developed and organized that they engulf the person in the institution which they erect. The rule, however, gives
expression to the minimum common norm which all members must
observe in order to be identified with the order. The limits set out
by the rule are those which define the minimal characteristics
specific to a given order: should a person be found lacking in this
minimum, he cannot claim to belong to the order.

Thus the purpose of the rule is to give scope for legitimate—and, therefore, limited—identification without sacrificing the person to the institution. Put otherwise, this means that the rule helps persons to pass from the state of isolated individuals to that of members of an order—this makes the common life—and it helps the collectivity of the individual members of an order to be members together of the Church. This collective membership in the Church determines, in its turn, the specific mission of an order within the Church: either a given form of charitable activity, or, in the case of the contemplative orders, the witness of a life.

This process of identification is not without certain risks. Some of these may arise from legislation which tends to encompass the rule, originally intended to provide a climate favoring personal spiritual growth, within a scaffolding of regulations. This institutionalization may lead to a certain pseudo-mystique called "observance." Other dangers may be created by the persons who are members of the order. Once they have become stereotyped in a certain rigid system of values, they lose their personality, give way to uniformity, conformity, exteriority, ritualism, rigidity, accepted mediocrity.

How may these dangers be avoided?

Identity Crisis and Growth in the Order

This new step in the spiritual evolutionary process leads from birth and maturity *of* the order to birth and maturity *in* the order, that is to say to the socialization of a person.

First, concerning the birth *of* the order. An order's capacity for growth and assimilation depends largely on the conditions existing at its origin. Some orders retain their pristine beauty, they continue to be attractive, they develop harmoniously and rapidly; others lose the charm which they had at birth, they fail to attract, grow slowly and with difficulty, they may even die out.

Secondly, birth *in* the order. This is not, as might be thought, a passage from an individual experience to a communal one. The order exists before the person; hence the experiential flow is from the general to the particular, from the communal to the personal.

It is this social process which allows the individual to learn insertion into the group, to identify himself with it by acquiring the spiritual attitudes which are approved by the group as being legitimate. This process of identification provides a lawful justification of the restrictions imposed by the order on the member's private life and right to private property, in so far as these hinder adequate identification. The test of authenticity lies in the extent of the member's development as a person: does membership of an order bring an individual to his full personal status? This is something which must be carefully attended to by the spiritual guide. His role is not confined to furthering insertion and assimilation, he must also ensure that an individual does not lose his personality by conformity with a group. It is wrong to reject a subject on grounds that "he has a personality."

Certainly, it is true that religious orders have a privileged position with regard to other groups such as the family and professional associations. Sociologists distinguish between "community" (*Gemeinschaft*) and "society" (*Gesellschaft*), the former supposing a certain vicinity of persons, the latter implying an association of interests. Other distinctions are made between the "primary group," founded on a face-to-face relationship as it were, and the "secondary group," the basis of which is more universal. A religious order is a group which is both primary and secondary.

In religious life, identification with the order is a process of socialization initiated by the subject's free choice. It leads to an integration because there is never perfect coincidence of the person with the group. The individual retains his personality. Within the religious groups the primary standards are not those of the order, but the common norms of Christianity.

The initial free choice, the choice to be a member of an order—which restricts identification to its legitimate limits and avoids the dangers of exaggeration,— must be continuous, constantly renewed and strengthened. Religious life is a life of inner crisis. This is often only minimal in the postulant; liberty and free choice should increase during the novitiate and throughout life. Hesitation, tension, temptation, lead to renewed choice, to acceptation and consent. A person who constantly criticizes everything in the order has not identified himself with the best interests of the order. On the other hand, the awareness of what must or ought to be is keener in the religious life than elsewhere by reason of the ideal of perfection which inspires the members, and—sometimes—on account of psychological conditioning occasioned by such factors as, for example, enclosure. We have to accept religious life as it is, not as it ought to be.

Affiliation and Achievement

The result of the process of integration, of limited socialization and identification should be the person's affiliation with the order: he must be accepted, not for what he does, but for what he is. It should lead to his personal achievement as an adult, a free and responsible being, not just a functional cog, someone who does something in the order. The test should be "who is he?" and not "what does he do?". And if he *is* a person, he will *act* as a person. The development of persons in the community and in the order furthers the very development of both community and order; it is then that the community fulfills its role as a community, and the members feel they are affiliated and have no need for mechanisms of compensation such as pets, hobbies and useless relations with people.

In religious life, a person should find achievement, fulfillment, satisfaction; having identified himself with the life of his choice, he remains free and becomes constantly more free in his relations with God and men for the service of the Church.

Jean Leclercq OSB

Clervaux Abbey,
Luxembourg

THE
WITNESS OF THE EARLY ENGLISH CISTERCIANS
TO THE SPIRIT AND AIMS OF THE FOUNDERS
OF THE ORDER OF CÎTEAUX

"THE CISTERCIAN REVIVAL of pure Benedictinism was ultimately a failure, but it was one of the most gallant failures in the history of the Church." This quotation from a booklet sold today at the ruins of Fountains Abbey continues: "At Fountains though the Church is still majestic and beautiful, it is roofless and derelict, and the floor is grass. It is a show piece now instead of a house of prayer."

Then it asks: "But would St Stephen Harding, Richard, its first Abbot, and his successors during the next seventy years, really have wept over the destruction of this wealthy house and her glorious church?"

"There is no evidence of corruption or abuse, but it is impossible to avoid the feeling that after the first seventy years there was a new set of values within the walls of Fountains; and the Cistercian ideal was so delicate, that whenever part of it was abandoned, the whole was put in jeopardy."[1]

One may not agree with this judgment; but there does seem to have been something quite special about those first seventy years, not only for Fountains but for the whole Cistercian Order in England. This paper is an attempt to say something of men like Aelred of Rievaulx who labored during those seventy years to make the reality of their own lives and the lives of their monks identical with the ideals of the Founders of Cîteaux.

1. A. M. Wilkinson, *The Fountains Story* (Ripon: Wakeman Press, 1961).

What were the ideals of early Cîteaux to which the English Cistercians were witnessing? When I began to write this paper, I was by no means clear as to what was especially "Cistercian" as distinct from "monastic" in the early days of the Order, and I was anxious to avoid fitting the English Cistercians into my preconceived ideas of Cîteaux. After some reflection on the writings and activities of the English White Monks, five themes in particular seemed to emerge:

1. Their regard for the evangelical aspect of the life, especially poverty.

2. Their regard for St Benedict, and the position of the Rule as a practical interpretation of the Gospel.

3. Their desire to taste and see how good God is.

4. Their desire to seek God by sharing their love for him and their common aims in a life lived in community.

5. Their realisation that charity was at the heart of the monastic life. (This last theme is so important that it will be discussed in a separate paper, and so I have not treated it explicitly.)

On consideration, I felt that these points taken together would contribute to form what I had always regarded as the Cistercian face of Christ.

Before discussing these themes, one should perhaps say something of the men upon whose witness we are going to draw, and the period in which they lived.

Cîteaux had been founded in 1098, and it was just thirty years later that the Cistercians came to England. St Stephen Harding was still alive, and St Bernard, with twenty-five more years as abbot before him, was at the height of his powers. Before his death in 1153 there were thirty-six Cistercian houses in England, all but four of which were descended from Waverley, Rievaulx or Fountains. To these may be added the thirteen Savigniac houses which joined the Order in 1147. When they came to England, the Cistercians would have found a native monasticism that had been given new life since the Norman conquest by such men as

L

Lanfranc, Anselm and Gundolf. And the effects of the literary culture and spiritual ideals brought by these men were still evident, at least in some houses of the Black Monks.

Politically these were often lawless times, especially during the Civil War between King Stephen and the Empress Matilda. It was during these troubled years that many of the new monasteries were founded, and there was constant danger from prowling marauders.

Among the men who governed these monasteries and guided the monks entrusted to them was Abbot William, St Bernard's English secretary, sent by him to found Rievaulx (1132); and his successor there, Aelred (1110–1167), previously steward at the Scottish court and finally father of a monastery of more than six hundred men.

Of the thirteen Black Benedictines who founded Fountains (1133), eight were later to become abbots, among whom were St Robert of Newminster, and Gervase, Abbot of Louth Park—the latter a monk for over fifty years and one of the great figures among the English Cistercians. (†1150).

There was Roger of Byland (1100–1196), a man of simple yet deep spirituality, and contemporary with him was Gilbert, Abbot of Swineshead, a disciple, in the spirit, of St Bernard and a man of intense prayer. Finally, towards the end of our period came Baldwin of Ford, later Archbishop of Canterbury, who had such a profound grasp of the meaning of community life.

It is of course a short list of witnesses to cover a period of seventy years from the foundation of Waverley (1128) to the end of the century. And we must remember that the material comes mostly from the preaching of abbots in chapter or from treatises carefully prepared by them. There is little from the rank and file, except for the Chronicle of Hugh of Kirkstall (written about 1207) which is largely based on the reminiscences of the old monk Serlo who had actually known the founders of Fountains.

1. *Their regard for the evangelical aspect of the life, especially poverty*
Hugh of Kirkstall relates that when the group of monks from Clairvaux founded the monastery of Rievaulx in the valley of the

Rye in Yorkshire, a rumor spread abroad that they were men of extraordinary holiness, really worthy of the name of monk. This report affected especially a group of Benedictines at York, who were eager for renewal. Led by Prior Richard and Subprior Gervase, they tried to explain to their Abbot that they wanted nothing that was novel but only the ancient Rule of their Father St Benedict, or rather the most ancient Gospel of Christ which transcends all Rules, and to observe this by God's grace with all their strength. Was the Gospel teaching, they asked, too hard or even impossible to put into practice? Then what about Savigny, or the monks of Clairvaux who had recently arrived and about whom everyone was talking? How clearly the Gospel had come to life again in them. Surely it would be more profitable to imitate them, than to read about the Gospel. These strangers were really trying to live out their profession, and their sincerity made them free. Unlike so many others, they were not attached to what they owned. They did not try to outshine their neighbors . . . but were content to cultivate the land and rear cattle. There were few who could say as they might: "The world is crucified to us and we to the world." A happy race of men whose diet, whose dress, whose whole life savor of the Gospel.[2]

Rievaulx, then, was a place where the Gospel was lived, and with the spirit of the Gospel went a spirit of poverty. When the group of York Benedictines—now adopted by St Bernard—was once established in the damp sunless valley of Skeldale, they too tried to make their own monastery of Fountains also a place where the Gospel was lived. For two years, by necessity, they lived under conditions of intense poverty. At first they had no shelter from the severity of the winter, except a poor shepherd's hut, and all slept under a great elm tree, covering themselves with straw and bracken. They got up to sing the night office, and during the day worked to build a chapel and tried to earn their living by plaiting mats and

2. "Chronicle of Hugh of Kirkstall," trans. A. W. Oxford in *The Ruins of Fountains* (Oxford: Oxford Press, 1910), Appendix One. Cf. W. Dugdale, *Monasticon Anglicorum,* 8 vols. (London: Bohn, 1817–1830), Vol. 5, pp. 231–239.

starting a vegetable garden. The chronicle reports: "They came hungry to table and went tired to bed, but there was no sign of gloom or grumbling. They blessed God with all their hearts, being poor in worldly goods but strong in faith"[3]—yet it was the poverty of the Gospel which bore fruit in charity, for even then they were already practicing that charity to the poor which was to reach its peak under Abbot Ralph (1190–1203). During the famine that occurred in his day, the poor gathered in great numbers at the gate of Fountains; the brethren made rough shelters for them, and the Abbot arranged for food to be distributed and for priests to attend the sick, give them the sacraments and bury the dead.[4]

Evangelical poverty that was real was certainly one of their ideals, as Roger of Byland was to write to a prospective postulant thirty years later: "Poor we follow the poor Christ, so that we may learn to serve him with minds that are free. We work, we fast, we keep vigil, we pray; Christ does not ask for gold and silver from us—only that we love and serve him with a pure heart and body."[5] Aelred too, when he was dying, used almost the same words—he had his Psalter, Confessions of Saint Augustine, the text of Saint John's Gospel, some relics and a little cross brought to him, then he told those around him: "I have kept these by me in my little oratory, and have delighted in them to the utmost. Silver and gold I have none—hence I make no will, for I possess nothing of my own. Whatever I have, and I myself, are yours."[6] This was the real poverty of Christ that liberated, because it allowed nothing to take God's place in his soul's devotion.[7]

But mere material poverty could also be a drawback. Fountains after two years was in such straits that the community appealed to St Bernard to find them a new site; and several other monasteries

---

3. Hugh of Kirkstall, trans. Oxford, p. 167.   4. *Ibid.*, p. 224.

5. "Roger of Byland's Letter to a Young Scholar," ed. C. H. Talbot, *Analecta S.O. Cist.,* 7 (1951), pp. 218ff.

6. W. Daniel, *Vita Ailredi Abbatis Rievalli,* trans. F. Powicke, *Life of Ailred of Rievaulx* (Nelson: London, 1950), p. 58.

7. *Speculum Charitatis,* I, 17: PL 195:520; trans. *The Works of Aelred of Rievaulx,* vol. 2, Cistercian Fathers XVII.

did not succeed on their original sites. Jervaulx, Whalley, Louth Park, Vaudey, Calder, to mention but a few. Generally the reason was poverty. The monks of Ford, for example, after a five year struggle, lacked even the necessities of life, and were actually on their way home to Waverley, when they were given new lands and enabled to make a fresh start.

Besides the often barren soil, there was always the English weather to contend with, which though it may be the best in the world, has its share of wet and cold, causing bad harvests and cattle diseases. The poverty which resulted could cause even well-established houses like Waverley or Meaux to disband for a while until things improved.

The poverty of the Gospel was not the same thing as economy, but it was closely linked with the economic life of the monastery, and the goal of the Cistercian economic life was to be self-supporting and have something over for almsgiving. The English Cistercians were hard-working enough and adapted themselves to local conditions. Jervaulx was famous for its horses, Furness for its ore mines, Fountains for its sheep, Rievaulx had sheep and probably linen. But it was in the field of poverty that the ideal first began to fade. According to the Little Exordium, the labor for this economy was to come from the monks, brothers and hired workers. Serfs were forbidden, as likewise the manorial system and ecclesiastical revenue.[8]

Gradually, however, serfs began to be acquired either by purchase or by gift with grants of land, and as early as 1157 the General Chapter took steps regarding the evasion of rules in respect to income from mills. Towards the end of our period a series of prohibitions had to be issued regarding the possession of churches, a practice that was involving the monasteries in lawsuits and rivalries.

It has been said, perhaps with some truth, that the English Cistercians were avaricious for land, both to buy and to rent. In the course of time they did acquire large estates; but much of it

8. A. Coburn-Graves, "Economy of English Cistercians," *Analecta S.O. Cist.*, 13 (1957), p. 3.

came to them through gifts and through their own work of clearing and draining. In the early years they were not rich. The great buildings raised to house the large communities of the twelfth century had to be paid for, and crippling taxes were often laid upon them. At times it was necessary for them to sell their wool crop for two or three years ahead, and any failure in this crop could place them in the hands of their creditors.[9]

Perhaps there was a decline because as the years went by, they had to adapt their economy to the social changes of their times. Naturally they had to go to market to sell their produce, and there was nothing wrong in having large quantities of wool for sale. But was it necessary for them virtually to own the markets and run the fairs; to act as middle men in the collection and selling of wool? One feels that when the spiritual structure had to be supported by such economic structures, then it was time for renewal.

At Fountains the change in spirit seems to have come right at the end of the century, between the reigns of Abbot Ralph and Abbot John. Both were good men, devoted to the Order and to the poor. Ralph was the ex-soldier, the mystic, drawn to Fountains by Our Lord asking: "Why don't you come, why are you delaying?"[10] John, on the other hand, was the well-born, large-minded man who planned the building of the great church and the beautiful chapel of the nine altars. The difference between the two is subtle, but with John's reign we seem to enter a period which has a new set of values. It is significant too that the chronicle which opens with enthusiasm for the humble beginnings of Fountains, ends equally satisfied with the splendid buildings later built on the site. We are further away from the poverty of the Gospel and immediately feel we are further from the ideals of the founders.

2. *Their regard for St Benedict, and the position of the Rule as a practical interpretation of the Gospel*

When Prior Richard of York was arguing his case for renewal, he

9. *Ibid.*
10. Hugh of Kirkstall, trans. Oxford, p. 219.

said they only wanted the Rule of St Benedict, because in this rule they were taught the truth of the whole Gospel and it was set out not in an allegorical interpretation, but by simple practice.[11] The account of the foundation of Fountains may perhaps be colored by later Cistercian polemic,[12] but nevertheless it does show how the English White Monks even at the end of the twelfth century regarded the Rule and looked on St Benedict as truly their Father.

Such teaching can also be found at Cluny under St Odo. The Feast of St Benedict had been chosen as the foundation day for Cîteaux, and the theme of St Benedict's spiritual fatherhood was developed especially among the Cistercians—by St Bernard, his secretary Geoffrey of Auxerre, Blessed Guerric, Odo of Morimond, and later Garnier of Cîteaux.[13]

To this list we may add above all Aelred of Rievaulx. For Aelred, to be a Father meant to transmit life, and this he felt is precisely what St Benedict had done—begotten his monks through Christ in the Gospel and passed on this Christ-life by his leadership, his mediation and his teaching. Aelred saw Benedict as a leader like Moses, who by means of his Rule,[14] led his monks, the special people of God, out of the bondage of sin and through the desert of this world to the promised land; out of Egypt not to the vision of the burning bush but to Jerusalem, the vision of peace, the vision of God himself. It was in fact the return journey to God (*reditus*). Christ had gone before, and had already crossed over (*transitus*): St Benedict followed. Like Moses, he was also mediator for his people at every stage of the journey. Whatever they possessed of purity or charity, or whatever progress they made in prayer was due, by God's grace, to his mediation. Aelred insisted that the totality came

11. *Ibid.*, p. 142.

12. D. Bethall, "Foundation of Fountains Abbey," *Journal of Ecclesiastical History*, 17 (1966), pp. 11–207.

13. A. Le Bail, "La Paternité de Saint Benoît sur l'Ordre de Cîteaux," *Collectanea O.C.R.*, 9 (1947), p. 111.

14. First Sermon for the Feast of St Benedict; PL 195:240bc; trans. M. B. Pennington, "St Aelred's Sermons for the Feast of St Benedict," *Cistercian Studies*, 4 (1969), n. 3, p. 71

through Benedict: *quidquid—omne—totum*,[15] because they were putting his teaching, his Rule into practice.

In his sermons on St Benedict and in the *Speculum*[16] Aelred explained that what St Benedict gave was not his own. He was a father who begot in Christ: his teaching was Christ's and led the monk into the life of Christ. The way he followed was Christ, and Christ had only one way—that of the cross. He was quite definite: to think otherwise would be to deceive ourselves, he said. Christ's cross was the complete contradiction of a comfortable way of life, yet if a monk who had professed the cross of Christ gazed at it, it would be like a mirror reflecting the way he had to live. *Ordo noster crux Christi est*[17]—i.e. the monastic way of life with its abstinence, vigils, work, doing the will of another, our putting obedience before all else, is the cross of Christ. He insisted that it was not just *the* cross or *our* cross, but Christ's cross. Living this life was the way in which the monk inserted himself into the saving act of Calvary.[18] That is why he had to love the cross, watch carefully that he did not turn away from it, or when placed on it do anything against it. "The cross of Christ is our glory, because it is our way." If, he asked, to follow this way means we will later follow Christ to the place he has gone to from his cross, how can we be so stupid as to say, contrary to St Benedict, that patiently preserving and sharing bodily in his sufferings is bad for our souls?[19]

Is not this also the teaching of William of St Thierry, that the monastic life was the fulfillment of the monk's crucifixion with Christ, through which he is united with the Father in the Holy Spirit?

There were some who tended to minimize the value of what we might call the accidental bodily austerities of the Rule because, they said, these things could be dispensed. If things like work, food,

---

15. *Ibid.*, 239ab. Cf. A. Hallier, *The Monastic Theology of Aelred of Rievaulx* (Cistercian Studies Series, II), especially Part Two.

16. *Ibid.*

17. First Sermon for Palm Sunday; PL 195:263f.

18. *Speculum Charitatis*, II, 6: PL 195:552b.

19. *Ibid.* Cf. the Prologue of the Rule of St Benedict.

beds, clothes, etc., were all subject to dispensation, surely this indicated that the essence of the Rule lay elsewhere: in whatever it was that gave these practices their worth, or in fundamentals like stability, conversion of manners, obedience.

Not at all, replied Aelred.[20] It was all these different practices that together made the Rule to which they were bound by their vows; and it was the way that these things were arranged and carried out that made the difference between one religious order and another. Observances could never be ignored, because at first sight they did not seem to be essential to the Rule. It was true that they could be dispensed, but he pointed out, that dispensation was according to the Rule, and should be carried out in such a way that the Rule was not destroyed or neglected even for the sake of the weaker brethren.

Aelred was no mere legalist, and he explained that the reason for dispensation was charity. Charity was the end, and ultimately the Rule was only a path leading to charity.[21] (This was borne out by his comments on the two abbot visitors who were down in the refectory checking the weight of the bread allowance, but over-looking the fervor of the choir—a story typical of his character.)

The Rule was something that had been chosen freely. Marriage, wealth, eating meat, drinking wine were all part of normal human life. They were God's gifts for which one had to be grateful and use as he intended.[22] But if a man decided freely to sacrifice them for the Gospel by taking on an austere monastic life, then he must leave these things behind and take the observances provided by his new life seriously, using them as means for progress in charity.[23] That is why he insisted that the monk should think well beforehand what he was about to do before he made profession.

William of Newburgh[24] and Serlo of Kirkstall[25] witnessed at

20. *Speculum Charitatis*, III, 35: PL 195:607.

21. *Ibid.*   22. *Ibid.*, 32:605b.   23. *Ibid.*, 36:613.

24. *Circa* 1193; quoted in D. Knowles, *The Monastic Order in England* (Cambridge: University Press, 1941), p. 259, note 3.

25. Hugh of Kirkstall, trans. Oxford, p. 186: "Good God, what perfection of life there was at Fountains! What a pattern of discipline! What rivalry in virtue! What zeal for the Order, which by God's grace remains to this day!"

the end of the twelfth century that the regular discipline at Rievaulx
and Fountains was still good. Were they referring merely to external observance? I think not. Men like Aelred had made it clear
that they regarded the Rule, spirit and letter, as a single whole, the
rectissiman viam by which they might enter the current of saving
history, and cross over to the great vision of God.[26] Stripped of its
accretions, there was a *sancta simplicitas*[27] about it, which meant it
could be so easily grasped that only seven years after the foundation
of Fountains one of its founders could be sent to establish a new
monastery,[28] which in turn could pass on the Cistercian-Benedictine
spirit to three daughter-houses founded within the space of nine
years.

3. *Their desire to taste and see how good God is*

When Ralph Hagget visited Fountains to consult Brother
Sunnulph about his vocation, the Brother promised to pray for him
and added: "Pray likewise yourself and be careful that your actions
do not stand in the way of our prayers." For Sunnulph, God,
prayer, and the actions of the "everyday" were not separate depart-
ments, but intimately bound together in one life.

Aelred's approach was similar. At first sight he does not seem
to speak about contemplation as much as one might expect, though
we know from Walter Daniel that he experienced it and that at
times his prayer was so deep that he forgot all about the regular
hours and times for meals.[29] The way to such prayer was in a sense
ordinary and accessible to all. He was guided and purified by the
Rule whose end was charity. Charity was the *sine qua non* for life
with God; it was that "good love"[30] which was chosen by a man
whose will was guided by reason, who did this or that simply

26. Aelred of Rievaulx, Second Sermon for the Feast of St Benedict:
PL 195:247b; 245d; trans. Pennington, *loc. cit.,* n. 8, p. 82; n. 4, p. 80.

27. Hugh of Kirkstall, trans. Oxford, pp. 131, 141.

28. Newminster founded in 1139 by St Robert; Pipewell, 1143; Sawley,
1146; Roche, 1148.

29. *Vita Ailredi,* 47, trans. Powicke, p. 50.

30. *Speculum Charitatis,* II, 7: PL 195:583d.

because he knew that God wanted it. It was something that required a man's energies and a desire to resemble as closely as possible the God in whose image he had been made[31]—yet it could not be attained by oneself alone. It showed itself in a readiness to suffer for the Beloved; and its effects could at times be visibly transforming, as Walter Daniel testifies.[32] Generally, however, its fruits were experienced briefly—almost too briefly. This might happen at any time to a man whose charity had made him spiritually free (*vacans*), who was "ready."

To describe such experiences, Aelred often uses the imagery of the Sabbath rest: joy, peace, tranquillity, the delight of resting with God.[33] In all this he seems to me, if I may say so, typically English, down-to-earth, intimate. He is a true forerunner of the later mystics, like Julian of Norwich and the author of the *Cloud*.

He speaks explicitly of contemplation in a sermon for the Assumption.[34] Contrasting Martha and Mary, he says: "If Martha must have a place in our home, Mary must be there too—free to take pleasure in the Lord's presence through reading, prayer or contemplation." Like St Bernard, Aelred insists that in this life these two women ought never to be separated. It would be a mistake, he says, to think that some of the community are Marthas and some Marys. They are two sisters, dwelling in the same house, in the same soul, complementing one another, each with her own rights and duties.

He is in the tradition of our early Fathers when he explains that the great model is the Blessed Virgin, *Domina nostra*,[35] in whom the two lives were perfectly blended, though like us she had to seek and contemplate in faith. As the Mother who gave Christ to men,[36] she stands at the very beginning of their ascent to contemplation,

---

31. *Ibid.*, I, 3:507d.

32. *Vita Ailredi*, 48, trans. Powicke, p. 50.

33. *Speculum Charitatis*, III, 6: PL 195:583.

34. First Sermon for the Feast of the Assumption of the Blessed Virgin Mary: PL 195:306–309.

35. *Ibid.*, 307a, 323a.

36. Sermon for the Nativity of the Blessed Virgin Mary: PL 195:327, 330.

which leads through his humanity to his divinity.[37] Her son is both our redemption and holiness; and though he exhorts his community to imitate her virtues, he implies that a man becomes holy not simply by practicing virtue, but rather by developing and living up to the gift of holiness he has already received when he was given Christ through her mediation.

With her help, and with that of Christ himself, the monk will gradually obtain that inward peace so necessary for contemplation. And so he comes to the Father, and that is what he waits for—the sight of God himself in the very substance of his Godhead (something given to no one in this life), a vision of inestimable beauty, giving an indescribable joy. Then, he says, we shall see how good he is and experience the loving kindness of him who came down to us in the womb of his blessed Mother.[38]

Seeking Christ, seeking the face of God, was perhaps the favorite theme of Gilbert of Swineshead, and he was at his best when describing the search for the Beloved.[39] Such a search was not merely emotional. It involved the intellect which had to be mindful of tradition, he said, while at the same time it investigated things that were new. Reason reached out, wanting to see, to test the things of faith, but it still depended on faith, for faith was the foundation. Meanwhile, the city in which the soul went out to search was not merely the Church, but the whole of creation, though he knew that the soul who was thirsty would never be satisfied with this creation, since it wanted to gaze on the Creator.[40]

When his community asked for rules to guide them in the search,[41] he warned them that success came not so much from their own efforts to find God, as from God spontaneously revealing himself. They, of course, had to cooperate. Self-knowledge, purification, inner peace and especially the desire for God would make them "ready" for contemplation. The intellect had done its

37. *Ibid.,* 327.   38. *Ibid.,* 335.

39. Sermon Four on the Song of Songs: PL 184:26ff., a trans. of these sermons will appear in Cistercian Fathers, XIV; Tract II: PL 184:253.

40. Sermon Four on the Song of Songs: PL 184:34.

41. Sermon Seven on the Song of Songs: PL 184:42.

part—now the will had to persevere[42] through dryness which might last all their life on earth; but if only they would wait, they would finally see. He added that if they did find and see the well-beloved, let them mention the love that their abbot had for him also.[43]

Nuns too followed his sermons on the Canticle enthusiastically, and he joked with them: "Do you think the Canticle was written for you alone? You turn the whole interpretation to the meaning of love. Everything must sparkle with sentiments of love and have the fragrance of charity!"[44] But it was he who encouraged them in this, and when they wanted something new, it was the New Commandment he gave them. "Others," he said, "have different duties to fulfill—your duty is to love, and the exercise of pure love is contemplation. Your motive should be to see God. There cannot be a more praiseworthy aim than to love and see God. It is an end in itself. It is the one thing necessary. Love begins here in faith, but leads to vision. So go out, daughters of Jerusalem, and see. Be what you are called: daughters of contemplation."[45]

Like Aelred whose friend he was, he maintained that one of the best places for contemplation was the cross.[46] Both men were singleminded in their rejection of the things of the world that were a hindrance, but they did not reject its needs. Aelred told his sister that her heart must be as wide as the world, like a Noah's Ark with a place for everyone, and Christ dwelling in the center.[47] Gilbert, speaking of the intervals after the night office when prayer can be made privately, said that such prayer sought nothing that was private in the sense of being selfish.[48] It was a prayer that was silent, because it had no need for words and was all the more penetrating

42. *Ibid.*

43. *Ibid.;* Sermon 46, 2. Cf. Aelred of Rievaulx, *When Jesus was Twelve Years Old;* trans. A. Walker and G. Webb (London: Mowbrays, 1956).

44. Sermon Seventeen on the Song of Songs: PL 184:87b.

45. Sermon Eighteen on the Song of Songs: PL 184:95.

46. Cf. E. Chenevière, *Nos Père par Eux-Même,* Vol. 3 (pro MS, n.d.), pp. 79ff.

47. "A Rule for a Recluse," trans. *The Works of Aelred of Rievaulx,* Vol. 1, Cistercian Fathers, II.

48. Sermon Twenty-three on the Song of Songs: PL 184:120, 121.

for that. But they were not to think of it as merely sweetness; it was like a fire that purified and prepared the soul for a deeper tasting of the Lord.[49] Such contact could entirely transfigure the soul which reflected the beauty of the God who filled it, and Gilbert never ceased to wonder at the affection of God the Creator which led to such a contact. The nuns might think they were on fire with love for the Lord but it was nothing compared to the love he had for them.[50]

John of Ford (†1220) continued Gilbert's sermons on the Canticle, and we find in them the same spirituality centered on love, which he says is comparable only to gold. The language of the Canticle was still the language of the interior life, but it was becoming less popular and I suggest that John was among the last great Cistercians to write in this way. He complains that "his monks are more ready, when they gather together, to talk about litigation, the progeny of bulls and the yield of crops, than Jesus and the Songs of Sion."[51] But though his form of teaching was possibly becoming outmoded, its content was perennial. He maintained that his monks were "seekers," and the result of their "search" would affect others and belong to others as much as to themselves (reminiscent of Aelred). Charity was John's special theme: it was necessary for pure prayer and directed it, while at the same time it was the fruit of contemplation. He wanted his monks to be sons of charity, and believed they could find this vocation in the Order; just as his Cistercian contemporaries, like Matthew of Rievaulx, were convinced that their Order was the "spiritual home of Christ."

The whole aim of these abbots was to develop in their monks that right kind of love, that charity which would make them more and more like God, more capable of possessing him, and so more capable of enjoying him.

49. Sermon Twenty-nine on the Song of Songs: PL 184:150.

50. Sermon Eighteen on the Song of Songs: PL 184:96.

51. John of Ford, Balliol MS 24, fo 257. Cf. C. Holdsworth, "John of Ford and English Cistercian Writings" in *Royal Historical Society,* Fifth Series, Vol. II (London: Royal Historical Society, 1961) and "Les sermons inédits de Jean de Ford sur le Cantique," *Collectanea O.C.R.,* 5 (1938), pp. 250–261.

4. *The importance of communion with Christ and the Brethren in the community life*

Both Aelred and Gilbert had a very high opinion of their communities, but when they speak of community life, Aelred is the more vivid. When he looks round the chapter house and says: "Some of you were once lions and leopards and wolves," one feels he is applying the text of Isaiah to his monks. But when Gilbert compares his community to the seeds of a pomegranate gathered together under a single rind, one feels that the community is being fitted to the text of the Canticle.[52]

However, he made some good points when he saw in the rind the regular life, dark-red with the passion of Christ—not oppressing, but helping. The seeds were united together by charity like the early Christians, who were bound not by the rules of an Order but by an instinct of love.[53] Since such a community could often obtain what one person could not find by himself, Gilbert encouraged his monks to seek as a community, bound to one another heart and soul. This unity was, he said, a witness to others that such a life was not merely useful and good, but a happy and joyful affair.[54] Perhaps most important of all was his comment that all this flowed from baptism—a realization that to be a Christian meant being a member of the Christian community.[55]

For Aelred this Christian community was the monastic community, which formed a little mystical body, as we might say. And as long as there were any of Christ's members on earth who were hungry or thirsty or tempted, then just so long must Christ be helped in them through vigils, fasting, manual work—all activities that take place within the monastery.[56]

Baldwin of Ford (Abbot, 1175–1180) was thinking of the Cistercian community twenty-five years later as the *Koinonia*, the communion of the early Church.[57] He insisted that in any life of

---

52. Sermon Twenty-five on the Song of Songs: PL 184:187bd.

53. *Ibid.*   54. *Ibid.*   55. *Ibid.*

56. First Sermon for the Feast of the Assumption of the Blessed Virgin Mary: PL 195:306bd.

57. *De Vita Coenobitica*: PL 204:543–562.

communion the important thing was love—for with love goes the
desire to share, and that is what communion is. People in love
want to pass on what they have, thinking that whatever is good
becomes better when shared, as far as this may be done. And if
they cannot share, they generally prefer to give rather than keep
for themselves. A person who loves wants to share not only his
goods, but also his love itself, and in practice this means he wants
to be loved in return. So if there is to be perfect charity in the
community, there must not only be love for the communion, for
the brethren, but also a communion, a sharing of love: and these
two should be inseparably joined.

Baldwin's whole approach is Trinitarian and he maintained that
our life of sharing was both a sharing in and a reflection of the life
of the Blessed Trinity, in which the sharing of life and love is
complete. It is the fact that we ourselves can communicate or share
in this life and love—through grace—that makes us gradually more
and more like God himself, and puts us in communion with one
another.

This is the sharing or communion that makes a common or
community life. The more a community is living as God wants it
to live, then the more deeply that community will be sharing in
his life, and the more the special qualities of Trinitarian life will be
present—unity and peace, together with the grace that those who
live in community may really be in communion with one another.

However, even in the closeness of the Blessed Trinity, where
there is only one life, there are three distinct Persons. Likewise,
however close a monastic communion may be, it is still a communion of persons. The community may possess the Gift of the
Holy Spirit as a community, but it must not be forgotten that he
has sealed each member individually—nor has he given the same
gifts to each. Baldwin suggested that it is only God who can really
give. Men communicate or *share* what they have been given; and
so with each gift goes the obligation of sharing it. Those who
receive and use it for God's glory and for others as well as for
themselves will receive more of the gift. But those who try to
keep it for themselves will lose it—selfishness of this kind is only

another form of avarice. Possibly he had in mind St Benedict's phrase which condemned private ownership in a monk, as "that most wicked vice."[58] For what is contrary to communion is contrary to charity.

Aelred had the same teaching[59]—all should contribute to the common effort; to withdraw from it in any way would be to act fraudulently. For their common unity based on the fellowship of each with the Blessed Trinity meant that whatever each possessed belonged to all, and whatever all posseessed belonged to each. So no one should be jealous of what he could do, as if it belonged to himself alone. The contribution of each would be different— fasting or work for one, reading, meditation or study for another. God could have made each one complete in himself, but he wanted each to have need of others and to find what was lacking in himself in others. Something that obviously required great humility and charity. But also something that, as he pointed out, united the community together, especially choir monks and lay brothers, into an integral body, members of one another.[60]

Obviously the advantages of such a communion in the brother- hood had to be paid for, and Aelred believed that the brethren were engaged in a fight to the death against a very astute enemy.[61] Each, whatever his position, had a responsibility to the community to fight both his personal temptations and those connected with his office and so maintain those ideals which had drawn them together.

It is perhaps here on the subject of community, that we are at the heart of the Cistercian witness, because here charity finds its concrete expression, and it is difficult to separate the teaching of one abbot from another. I think they would have made their own the thought of Martin Buber who said that though a real community need not consist of people who are perpetually together, it must

58. Rule of St Benedict, 33:4.

59. Second Sermon for the Feast of All Saints: PL 195:347d.

60. Third Sermon for the Feast of St Benedict: PL 195:249a c; trans. Pennington, *loc. cit.,* nn. 7f., pp. 85f.

61. Sermon on the Feast of Sts Peter and Paul: PL 195:294ff.

M

consist of people who are ready for one another.[62] A "readiness" that teaches tolerance of the infirm and compassion with others in their needs—this was the special and supreme glory of Rievaulx.[63] A "readiness" which at Fountains bore fruit in unity and peace;[64] a "readiness" which at Ford shared in the everyday joys, sorrows . . .[65] yes, and the merits of others, and brought the monk into contact with a common charity that was so broad and wide that he could not possibly be shut in by the limits of his own holiness; a charity which would lead to the *Koinonia* of heaven—the communion towards which both as "person" and as "community" the monk is moving forward.

It is perhaps under the heading of "community" that we should mention the relationship which existed between monks and abbot. It was certainly a very close relationship. When Richard, the second Abbot of Fountains, wished to resign he was reminded that there had been no division in the community since the foundation of the monastery. "Head and members," he was told, "were joined by a bond that was so tight that it did not know the sword of division. We are your monks; we know no other abbot; while you live, we will admit no other. Our resolve stands firm, by no means will we suffer you to be torn from us."[66]

He was not the only one who encountered difficulties when he wanted to resign. Roger of Byland,[67] a fine man with a gift for understanding the young, began to feel old and infirm after he

---

62. M. Friedman, *Martin Buber* (Chicago: University Press, 1955), p. 217.

63. *Vita Ailredi,* 29; trans. Powicke, p. 37.

64. Hugh of Kirkstall; trans. Oxford, p. 194: a speech made in the chapter by Hugh de Mathan.

65. *De Vita Coenobitica:* PL 204:551.

66. Hugh of Kirkstall; trans. Oxford, p. 194.

67. Cf. Roger of Byland, *op. cit.*: "It is given to few men to pursue a life of self-sacrifice for so long a time. He had been with his community on four different sites, and the ultimate spiritual and material prosperity of his house was due to his government." Cf. Dugdale, *op. cit.,* p. 354 and Gilbert of Swineshead, Tract Seven: PL 184:276. Roger was also a witness to devotion. to Our Lady: "Love Mary, the holy Mother of God and Mother of mercy above everything."—*op. cit.*

had been superior for about ten years; he consulted St Bernard about retiring. St Bernard urged him to continue (though he commented that his successor ought not to maintain such a large estate). Roger returned home, and remained Abbot for another forty years, finally resigning three years before his death at the age of ninety-six.

Gervase, Abbot of Louth Park, had already been a monk for thirty-two years when he went with the original founders to Fountains. Six years later he was sent to found Louth Park.[68] (He did not write much himself, but was in contact with the literary men of his time, encouraging them in their work.) The erroneous attribution to him of the Preface to St Aelred's *Speculum* shows the esteem in which he was held.[69]

As Abbot, he always desired to be treated as one of the brethren, rejecting the honour due to his dignity. A single-minded man, intent on the things of God, he was loyal, merciful, a lover of the Order, of truth, of charity, devoted to the common life, to silence and to the choir.[70] He was always approachable and possessed that quality which made him at the same time both a father and a friend.

After about ten years as Abbot, and a year before his death, he resigned; not, he said, because of any ill will of the community, but because they had grown in numbers from twelve to one hundred, and he felt he was a hindrance to the progress of the house.[71] He was always anxious for the spiritual well-being of his monks, and in this he resembled Gilbert of Swineshead who maintained that it was in prayer that an abbot came to understand the needs of his monks, and learn to have compassion on their weaknesses.

That was why the community should respect this need of the superior and not consider that the time given by the abbot to prayer

---

68. C. H. Talbot, "The Testament of Gervase of Louth Park," *Analecta S.O. Cist.*, 7 (1951), p. 36.

69. *Ibid.*

70. Gervase of Louth Park, "Lamentation, Letter of Resignation, Testimony of Monk-Disciple," ed. C. H. Talbot, *Analecta S. O. Cist.*, 7 (1951), pp. 34–45.

71. *Ibid.*

was lost to the community; without it, the superior could not help them. For it was in prayer that the heart of a superior was fashioned to the likeness of the heavenly Father.[72] Gilbert was Abbot for about twenty years before he resigned, but his superiorship weighed on him like a burden, and at times he felt he was being asked to share his very soul.

Finally we return to Aelred, who was above all a Father Abbot. But in his *Pastoral Prayer* we can see the incapacity which even he felt when faced with the responsibility of guiding and caring for the souls of his very large community. As he turns in anguish to the Good Shepherd, we see how he regards the community. It is Christ's family, a special people whom God had created, redeemed and gathered together into that house. In this family, he wants to be a power for good, so he asks for courage and wisdom. "My God, you know what a fool I am, therefore I ask for wisdom, to direct all my thoughts, deeds and plans for their advancement and my salvation. You know that whatever you give me shall be entirely devoted to their service. My work time, and my leisure, my doing and my thinking, each single thing that makes me what I am."[73] And what was he? A man whose greatest joy was to love and be loved; and the love he gave and sought was the finest kind of love that a man can give. That which comes from a man acting as a whole person, when feelings, reason, will and grace collaborated. The only thing he asked, and this was perhaps the key, was that it should be a love where Christ was really present.

It is Christ who is the key to the whole of the witness of the early English Cistercians. They only wanted the Rule and the Gospel teaching as means to follow him. They wanted the community life of sharing, because it put them in contact with him.

Or perhaps to put it better, it was because they were in contact with him and wanted to seek him in this particular way, that they

72. Gilbert of Swineshead, Sermon Fourteen on the Song of Songs: PL 184:71cd.

73. "The Pastoral Prayer," trans. *The Works of Aelred of Rievaulx*, Vol. 1 (Cistercian Fathers Series, II).

were in contact with one another and could go as a community with him through the Holy Spirit to the Father.

In conclusion one might well ask again if there was anything specifically English or Cistercian about the five points I listed. Perhaps nothing English, though the sixty-six houses in England at the Reformation were a witness to the attraction such a life had for Englishmen; perhaps also nothing Cistercian, if the points are taken separately. But I think that if they are taken together and viewed within the framework of "the Cistercian simplicity,"[74] then one might say that the life in these monasteries out in the wilds was different. It made them places where a man could respond more fully than elsewhere (at least in England) to the personal call of the Gospel to seek the one thing necessary.

That there should always be such places is important, for God will utter this call as long as there are men with hearts to love him and wills to seek him. And it was another Englishman who later said: "To be a seeker is to belong to the next best sect to that of a finder, and indeed a finder shall every faithful humble seeker be at the end. Happy the seeker—happy the finder."[75]

Paul Diemer ocso

Mount Saint Bernard Abbey,
Leicester, England

74. Especially from the point of view of economy, the Cistercian monastery with granges organized as a unit with the monks doing manual work was basically more simple than a house of Black Monks with the obedientiary and manorial systems.

75. Oliver Cromwell.

AELRED OF RIEVAULX

HIS RELEVANCE TO THE POST-VATICAN II AGE

IN HIS MASTERLY WORK, *The Monastic Order in England*, David Knowles remarks that "no other English monk of the twelfth century so lingers in the memory" as Aelred of Rievaulx.[1] This is very true; in English minds, Aelred is the English Abbot par excellence. But it would be a mistake to think that the attractive "Bernard of the North" was nothing more than a fragrant memory embalmed from the past, a figure that is *passé* in every sense of the word. Nothing would be further from the truth. On the contrary, Aelred is astonishingly relevant to the modern age. He speaks to us today with almost as much pertinancy as a Jean Leclercq or a Thomas Merton. Of all our Cistercian Fathers perhaps none is more vitally relevant to the monks of the post-Vatican II era than Aelred of Rievaulx. In passing we may add that his relevance is far from being confined to monks. If we except the occasional references in his *De Anima* to physiology, which strike us as being rather ludicrous but which were the accepted opinions of the physicians of his own time, there is a modern ring about practically everything he says. Or, to put it the other way, some of the modern things we are saying are far more traditional—truly traditional—than may at first sight be realized.

Theological Approach in the Schola Christi

Love was the lodestar of Aelred's life, as it is the keynote of all his teaching. It has been said that "never did so many talk so much

1. David Knowles, *The Monastic Order in England* (Cambridge: University Press, 1941), p. 240.

or so well of love as in the twelfth century. Never was love studied with such enthusiasm or fathomed with such penetrating keenness."[2] The twentieth century might be said to equal the twelfth in its interest in and preoccupation with love, if not always in the high standard of its analysis and penetration of the subject. Among the present-day generation there is a very genuine awareness of the need to love and to be loved, a need that is inherent in man's nature. Everyone today talks about love (no word in the English language, perhaps, has been extended to cover such a wide spectrum or meaning as the word *love*), but for all the talk, those who really know how to love are rare enough.

Aelred shared fully the prevailing interest of his age. It is from the standpoint of love that he approaches the mystery of monastic life. Love is the axis on which his whole doctrine turns. It is so clearly the thread running through all his monastic theology that he has been justly styled "the doctor of spiritual love."[3] This was no abstract concept for him: it was something that had been lived, had been experienced in his own life. In his *Mirror of Charity* and *Spiritual Friendship* this monk is giving us the fruits of his own rich experience. The reader can catch a warmth of feeling still pervading the written word he has left us. His theology is, in the best sense, existential and in this it cannot but have an immediate appeal to the monks of our day who are turning away dissatisfied from the desiccated and desiccating rationalizing and speculation of the manuals to the vivid, concrete, living theology of the Bible. Not only the monks, but the theologians also who are not monks are looking today for a more authentic theology, that is to say, a more spiritual theology. The Second Vatican Council, in its decree on the training for the priesthood, states that the Bible must become the soul of theology.[4] It certainly is so in the theology of Aelred as of

---

2. G. Dumeige, *Richard de Saint-Victor et l'idée chrétienne de l'amour*, p. 3.

3. A. Le Bail, art. *Aelred* in *Dict. Spir.* 1 (1937), col. 234.

4. Decree *De Institutione Sacerdotali*, no. 16: "The teaching of theological subjects . . . should be carried out in such a way that the students can derive Catholic teaching accurately from divine Revelation, understand it in depth and make it their spiritual sustenance. . . . Students should be trained in the

all our Cistercian Fathers. For him theology meant an ever-deepening, experiential, living knowledge of Scripture and the mysteries of faith, a knowledge that is translated into living terms in a monk's life. I venture to suggest that a theology on the lines of Aelred's monastic theology would correspond admirably with the demands of the Council for a renewed theology.

The monastery is, in St Benedict's phrase, a *schola Christi*, a school of Christ. But in the twelfth century it was quite clearly differentiated from the great non-monastic schools, such as Laon, Paris and Chartres. In the latter establishments emphasis was on the intellectual investigation of truth. Aelred himself had attended such schools, at Hexham and Durham, but had not remained long enough to acquire a completely scholastic education. His humorous remark that he was a graduate of the kitchen rather than the schools had more than a grain of truth in it.[5] In the monastic schools, on the other hand, the stress was put on experience of the truth, which, in the last analysis, is experience of *the* Truth, which is God. This is a process in which not merely the intellect was committed but the whole man. Knowledge and experience were closely wedded in the monastic school which was Aelred's Rievaulx, where men were apprenticed to a life of love rather than introduced to the subtleties of speculation. Knowledge that did not influence one's life was sterile and did not make sense to a spiritual man like Aelred. His own spiritual knowledge had been culled, not from dry scholastic tomes, but from contact with the living God. Consequently the theology which the Abbot of Rievaulx taught his monks did not stop short at purely intellectual research, however valuable this may be, but aimed at true spiritual experience.[6]

---

study of Sacred Scripture with that very special care which is its due as the vital principle of all theology."

5. *Epist. S. Bernardi*, PL 195:501–502. The reference to the kitchen is an allusion to his office as seneschal at the Court of King David I of Scotland.

6. Cf. *When Jesus Was Twelve*, ch. 6–7: "I leave this for those to discuss among themselves who revel in arguing about such things. But you did not ask me for theories and arguments, dearest son. You want my words to bring you the beginnings of devotion to raise your mind to God."; trans. *The Works of Aelred of Rievaulx*, Vol. 1, Cistercian Fathers, II.

Theological reflection was only a door that opened on to union with God. It was a theology for life of the highest order. The theology we give our monks today should have no less an aim than that.[7]

Aelred's Monastic Ideal

Men enter a monastery to seek God, or to be more exact, to return to God. Aelred shows them the way, the one and only way that leads to that goal—the way of charity. We have his monastic ideal summed up for us in his *Mirror of Charity* which St Bernard, who had commissioned it, regarded as a kind of spiritual directory for Cistercian monks. In reality it is a guide to the ways of divine love. Let us briefly sketch out Aelred's teaching on the subject.[8]

The monastic life is essentially a relationship of response by man, who is a member of a community, to God's love-invitation in Christ. The God who is love has revealed or communicated himself to man in Christ. This communication of God is at the same time an invitation to man to respond in love by giving himself to God and so sharing divine life. Man's self-giving and sharing, like God's communicating and inviting, is achieved in Christ. Thus there are three focal points in Aelred's monastic theology—God, man, and Christ. To start with the second of these three poles—what is man?

Aelred possessed a sound anthropology.[9] The book of Genesis supplies the Abbot of Rievaulx with the key to the meaning of man. "Let us make man in our image, in the likeness of ourselves,"

7. I recall Dom Gabriel Sortais once (about ten years ago) quoting the Rector of San Anselmo, Rome, who described the ideal of monastic studies as—*ut non tantum sciatur sed ut vita divina communicetur.*

8. Those who are acquainted with Amédée Hallier's work: *The Monastic Theology of Aelred of Rievaulx* (Cistercian Studies Series, II) will realize my indebtedness to Fr Hallier in this presentation of Aelred's monastic ideal.

9. Aelred wrote a treatise *De Anima,* chronologically the last of his works and in fact death claimed him before he had finished it. But there is, besides, copious matter for an anthropology scattered throughout his other works and sermons.

said God.[10] This creative word of God makes man what he is, namely, a divine image that is, at his creation, also a likeness of God. This image, which is something in-built in his very nature, makes man *capax Dei*, open to God, capable of receiving God's love and returning it to him, susceptible of perfect happiness by going out to God in self-giving and love. In this out-goingness consists his likeness to God. Since this is an openness, a capacity for God, it is, in a sense, infinite. Only God can fulfill this capacity in the human person, and, since God is love, this capacity is fulfilled by man's responding totally to God's love, or, as Aelred puts it, by consenting to it. *Consensus*, an act of the will fully accepting and responding to God, is a keyword in Aelred's theology. The human person has freedom and consequently can consent, with the help of God's grace, to accept his love, or he can refuse it, in spite of grace.

As a matter of fact the first man did refuse to consent, to fit in with God's plan for his happiness. He rejected God's offer of love and his invitation to return his love. In so doing he lost his likeness to God and took the first downward step in the history of salvation. Aelred's doctrine of love must be studied in the context of salvation history. This is a good example of a contemporary idea that is in reality a very old idea, a traditional idea, certainly an idea that is a salient part of Aelred's theology. He was acutely conscious of salvation history which comprises two movements, a downward and an upward movement, or a withdrawal from God and a return to him.

The image of God in man continually urges him to transcend himself. Every man is faced with the choice confronting Adam. All his life every man will have to choose between responding to God's love or refusing it, and so he will live out his own history of salvation. He must go out of himself if the divine image in him is to remain true, or more correctly, if the image is to become a likeness again. The image in man becomes a perfect likeness when he responds totally and unconditionally to God's love. But instead

10. Gen 1:26.

of responding and opening himself to God, and this will involve openness to his fellowmen as well, man can close in on himself. In place of self-giving to God and others, he can want to get others for himself, to use things and persons for his own selfish purposes. By turning love into selfishness, man contradicts the divine image in himself. If he turns the impulse to love to God, he becomes free. If this natural impulse turns in on itself and becomes its own object, he ceases to be free. Freedom and true love are inseparable. Only the monk who loves authentically, that is, who gives himself generously to God and his fellowmen, is genuinely free. For Aelred the whole purpose of the monastic life is to educate the monk to true freedom by way of genuine and authentic love. The school of Christ thus becomes a school of love, where monks learn to respond to God's love. But a man cannot do this of himself. Just as God's invitation to love came through Christ, so must the response of love go back to him through Christ. The very love to respond can only be found in him. The human race has made its perfect response to God's love through the God-man. He is the perfect likeness of the Father and it is only in so far as we participate in his love, put on Christ as Saint Paul says,[11] that the divine image in us is restored to divine likeness. United to him, our love is made perfect, because it is now Christ's love with which we love the Father. And in loving God in Christ we share the life of God who is love, and we attain authentic freedom.

We also attain our authentic personality. Here, in germ, is to be found the solution, the only solution, to a problem that agitates the contemporary generation. Religious today are concerned about their self-development and the cultivation of their personality. Obviously this can get out of hand and grow into a cult of self,[12]

---

11. Gal 3:27.

12. Fr E. F. O'Doherty, Professor of Psychology at University College, Dublin, wrote concerning aspirants to the priesthood: "With regard to motivation, applicants can be sorted into three groups, according as they seem to be seeking an escape from a problem-situation, a solution to a personal problem, or a life of sacrifice. It cannot be too often stressed that sacrifice is

but the basic desire to grow as a human person is good and laudable. The trouble is that too many people today are going about their personality development in the wrong way. Personality develops best the less one tries directly to develop it. The less we concentrate on what we call our "self" and the more we concentrate on Christ, the more does our real self develop. It is he we have to think about if we are to find our true self. In a very true sense there are no real personalities outside of Christ. Hence if we are looking for our personality it is to him we must go. If we look for it anywhere else, above all if we look for it in ourselves, we shall not find it because it is not there. Our real new self will begin to grow as soon as we go out of ourselves to Christ and through him to God. Our authentic personality is to be found in no other way. If we insist in cultivating it in our own way, we are doomed to fail: we remain stunted and warped and unfulfilled.

It is worth noting that we must not go to Christ just for self-development. If this is the purpose of our going to him, then we are not really going out to him at all. Christ himself is only being used for a selfish purpose and thus we remain turned in on ourselves still. For a genuine going-out of self we have to forget self as much as possible. Certainly if self-interest, in the form of personality development, is our motive, no out-going movement is possible. It all comes back to the principle laid down in the Gospel, that a man must lose his life before he can find it. To spell out this principle in the present context, a man must lose his own self if he is to find his real self. His real self, which is Christ's, becomes his when he goes to God in Christ. All this is only another way of saying what Aelred said eight centuries previously—that man, the image of God, is re-created in the divine likeness through Christ; man becomes most truly himself when he becomes most God-like.

---

the prerogative and defining function of the role of the priest. If, therefore, self-fulfillment is the dominant or even a markedly prominent feature of the motivation, the candidate should be discouraged"—*Doctrine and Life*, Vol. XVII (1967), p. 481f. This can be applied equally well to aspirants to the monastic life.

Community Spirit

This progressive turning of the divine image in man into a like-ness, which is the aim of the school of Christ, is obviously a pro-cess that affects the monk deeply and personally, but it is not an individualistic process. It takes place in the setting of a monastic community. The school of charity teaches, and must teach, a theology of community. The monk is a member of a community, a People of God, and it is precisely as such, and not as an isolated individual, that he goes to God and advances in charity. His quest being a community one, he must always be aware of his solidarity with his brethren.

The monastic community is the picked company[13] with whom the monk journeys through the desert to the promised land; it is the milieu in which his return to God takes place. Consequently the community spirit is, to Aelred's mind, an essential aspect of monastic living. Man being a social animal, it corresponds with his nature. But there is more to it than that: there is a gracious divine plan behind it. The community life of the Godhead, that communi-cation of knowledge and love between the three divine Persons which is beyond description, is the pattern of man's life on earth, as it will be of his life in heaven. Men bear witness to God, show forth resemblance to his goodness, when there is loving interchange between them. Moreover the restoration of the divine image in man necessarily leads him to an opening out to the other images of God. Love of self, love of God and love of neighbor progress together. No true love of God or self can exist without love of neighbor. The ideal of community life is the sabbath of fraternal

13. The community is a picked company in the sense that the members of it are of God's choosing, not in the sense that it is an exclusive gathering of select souls. At least Aelred did not regard it as such. He accepted all and sundry, as Walter Daniel tells us in the *Life of Aelred,* p. 37–38: "Whoever came there in his weakness and did not find a loving father in Aelred and timely comforters in the brethren? When was anyone feeble in body and character, ever expelled from that house, unless his iniquity was an offense to the community or had destroyed all hope of his salvation? . . . The house which withholds toleration from the weak is not to be regarded as a house of religion."

charity when a man experiences how good it is for brothers to live together: "Each one feels in his soul how he is bound by love to each one of his fellowmen . . . we embrace and cherish them so as to have one heart and one mind with them all."[14]

Aelred's teaching never lets us forget the community dimension of monastic life. Like the Church, a monastery is a body composed of many members. Each has his particular function in the body, depending on his qualities and talents. The community benefits from the use of the gifts each one brings to it, and in turn the gifts themselves are perfected by the use they are put to for the good of the community. As Aelred saw it, community life offers ample scope for mutual service and mutual enrichment. In one of his sermons for the Feast of St Benedict he said:

> One is able to offer more toil, another more watching or more fasting, more prayer or more *lectio*. . . . As (in the book of Exodus) all contributed to the construction of a single tabernacle . . . so, in our case, all is to be done for the good of the community. . . . No one is to behave as though the gift he has received from God were merely for his own use . . . no, he must regard it as belonging to all his brethren. On the other hand he cannot envy his brother if he is convinced that he benefits by whatever gift his brother has.[15]

This cooperation is not motivated by regard for the mere external regulating of a group of men living together, nor by human prudence, a kind of *quid pro quo*. It must be the expression of the monk's love of God and of his brother in God. This brotherly sharing is part of God's plan of salvation: "Almighty God could no doubt grant instant perfection to everyone and bestow all the virtues on each of us. But his loving arrangement for us is that we should need one another."[16] This service of the brethren is turned into praise of God and bears witness to the inner vital principle that animates the monastic community and unifies it.

It was Aelred's dearest wish to make such a spirit flourish in his

---

14. *Mirror of Charity*, 3, 4; PL 195:579bc (References to Aelred's works are to PL 195 unless otherwise noted.); trans. Cistercian Fathers, XVII.

15. *S. Temp.*, 7; 249a.   16. *Ibid.*, 249b.

beloved Rievaulx. How well he succeeded may be gauged from the spontaneous remark of a novice who had just entered the community and was immediately struck by the wonderful, warm fellow-feeling that pervaded the place: "Among the brethren there is such unity, such perfect harmony that everything belongs to everyone. And what I love above everything else is that there are no preferences, gentle birth counts for nothing. Necessity alone makes for diversity."[17]

Rievaulx under Abbot Aelred had a family spirit that was warm and homely and humanly attractive, and it is this which did so much to give the famous Yorkshire abbey its unique atmosphere.[18] Such a family spirit is essential if a monastery of monks is not to turn into a club of eccentric bachelors, isolated individuals acting and living in complete independence of their neighbors. The common goal of a monastic community—the collective quest of God—can hardly be attained without a common spirit, an esprit de corps which should be the special charm and mark of a community. This family spirit is an elusive thing to define, but not nearly so difficult to detect. Like any other spirit it cannot be legislated for; it must come from within the community itself and be the expression of its own life. In this the influence of the abbot is of paramount importance. Like abbot, like community.[19]

Abbatial Charism

The office of abbot cannot be defined in terms of authority or administration. Without a doubt, authority is his and he must exercise it; the burden of temporal responsibility is his and he must discharge it. But his essential role is to be the father and leader of the community entrusted to his care. The abbot has got to be at

17. *Mirror of Charity*, 2, 17; 565a.

18. D. Knowles, *op. cit.*, p. 645.

19. Cf. Pope Pius XII to a Congress of Superiors General at Rome in 1952: "The religious Order must take the place, as far as possible, of the family (which their sisters had renounced) and it is you, the Superiors General, who are expected in the first instance to breathe the warmth of family affection into the community life of the sisters." A.A.S., Vol. XLIV (1952), p. 825.

the center of the community, guiding them, inspiring them, leading them. As we are realizing so clearly in these post-Vatican II
days, the abbot's role is a charismatic one. An abbot must himself
be a man of the spirit if he is to make his monks men of the spirit.

Aelred had the charism for abbot in a marked degree. By nature
he was ideally suited to be a guide and leader of men. Gentleness
of manner, a warm approachability, a deep, radiant sympathy and
fellow-feeling are not qualities one would automatically associate
with the early Cistercians, when one thinks of their austere discipline, their severity in art and architecture and their relentless
determination to effect and carry through their reform. But these
were the outstanding natural qualities Aelred possessed which made
him the abbot par excellence. It is interesting to note in passing
that these tender qualities of heart did not unfit him for the material
duties of his office. He possessed a good head for business affairs as
well, and his skill and shrewdness as an administrator can be gathered
from the undeniable fact that Rievaulx under him prospered in
temporal matters.[20] But for Aelred this side of his office was
definitely secondary. He had one primary aim—to help his monks
grow in God, to form them in the likeness of Christ. Because
Aelred was, above all things, an educator of monks. For the title
of his synthesis of Aelred's doctrine Fr Amédée Hallier chose the
apt phrase—*un éducateur monastique*.[21] This is exactly what Aelred
was. His predominant aim, first as novice-master and later as abbot,
was to educate his monks in the fullest sense of the word—to lead
them to open themselves up to the creative influence of God's love
and to be free with the freedom of the lovers of God.

The good teacher or educator has to be totally dedicated to
those in his care and to love them with an intimate, personal love.
Unquestionably the Abbot of Rievaulx had such dedication and
such love for his monks. One of the most touching documents he
has left us is his *Pastoral Prayer*,[22] in which we can almost tangibly

---

20. D. Knowles, *op. cit.*, p. 258.   21. Amédée Hallier, *op. cit.*

22. *Oratio Pastoralis*, edited and published by A. Wilmart in *Auteurs spirituels et textes dévots du moyen âge latin*, pp. 291–298; trans. *Works of Aelred of Rievaulx*, Vol. 2, Cistercian Fathers Series, II.

feel his tremendous affection and devotion. In Dom Wilmart's opinion, this prayer is one of the "finest writings that express the piety of medieval monachism."[23] It is worth quoting passages of it verbatim, because no analysis or paraphrase of it could reveal Aelred's lovely qualities of soul and charisms as abbot so well as these words of his do. He simply must be allowed to speak for himself:

> You know well, Lord, how deeply I love them; you know that I have given my heart and all its tender affection to them. . . . I pray that all you have given me I may give to them without reserve. I will spend myself completely on their behalf. . . . All that I am, my whole life, my experience, my knowledge, may it all belong to them. . . . Grant me to accommodate myself to the character, the manners, the disposition, the gifts—or lack of gifts—of each one; to do as circumstances demand and as you see best. . . . You know, O Lord, that I do not rule over them in a spirit of severity or domination, that I desire to be of service to them in charity rather than to lord it over them, to be their humble servant and to be in the midst of them as one of themselves. . . . Grant them, Lord, to think and feel always towards me, your servant and theirs for your sake, as best serves their spiritual welfare. Let them love me and fear me but only in so far as you see is for their good. . . . May they, through the influence of your Spirit, Lord, have peace in themselves, among themselves and with me; may they be well behaved, kindly disposed; may they obey, help and bear with one another.

We have to be on our guard against imagining that all the monks at Rievaulx were as gentle-natured as Aelred, or that it cost him nothing "to accommodate himself to the characters" of all his monks. The picture is quite otherwise. Many of those who entered at Rievaulx were rough, illiterate men, "men of no refinement or intellectual gifts."[24] Aelred had his "problem" monks as much as, and even more than, other abbots, such as the troublesome cleric

---

23. A. Wilmart, "L'Oraison pastorale de l'abbé Aelred" in *Revue Bén.* 41 (1929), p. 74.

24. D. Knowles, *op. cit.*, p. 259.

N

who ran away from the monastery,[25] and, perhaps the most extreme example of all, the monk, "a bovine creature of criminal aspect,"[26] who seized Aelred as he lay dying and threw him on the fire! The Abbot was saved from a death similar to St Lawrence's by some of the brethren who heard his cries and rushed to his rescue. He then saved his near-murderer from being torn apart by the brethren, kissed him, blessed and embraced him and gently sought to soothe his senseless anger against himself.[27] Is it any wonder that Gilbert of Swineshead could say of Aelred: "He would put up with annoyances caused by others, but he himself was a nuisance to none . . . his patience enabled him to bear with everything. . . . If I cannot say that he was slow to lose his temper, it is because that would be tantamount to saying that he did sometimes lose his temper; but in fact he never did."[28]

More and more today authority is conceived as a service of those over whom one is placed. No more beautiful image of such a concept of authority could be found than in Abbot Aelred's *Pastoral Prayer* which was a faithful echo of his own life.

Dialogue

The Abbot of Rievaulx was a master of the delicate art of dialogue, another feature which makes him appear extremely modern. By *Perfectae caritatis* religious superiors are required to consult their religious, to listen willingly to their views on all matters pertaining to the life and activities of their communities.[29] This is a new idea in as much as we have had very little of it before the Council, which shows to what an extent we had forgotten Chapter Three of the Holy Rule. Aelred had not forgotten that particular chapter and the dialogue he held with his monks and novices is one of the most charming features of his monastic education. Walter

---

25. *Life of Aelred*, edited by F. M. Powicke (Nelson: London, 1950), pp. 24–25.

26. *Ibid.*, p. 79.   27. *Ibid.*, p. 80.

28. Gilbert of Swineshead, *Sermo XLI in Canticum Salomonis*, PL 184:216; trans. Cistercian Fathers Series, XIV.

29. Decree *Perfectae caritatis*, nos. 4, 14.

Daniel, who wrote the *Life of Aelred*, tells us how the novices came to him when he was their Father Master for impromptu talks on spiritual things.[30] On becoming abbot he kept this practice up. Some of his writings, the *Mirror of Charity* and *Spiritual Friendship* for example, actually describe some of these informal and spontaneous dialogues. Toward the end of his life, when he was confined to the little cell near the infirmary, they were a daily occurrence. We get a delightful and homely picture of them from Walter: "The construction of this cell was a great source of consolation to the brethren, for every day they came to it and sat in it, twenty or thirty at a time, to talk together of the spiritual delights of the Scriptures and of the observance of the Order. There was nobody to say to them, 'Get out, go away, do not touch the Abbot's bed'; they walked and lay about his bed and talked with him as a little child prattles with its mother."[31] There is a touch of humor in the remark of a monk at one of these dialogues: "The Procurator is coming. If he gets in, that will put an end to our talk. I'll watch the door, Father, while you carry on."[32]

We are reviewing at present the formation and education to monastic life, which we are giving our young monks and nuns.[33] A great deal of valuable aid would be provided by a study not only of Aelred's doctrine but of his method of education. The Socratic method, which is at the basis of many of our modern educational techniques, found its place at Rievaulx. In the *Mirror of Charity* there is a lengthy but interesting digression in which Aelred reveals the sure touch of the good teacher.[34] A novice confides to Abbot Aelred that his spiritual life has gone flat and empty. Out in the world he felt he loved God fervently, felt sorrow and compunction for having offended him, but here in the monastery he feels nothing

30. *Life of Aelred*, p. 40.

31. *Ibid.*

32. *Spiritual Friendship*, PL 195:687.

33. Cf. Report of Commission on Formation, Monte Cistello, November, 1968.

34. *Mirror of Charity*, 2, 17–20.

at all like that, and he is worried and discouraged. He cannot understand why he does not love God as much now. Aelred handles his problem, a fairly common one among young religious, with consummate tact and sympathy. In a dialogue with him he gradually leads him to a clearer understanding of the meaning of the sentiments of fervor and devotion he experienced and to a truer estimation of real love of God. In this dialogue Aelred tactfully guides the novice into discovering the truth for himself, which is the ideal way of ensuring that the truth will really go home to him.

In this modern age when we pride ourselves on our educational facilities, is there a danger that we may forget the very first principle of pedagogy? If we have to teach in any capacity, the most necessary requisite is not to arm ourselves with degrees in the subject we are going to teach, in other words, it is not to know our subject well (though this is, of course, necessary); it is to know well the person we are going to teach. The personal relationship between teacher and pupils, abbot and monks, novice-master and novices, etc., is of primary importance. Without it all the skilled knowledge in the world would be of little use. A deep, personal interest in and concern for the human person we are dealing with is absolutely essential for all who are charged with the formation and education of our monks and nuns. In this is to be found the secret of Aelred's amazing success as a monastic educator.

Aelred's Humanism

This brings us to one of the chief characteristics of this many-sided monk: he was a humanist, one of the greatest humanists of the first half of the twelfth century when humanists reached a peak.[35] He was not the only Cistercian humanist of his day, but he was undoubtedly the most remarkable. He was so thoroughly typical of the humanism of his age that he found himself classed with Abelard and Héloïse—rather surprising and perhaps embarrassing company for the gentle Abbot of Rievaulx—as "personalities of

---

35. D. Knowles, "The Humanism of the Twelfth Century," *Studies,* Vol. XXX (1941), p. 44.

the early twelfth century whose lives and words will continue to attract and move the minds of men throughout the ages."[36]

Aelred was a humanist in almost every sense of the word.[37] He was intensely interested in everything human.[38] His flair for psychology made him a penetrating observer of the whole range of human emotions and affections, and his analyses of these human sentiments were so accurate that they stand up to the test of twentieth-century standards.[39] For Aelred the human personality was one of absorbing interest, and we find this same interest coming through even in his study of the Bible.[40] He concentrates, not so much on biblical theology or exegesis, as on the men and women in the Bible. These he grew to look upon as his friends. They were not historical figures to him; they were as living as the monks in his own monastery.

According to David Knowles, "the quintessence of the humanism of the twelfth century" was to be found at Rievaulx.[41] One of the chief notes of this humanism is "the high value set upon the individual, personal emotions, and upon the sharing of experiences and opinions within a small circle of friends."[42] These are values that are rated highly by the men and women of the mid-twentieth century. The young people who come to our monasteries today are definitely concerned about the human values which they have learned to appreciate intensely before their entrance. One of the important tasks facing the Order at present is to ensure that these young people will be able to find within our communities a

36. D. Knowles, *art. cit.,* p. 48.

37. Cf. L. Bouyer, *The Cistercian Heritage* (Westminster, Md.: Newman, 1958), pp. 125–127.

38. The Pastoral Constitution, *Gaudium et Spes,* of Vatican II might aptly be called a charter of Christian humanism. Its opening words fit Aelred to perfection: "The joys and hope, the sorrow and anxiety of the men of our time, especially of the poor and of those who are suffering in any way, these Christ's disciples make their own and there is nothing human that does not find an echo in their hearts." Cf. also *Populorum Progressio,* Nos. 20 and 42.

39. Cf. J. Chatillon, *Cordis affectus* in *Dict. Spir.* II, 2294.

40. Cf. L. Bouyer, *op. cit.,* p. 126.   41. D. Knowles, *art. cit.,* p. 53.

42. *Ibid.,* p. 46.

meaningful form of monastic life that will respect these human values and integrate them into their monastic formation.[43] Aelred of Rievaulx achieved this admirably in the monastic education he gave his monks, which assimilated human values into the scale of Christian values. His attractive monastic theology would make a profound impact on the contemporary generation of monks and nuns if they were put in touch with it. For Aelred the monastic ideal of seeking God and responding to his love did not exclude the cultivation of what was best in human nature, for example, the development of human relationships. Indeed it could even be said that he set as much store by relationships with other persons as he did by what might be called the strictly spiritual exercises in attaining that ideal.[44] Because Aelred had the true contemplative's vision of God's presence in all things, above all, in all persons. To love his brother with all his human dimensions is to love Christ. When God brought a human love, a human friendship into this life, Aelred knew that he was not subtracting some of his love from God, but rather that God was giving him something more to love him with, was asking something more, not less. Every human relationship was an added way of loving and worshiping him, a gift to give back to him. This led Aelred to emphasize what is, perhaps, most characteristic of his theology, namely, his doctrine on friendship.

43. The criticism is sometimes leveled against the religious life in general and the monastic life in particular that they have produced a spirituality which not only has no place in its program for human and temporal values, but positively despises and condemns them. Thus, for example, D. F. O'Callaghan, writing in *The Irish Ecclesiastical Record,* Vol. CV (1966), p. 50, says: "The annals of Christian spirituality . . . give too many instances of pessimism and distrust of the corporal and temporal. . . . Mother Church may have turned a blind eye to many of the goings-on of the Fathers in the desert, approving their generosity of spirit if not the extremes of expression and practice, but the hostility to human and secular values inherent in their spirituality and formulated in many treatises *De fuga mundi* and *De laudibus eremi* came to be accepted as the genuine party-line of Christian ascesis." To which it may be replied that a study of Aelred of Rievaulx would reveal a different note from that sounded by the party-line, if such exists.

44. Cf. L. Bouyer, *op. cit.,* p. 126.

Friendship

Aelred's teaching blossomed into a theology of friendship and for friendship. The monastic life, when lived to the full, should open men up to friendship with God and friendship with their fellow-men which is, in a true sense, a manifestation of their love of God. "The Christian life is, for Aelred, simply the full flowering of freedom and consent in the perfection of friendship."[45]

By nature Aelred was predisposed to be a great maker and cultivator of friends. He possessed a warmth of feelings, a rare delicacy of perception and the quality of self-revealing intimacy. Even "when I was still a boy at school," he tells us himself, "and took great delight in the charm of the companionship of those around me, it seemed good to me to give myself up unreservedly to my heart's leading and to dedicate myself to friendship. Nothing seemed to me more delightful, more sweet, or more profitable than to love and to be loved."[46] This love had to be properly channeled, not choked off completely, and it was channeled in the right direction when Aelred found his true spiritual home at Rievaulx. To the end of his days he retained his warm, spontaneous readiness to give and to receive love. So he was ideally suited to produce a Christian version of Cicero's *De Amicitia* which had made a profound and lasting impression on him.

Aelred is probably best known by outsiders for his treatise on friendship. We could hardly do better than put this famous work of Aelred's in the hands of our young monks. It will get across to them immediately. It may need, indeed it will need, to be properly interpreted for them, but they will recognize instantly that it speaks to them of a need that lies deep in their human nature, a need they do not want to have repressed or suppressed when they come to join our communities, a need which they feel can be, and should be, taken up into the new creation that is Christ's life in us. Aelred would applaud this concern of theirs for friendship, for he said that

45. Thomas Merton in Preface to *The Monastic Theology of Aelred of Rievaulx*, Cistercian Studies Series, Vol. 2.

46. *Spiritual Friendship*, Prologue, 659–660.

if you shut out friendship you shut out the sunlight of human life.[47] And even more bluntly: "To live without friends is to live like a beast."[48]

To be sure, the friendship of which Aelred speaks is not everything that goes by the name of friendship today. There are bogus kinds of friendship as there are bogus kinds of love.

The mystery of God's trinitarian life is at the basis of Aelred's doctrine on friendship, this indescribable life of love between the three divine Persons which St John sums up as "God is love," and which Aelred would be tempted to interpret as "God is friendship" but for his great reverence for the word of God. Nevertheless he will go so far as to say that he who abides in friendship abides in God.[49] This God of love has written deep in the nature of every creature a desire for unity in peace and love. This natural impulse is of cosmic dimensions. Hence, for Aelred, every human friendship is, in germ, a participation in that love that is the very essence of God, and so it has of itself a religious and supernatural value.[50] He is quite prepared to tolerate an inferior form of friendship, an over sentimental one for example, and use this as a starting point for attaining a more holy friendship.[51] Far from hindering one's life of union with God, true friendship furthers it. "Suppose you are praying to Christ on your friend's behalf," says Aelred, "so easy and inevitable is it for your affection to pass from one to the other that in no time Christ himself has become the object of your love and desire."[52] Christ is the meeting ground of true friends and hence Aelred is insistent that friendship can only exist between good men: "Here we are, you and I, and Christ, I hope, is the third that unites us."[53] "A friend goes forward with his friend to Christ's friendship and to becoming one spirit with him."[54] "The beginning and end of all spiritual friendship is Christ, its progress is his doing."[55]

47. *Ibid.,* 676b.   48. *Ibid.,* 676c.   49. *Ibid.,* 670a.

50. Cf. G. Raciti, "L'Apport original d'Aelred de Rievaulx à la réflection occidentale sur l'amitié," *Collectanea Cisterciensia,* 29 (1967), p. 95.

51. *Spiritual Friendship,* 692a.   52. *Ibid.,* 701a.

53. *Ibid.,* 661a.   54. *Ibid.,* 672d.   55. *Ibid.,* 662c.

There is nothing naturalistic about Aelred's concept of love and friendship. Nowhere does he quote St Augustine's famous phrase: *Ama et fac quod vis* (though he is heavily indebted to him for much else), perhaps because he realized that such an epigrammatic sentence can too easily be caricatured and robbed of its true meaning. But also because he was too firmly convinced of the value and necessity of the *disciplina Ordinis*—the Cistercian observances. The monk is not left to his own devices, to do what he likes; he comes to the monastery to take up and be moulded by the monastic observances. These have value, not in themselves, but because they purify him and make charity grow in him. Their spiritual value and sanctifying power derive from their orientation towards charity.[56] They are the *dura et aspera* of the Rule, but the qualifying phrase St Benedict uses is significant: *per quae itur ad Deum*,[57] the hardships and trials which lead to God and without which the monastic life would be no true approach to him.

Aelred never lets us forget that man, the image of God, is a fallen creature, a distorted image. The innate dynamism in him which we call love has to be purified, to be repaired, to undergo a painful process of restoration if it is to become true love or charity and if this love is to flower into friendship. In fact the complete process of restoration will be achieved only in heaven where friendship will then be universal.[58] On earth Aelred admits that it can only exist among the few.[59] During the whole of one's earthly life a struggle will have to be kept up between the perversion of love which is cupidity and true love which is charity. "He who shirks

56. Cf. P. Salmon, "L'ascèse monastique et les origines de Cîteaux" in *Mélanges Saint Bernard* (Dijon, 1954), pp. 282–283.

57. Chapter 58. Cf. Erich Fromm, *The Art of Loving*, p. 110: "With regard to the art of loving, this means that anyone who aspires to become a master in this art must begin by *practicing* discipline, concentration and patience throughout every phase of his life," quoted by Fr Raphael Simon ocso in his paper *The Adaptation of our life to the psychological condition of the religious and candidates of our times*, read to the Regional Conference of the United States, Genesee Abbey, May–June 1968.

58. *Spiritual Friendship*, 702b.

59. *Ibid.*, 690c.

spiritual warfare," says Aelred, "has no right to be called a man."[60]
The monk who thinks he can share Christ's friendship without
submitting to a stern discipline is under an illusion. By their profession Christians are "heralds of the cross of Christ."[61] "In the
cross of Christ there is no room for softness, flabbiness, daintiness,
for what flatters flesh and blood . . . Our Order is the cross of
Christ."[62] As Aelred taught it, love is anything but soft and sentimental; it is, as in Dante, "a lord of terrible aspect."

If Aelred's concept of friendship was not naturalistic, neither was
it angelic. He never ceased to put before his monks the highest
ideal of spiritual friendship, but he never forgot that man is a unity
of soul and body and that the bodily side of man enters into man's
personal relationships and friendships. Man does not love with his
soul or mind alone, as a disembodied spirit, but as a human person.
Hence friendship will involve both the body and the mind. Our
human *affectus* will have to be in accord with right reason and informed by charity,[63] but these *affectus* will still form part of the
human friendship. Grace does not replace nature or become a
substitute for it. On the contrary, here more than anywhere else,
grace builds on nature, perfects it,[64] transmutes something that
belongs to the body and uses it as an instrument for bringing God's
love and friendship to men. The life of grace is not superimposed
on a Christian regardless of the human life that is its basis. Grace
follows the special contours of the human life so intrinsically that
one cannot determine where nature ends and grace begins. Péguy

60. *S. Temp.* XV, 294d.   61. *S. Temp.* IX, 263c.

62. *Ibid.*, 263cd.   63. *Spiritual Friendship*, 679d.

64. Cf. Pope Pius XII, addressing Professors of the Carmelite Order at
Rome in 1951: "If it is true, as indeed it is most true, that nature is perfected,
not suppressed, by supernatural grace, then the edifice of evangelical perfection
must undoubtedly be raised upon the foundation of the natural virtues. If the
young religious is to become an exemplary member of his community, he
must first strive to become a perfect man in ordinary things and everyday life;
he cannot scale the mountain peaks unless he is able to walk freely on the
level ground . . . as far as possible the religious house will endeavor to become
a loved family home for each member of the community." A.A.S., Vol.
XLIII, p. 735.

suggests this interlocking of the natural and supernatural in the lines:

Car le surnaturel est lui-même charnel,
Et l'arbre de la grâce est raciné profond.

Aelred was clearly aware of the danger involved in accepting the emotional content in friendship.[65] The cautious Walter Daniel, who could not see beyond these dangers, felt that it would be better to have no friendships at all than to run such risks. But Aelred cordially disagrees with him on this point—to live without friendship is not to live a human life at all.[66] But it is more than that, it is to refuse that for which God made his creatures.[67]

The tender, human, loving side of Aelred is evident in everything he wrote. His pet word was *dulcis*; the word was so often applied to himself. The love that he gave and received and that he taught his monks to give and receive at Rievaulx was no cold, abstract, purely "spiritual" love. He took a personal interest in each of his monks: he loved them, we are told in the *Life*, as a mother loves her children.[68] Every human being, the monk and nun no less, has need of a love that is truly human. In point of fact it is only men and women who know by experience what human love is who are in a position to understand divine love.[69] Some people actually think that they love God because they love no one else— what a caricature!

Charity can only gain, not suffer, if monks have warm, genuine, balanced human relationships with one another. A community which is knit together by a network of friendships is more likely to be advancing in genuine charity than one in which friendship is

---

65. Cf. *Mirror of Charity*, 3, 31: "Friendship is the most potentially dangerous of all our affections."

66. *Spiritual Friendship*, 676ac.   67. *Ibid.*, 690b.

68. *Life of Aelred*, p. 58.

69. Cf. Ladislas M. Orsy, *Open to the Spirit* (Washington: Corpus, 1968), p. 94: "There cannot be a healthy relationship with God without a healthy relationship with human friends."

discouraged. To the individual monk in a community it is no small blessing to know that he has someone to whom he can turn as a close friend. Chastity, too, benefits from such a situation, as the Council reminds us: "chastity has stronger safeguards in a community where true fraternal love thrives among its members."[70] "Surely if celibacy means anything at all," says Fergal O'Connor OP, "those who practice it should be models of all these qualities of human love. In them we should be able to find an example of how to cultivate friendship, how to maintain friendship, and how to sustain friendship against all odds and all difficulties."[71] To use the very beautiful expression of Aelred, friendship is "the kiss of Christ" who breathes this holy affection into those who really love each other.[72]

Conclusion

This brief study has tried to bring out some of the chief traits of Aelred's methods and principles of monastic education, which made his contribution to the spirit and aims of our Cistercian Fathers something special and even unique—the living and experiential aspect of his theology which reads like a personal testimony of his own experience of God; the charismatic qualities that made him an outstanding abbot; the family spirit he created in his beloved community at Rievaulx; the delightfully informal dialogues of which he was the center and which appear to be unique to the Rievaulx of his day; the keenly developed appreciation of human values he had and his ability to assimilate and transpose these into the monastic way of life; finally his magnificent doctrine and example of friendship. These are traits which cannot but make him an attractive figure to contemporary monks and nuns. Here is a monastic theologian whose writings have lost none of their magnetic charm. If Aelred's works are placed in the hands of the monks

70. *Perfectae caritatis*, no. 12.

71. Fergal O'Connor OP, "Sexuality, Chastity and Celibacy" in *Celibacy and Virginity* (Dublin, 1968), p. 44. This whole essay by Fr O'Connor is worth reading.

72. *Spiritual Friendship*, 673c.

of our age, the appropriate epitaph, that was inscribed on his tomb, will surely be verified now as much as ever before: *Et cito quam legitur tam cito relegitur*—No sooner have you read him than you want to read him again.

Columban Heaney ocso

Mount Melleray Abbey,
Cappoquin, Ireland

THE ORIGIN AND EARLY EVOLUTION OF THE CISTERCIAN ANTIPHONARY[1] REFLECTIONS ON TWO CISTERCIAN CHANT REFORMS

MANY OF YOU will recall that in Tolstoy's *Anna Karenina*, Anna's bureaucrat of a husband, Alexei Alexandrovitch, is portrayed as a man several stages removed from real life. One of the ways poor Alexei manifests this is by his irritating habit of trying to reduce each complex, real-life situation to a clearly defined, well ordered object which can be studied according to its various logical aspects. And, as Tolstoy tells us, "To all these questions there were answers admirably stated, and answers admitting of no shade of doubt. The answers were all based on official data . . . and so they were unhesitating and certain."[2]

I mention Alexei Alexandrovitch Karenin at the beginning of this paper so as to assure you that I am well aware of the risk we all run in a symposium of this sort, where we study a complex, only imperfectly documented situation according to various aspects. It is probably in the logic of things, I suppose, that someone should study the spirit and aims of the early Cistercians from the aspect of their *liturgy*. But if we isolate this area of research as something

---

1. "Early evolution" is a rather vague formula. As a *terminus ad quem* we may take a date marking more or less the mid-point of the twelfth century. Though the antiphonary continued to evolve by way of successive additions, its substance and shape had been definitively determined, as we shall see, towards the year 1147.

By "antiphonary" I mean the choir book thus designated in the relatively modern acceptation of the term, i.e., the book containing texts and melodies of the antiphons, responsories, and similar chants used in the choral celebration of the Divine Office.

2. *Anna Karenina*, Part IV, Chapter VI.

self-contained and clearly distinct from other similar areas of research, we shall be a bit like Alexei Alexandrovitch. The experience
of those first Cistercians at the New Monastery was deep, and it
found expression not only in their liturgy, but also in their legislation, their usages and institutions, their writings, their general style
of life. Their cultural environment sprang in large measure from
their spiritual experience; and it is precisely this experience which
provides the background against which the monuments of Cistercian culture and Cistercian institutions become understandable, and
enter into a living, organic relationship, in which clear lines of
demarcation become blurred. The Mystery of Christ as lived by the
early Cistercians is something deep, something rich and living. It
is only as an expression of this experience of Christ that their liturgy
makes sense. But at this level of understanding, are we not perhaps
right to be a bit suspicious of overly clear solutions and unhesitating,
certain answers based on official data?

The early Cistercian liturgy in general is much too broad a
subject. So I wish to focus my attention chiefly on the earliest versions of our present-day antiphonary. I believe that the essentials of
the early Cistercian liturgy can be grasped by a study of just this
one book.

Recent Research in the Field of Cistercian Chant

Ten or fifteen years ago, the reform of our Order's chant books
became a much agitated question.[3] Contact with Solesmes and a

---

3. In the first *post bellum* General Chapter held by the Strict Observance in
1946, indications of a new orientation were already in evidence. The Chant
Commission appointed on this occasion was charged with the task of studying
the state of the Order's chant with a view to the possible future revision of the
same:

Ad mentem Capituli Generalis huius commissionis munus est investiga-
tionem instituere circa statum cantus in Ordine, circa methodum quoque
eum efficacius colendi et circa varia problemata, quae cantus Cisterciensis
traditionem eiusque forsan in futurum revisionem spectant.

These are the directives formulated in the report of the Chant Commission,
"Conspectus historicus de cantu in Ordine Cisterciensi," in *Collectanea O.C.R.*
12 (1959), p. 216.

better knowledge of chant theory and practice helped to make many of us somewhat sensitive to the imperfections of our particular kind of chant called Cistercian. Others of us were, on the contrary, quite happy with our particular chant tradition dating back, for better or worse, to the time of St Bernard.

It would be a great mistake simply to think of the dissatisfied monks and nuns as interested only in aesthetics, or paleography, or historical studies. I found myself among the dissatisfied brethren, and my own position was typical: a chant repertory more faithful to authentic sources would better ensure a more fruitful experience of our prayer in common. It was essentially a question of our contemplative vocation, a question of our contact with the word of God. After all, it was St Bernard himself who had written that the function of the chant is "not to void the meaning of the text, but to make it fruitful."[4]

I am quite *sure* that everyone was interested in contact with the word of God, no matter what his position with regard to the chant. I am likewise sure that opposition to a reform of our chant tradition stemmed usually from the conviction that, really, the chant simply was not that important, or that any reform would be in the direction of elaborate melodies and complicated neums. Unfortunately, appeal was usually made to our 800 year old chant tradition, stabilized under St Bernard's personal aegis toward the year 1147.[5]

---

4. Letter 398.—PL 182:611a. In this letter addressed at an uncertain date to Abbot Guy of Montiéramey (1137–1163), and accompanying his Office composed in honor of St Victor, St Bernard presents his views concerning the nature of music in the monastic liturgy. The letter deserves serious attention on the part of anyone studying the chant reform linked with St Bernard's name. A trans. of both the letter and the Office of St Victor can be found in Cistercian Fathers, I.

5. The date 1147 represents the *terminus ad quem* for the reform in question. It is arrived at by the following rather dense line of argumentation. In 1147, the independent monastery of Obazine (near Limoges) was incorporated into the Order in the line of Cîteaux. Consequent upon this affiliation was the reform of the liturgical books of Obazine. Such a reform came as a surprise to the Obazinites, since, as early as 1142, they had *already* received a complete set of Cistercian liturgical books from the nearby monastery of Dalon (itself not officially Cistercian, but Cistercian with regard to usage from around

How could we possibly think of rejecting a tradition established and confirmed by our Father St Bernard?

Our answer to this argument from Cistercian tradition was that the tradition in question was a very bad one, and that the whole chant reform associated with St Bernard's name had been a terrible mistake.[6]

St Bernard and the Cistercian Chant Reform: the "Prologus" to the Antiphonary

Perhaps the best way of getting the background of the chant reform carried out under St Bernard's aegis will be for us to read together one of the several documents closely linked with the reformed antiphonary, which to this day provides the substance of our own antiphonary. I spoke of *several* documents. The first

---

1120 onwards). The chronicler explains that the 1142 version ante-dated the reform which evidently was promulgated in or before 1147. The extent of the revisions varied according to the book in question. The pertinent passage is found in the *Vita beati Stephani abbatis monasterii Obazinensis*, written in the second half of the twelfth century by a disciple of the first abbot and founder of Obazine, and first edited by Etienne Baluze in 1683. The following extract is from the same scholar's reprint in *Miscellanea* I, Lucca, 1761, p. 161. Chapter 13 of Bk. II reads in part:

". . . illud certe molestissimum videbatur, quod libros, quos secundum ordinem monachorum (i.e., Cisterciensium) nuper multo labore confecerant (i.e., ca. 1142), deponere cogebantur et ad formam Cisterciensium revocare. Itaque alios in ipsis a fundamentis incipiebant, alios radebant et denuo rescribebant, alios ex integro dimittebant, alios paucis immutatis sibi iterum retinebant. Sed cum et ipsi primitus per Dalonenses a Cistercio fuissent delati, mirum videbatur quod tam discordes inter se tamque dissimiles esse potuerint. Sed sciendum quod libri quibus primo Cistercienses in divinis officiis usi sunt, valde corrupti ac vitiosi fuerunt, et usque ad tempora sancti Bernardi permanserunt. Tunc enim Abbatum communi decreto ab eodem sancto Abbate ejusque cantoribus sunt correcti et emendati, et sicut modo habentur dispositi. Unde constant eos ante hanc emendationem a Dalonensibus expetitos; qui etsi de ordine tunc non erant, secundum ordinem tamen vivere gestiebant, et consuetutines scriptas sibimet deferebant."

6. The groundwork for the refutation of the "argument from tradition" had been done by Fr Dominique Delande OP, in his book *Le Graduel des Precheurs* (Paris, 1949). Since the reformed Cistercian gradual underlies the further re-worked Dominican version, Fr Delande's study of the sources of

is designated as a *prologus* by all the ancient manuscripts,[7] though in reality it is an official act of promulgation. The second is a brief treatise explaining the reasons for the revision of the texts and melodies;[8] and I shall refer to it by its incipit, *Cantum quem Cisterciensis.* The third document is designated in the manuscript as a *Tonale.* It is, in effect, a practical catechism of the reformed Cistercian chant.[9] All three documents were meant to be included in every manuscript of the reformed antiphonary.

The *prologus* is, as I have said, an official act of promulgation, and its structure is easily discernible: a brief *initial protocol*, in which Bernard identifies himself and his addressees, namely, all those who are either to transcribe the reformed antiphonary, or are to sing from it; and the *text* in the strict sense of the word, made up of two essential parts, the *exposé* (which gives the historical events,

the Dominican gradual necessarily brought him face to face with the Cistercian gradual and the Cistercian chant treatises which explain the features proper to this version. Fr Delande's analyses and methodology were later exploited and developed by Fr R. Solutor Marosszeki s o cist, in his doctoral dissertation, *Les origines du chant cistercien, Analecta S.O. Cist.* 8, (Rome, 1952), as well as by Fr Maur Cocheril ocso, whose many monographs were a significant contribution to the study of our twelfth century chant. Unfortunately, his major work, *Le graduel de Cîteaux et la tradition gregorienne* (Port-du-Salut, 1955), was never published. Important among his many articles are his study of our Kyriale, i.e., *L'évolution historique du Kyrieale cistercien* (Port-du-Salut, 1956); and his study of the Cistercian Tonale, i.e., "Le 'Tonale Sancti Bernardi' et la définition du 'ton'," in *Cîteaux: Commentarii Cistercienses,* 13 (1962), pp. 35–66.

7. Critical edition by Dom Jean Leclercq osb, and Dom H. M. Rochais osb, in *S. Bernardi Opera* III, Rome 1963, pp. 511–516. The edition in PL 182:1121–1122, though not a critical edition, is quite good. An English trans. can be found in Cistercian Fathers, I.

8. The most accessible edition is that by Dom Mabillon, re-printed in PL 182: 1121–1132. It is, unfortunately, a rather bad edition filled with typographical errors.

9. The Tonale is also found in PL 182:1153–1166, re-printed from Dom Martin Gerbert's poor edition in *Scriptores ecclesiastici de musica* II (Typis San-Blasianis, 1784), p. 265ff. The Tonale exists, as a matter of fact, in *two* recensions. The second, interpolated recension reproduced in PL 182, is from the pen of a chant enthusiast only partly satisfied with the reform effected under St Bernard's aegis. We have need of a critical edition of the theoretical treatises written in the context of the Cistercian chant reform.

the circumstances, the motives which have occasioned this official act) and the *dispositio* (in which the object of the act is clearly set forth). We shall limit our exegesis almost exclusively to the *exposé* (lines 6–20 in the critical edition referred to in Note 7):

> Among other things for which our fathers, that is to say, the founders of the Cistercian Order, were very rightly zealous, was this: that they should sing in the divine praises only that which would prove to be the more *authentic*, and to this end they zealously took pains with all devotion.

Bernard is lavish with his superlatives: *studiosissime et religiosissime;* and he obviously approves the zeal of the Fathers of Cîteaux: *optime aemulati sunt.* The key word of the sentence is, however, the word *authenticum.* It is certainly correct to translate it by "authentic," but authentic as understood in its original, technical sense. Nowadays we speak of "an authentic spiritual life" or "authentic poverty" meaning simply genuine or meaningful. In our twelfth-century context, however, and in a passage dealing precisely with our Fathers' search for an exemplar of the so-called Gregorian antiphonary, authentic can be understood only as meaning authoritative, because of its conformity with the original.[10] In brief, Bernard describes our Fathers as desirous of using in their Office only that which enjoys the most unimpeachable authority:

> They accordingly sent (scribes) to transcribe and bring back the Metz antiphonary, for this was said to be Gregorian.

---

10. On several occasions Fr M.-D. Chenu OP, has had occasion to treat *in extenso* of the word *authenticum*. In his *Introduction à S.-Thomas* (Montreal-Paris, 1950), pp. 110ff. he has traced the origins and evolution of the term. If it be objected that this view is determined by his thirteenth-century subject, the reader may consult the same author's *La théologie au douzieme siècle, Etudes de Philosphie Médiévale*, 45 (Paris, 1957), pp. 351–365, where the point of reference is closer to our own period. The notes provide an abundance of lexicographical material and bibliographical references. Even in our own day, Webster continues to give, "having a genuine origin or authority." as the first meaning of "authentic."

No serious scholar nowadays would care to link Pope St Gregory I's name *too* closely with the corpus of chant for centuries associated with this great pontiff. But, remember, we are in the historically naive early twelfth century, when scribes were still depicting St Gregory seated at his writing desk, and taking down melodies sung into his ear by the Holy Spirit under the form of a dove.[11] Needless to say, neither the twelfth-century Cistercians nor any of their coevals were so much as even aware of the existence of a "Gregorian problem." For them, authentic antiphonary and Gregorian antiphonary were obviously convertible terms.

Question: If our Fathers wanted an *authentic* Gregorian antiphonary, why did they go to Metz in preference to Rome, or to St Gall's Abbey in Switzerland, so famous for its manuscripts of

11. It was only in the latter part of the seventeenth century that the "Gregorian problem" was raised. In 1675, Pierre Goussainville, in the preface to his Paris, 1675, edition of St Gregory's *opera,* called into question the traditional opinion that St Gregory I had authored, in the strict sense, the antiphonary attributed to him by generations of Christians. A half-century later, Georg von Eckhart went still further, and in his *Commentarium de rebus Franciae orientalis,* I (Wirceburgi, 1729), p. 718, attributed to Pope St Gregory II (715–731) much of the liturgical work up to that time invested with the prestigious authority of Gregory the Great. No one rallied to so novel a theory; and in 1781, when P. Zaccaria published his "Dissertatio de Antiphonarii et sacramentarii Gregoriani auctore fueritne S. Gregorius I and II?" (in *Bibliotheca ritualis* [Rome, 1781], T. II, pars 2da, ccxi–ccxxviii), this defender of tradition was able to invoke in support of the common doctrine names as illustrious as those of Pamelius, Rocca, Menard, Mabillon, de Ste-Marthe, Georgi, Tommasi, Vezzozi and Muratori.

And so things stood for more than a century. It was the Belgian musicologist F.-A. Gevaert, who, on October 27, 1889, startled the scholarly world by proposing, in a conference delivered before the Académie de Belgique, that the *real* Gregory of tradition was not the First, possibly not even the Second, but quite probably the Third, i.e., Gregory III, who reigned from 731 till 741. Almost straightaway Dom G. Morin osb, rose to the defense of Pope St Gregory I, and in 1890 fulminated against Gevaert a series of no less than four separate articles, all of which were published in rapid succession in *Revue Bénédictine:* "Le rôle de saint Grégoire le Grand dans la formation du répertoire musical de l'Église latine, à propos d'un récent discours de M. Gevaert," pp. 62ff.; "En quoi consista précisément le réforme grégorienne du chant liturgique," pp. 193–204; "Les témoins de la tradition grégorienne," pp. 289–323; "Examen du système substitué par M. Gevaert à la tradition grégorienne," pp. 337–369. (These last two articles later appeared under the title, *Les*

chant, or to some of the other great schools of music such as flourished at Liége, Chartres, or Montpellier?

Rome: Abstracting completely from the political chaos rampant in the Rome of our period, and leaving aside the personal reputation of Paschal II, whom many a monk and ecclesiastic reproached for weakness in the *sacerdotium/imperium* battle, Rome would surely have been the last possible place to go in search of an antiphonary of the same type in current use in Burgundy or elsewhere north of the Alps. On the basis of the manuscript evidence at hand, it is clear that Rome had its own very strange local chant (vestiges of which appear in parts of central Italy, and perhaps even in the British Isles prior to 1066).[12] It is quite likely, even probable, that our standard so-called Gregorian chant co-existed with the reper-

---

véritables origines du chant grégorien, Maredsous, 1895 and 1904.) Dom Morin had the support of scholars of the stature of Dom Cagin osb, W. H. Frere, Dr P. Wagner, A. Gastoué, Dom J. Leclercq osb.

Since the time of Dom Morin, however, the acquisitions of modern scholarship have thrown much new light on the extremely complex question of the origins of the chant we call "Gregorian." An imposing mass of analytical, comparative, musical, and historical studies converge to demonstrate convincingly that the "Gregorian" repertory is not so much the product of any one given period, but the result of a long-term evolution begun, surely, before St Gregory († 604) and continued for centuries after his death. Either personally or through his subordinates, Gregory himself could well have played a major role in the shaping up of an early seventh-century Roman corpus from which ours in part derives. But this would have marked only one moment (though a decisive one) in a long organic development. For a number of penetrating insights into the complexities of the question, see the important series of articles by Dom Jean Claire osb, starting with the 1962 issue of *Revue Grégorienne* (40/5), and continuing until the demise of this revue. Also the following: Dr H. Hucke, "Die Einstehung der Überlieferung von einer musikalischen Tätigkeit Gregors des Grossen" in *Musikforschungen* 8 (1954), pp. 259ff.; W. Lipphardt, "Gregor des Grosse und sein Anteil am römischen Antiphonen" in *Atti del Congresso Internazionale della Musica Sacra: Roma, 1950* (Rome, 1951), pp. 248ff. [=*Actes du Congrés international de musique sacrée: Rome, 1950*, Tournai, 1952]; W. Apel, "The Central Problem of Gregorian Chant" in *Journal of the American Musicological Society*, 9 (1957), pp. 118ff. See also the greater number of studies referred to in the following footnotes 12–14.

12. Cf. M. Huglo, "Le chant vieux-romain: liste des manuscrits et témoins indirects" in *Sacris Erudiri*, 6 (1954), pp. 96–124.

tory usually dubbed "Old Roman," but the positive evidence in favor of this is admittedly meager.[13] I have no intention of discussing here the physiognomy of this strange music; still less can we discuss its relationship with our own standard chant.[14] We must conclude from the manuscript evidence at hand, however, that anyone in search of a pure form of the chant sung in Burgundy would have been embarrassed by what he found in Rome. Perhaps it should be pointed out in passing that even the papal chapel stood in constant need of reform, and accounts of the state of affairs around 1105, when Paschal II imported a group of Canons of St Fridian to help alleviate the scandal, indicate that the attempted reform merely fostered further chaos.[15]

St Gall: Rightly or wrongly, the celebrated Swiss abbey claimed

13. Dom Georges Frenaud osb, "Les témoins indirects du chant liturgique en usage à Rome aux IXᵉ et Xᵉ siècles" in *Etudes Grégoriennes* III (1959), pp. 41–74. The author claims that several of the MSS studied by M. Huglo (see above, Note 12) attest to the presence of the "standard" repertory in Rome of the ninth and tenth centuries. In view of the cosmopolitan nature of Rome, this would not be surprising. But Dom Frenaud's hypothesis rests, to date, on no direct evidence.

14. Scholars are reasonably unanimous on two points: 1. Though the "Old Roman" repertory is clearly related to our "standard chant" (which derives from the former), the two repertories belong to two different musical milieux, and bear the characteristics of two essentially distinct epochs; 2. Although the "Old Roman" chant MSS clearly represent an *evolved* stage of development, the substance of this chant is definitely anterior to the standard "Gregorian" corpus. There is less unanimous agreement, however, on the widely held theory that the standard repertory is a re-working of the "Old Roman" chant, effected sometime in the course of the Carolingian reforms in a Frankish milieu, and under the influence of Byzantine musical theory (more or less badly understood).

To the best of my knowledge, the most helpful introduction to the question in English is the chapter by Robert Snow, "The Old-Roman Chant," in Dr Willi Apel's *Gregorian Chant* (Bloomington, 1958), pp. 484–505. Excellent bibliographical references and a clear presentation of the *status quaestionis* are given in the recension of *Zweiter internationaler Kongress für katholische Kirchenmusik: Wien, 4–10 Oktober, 1954*, signed J. H. [=Dom Jacques Hourlier osb], in *Etudes Grégoriennes,* III (1959), pp. 187–192.

15. Cf. the highly readable exposé of "The Twelfth-Century Offices of the Lateran" in Fr S. van Dijk ofm, and J. Hazelden Walker, *The Origins of the Modern Roman Liturgy* (Westminster, Maryland—London), pp. 67–87.

to be the depository of the most authentic Gregorian chant tradition.[16] Certainly, the paleographical remains are extant to demonstrate that at an early epoch, the chant tradition at St Gall's must indeed have been glorious. By the twelfth century, however, the glory of the abbey had indeed fallen low. There were not only illiterate abbots, there were abbots and anti-abbots. Still worse, in the conflict between Pope and Emperor, St Gall's gave its allegiance to the crown.[17] All in all, it was a wild situation, and rather frightening, I suppose, for a group of monks whose chief guarantee of peace lay precisely in their attachment to the Holy See.[18] Besides, the St Gall scribes were frightfully conservative in their notation. They persisted in the old way of writing melodies without staff (and therefore without precise melodic indications), so that their tradition could have been transplanted to the New Monastery only by recourse to rote memorization technique.

As for *Liège*, *Chartres* or *Montpellier*—these centers of chant were noted more for their *new* developments in music: precisely what was of least interest to the first monks of New Monastery in search of St Gregory's antiphonary!

What, then, were the credentials of *Metz*? Metz had enjoyed a privileged role in the propagation and maintenance of Roman chant in the Frankish kingdom of the eighth and ninth centuries. As part of Pippin's (751–768) policy of close fellowship with the Holy See, Metz, a very ancient see, and one-time seat of the court of Austrasia, had been thoroughly "romanized." In a pamphlet written around 783 in gratitude for his own short stay in Metz,

16. Dom Mocquereau OSB, elaborates on Ekkehard IV's account, in the Introduction to the first volume of the *Paleographie musicale* series (Solesmes 1889). The story wins less credence now than it did a century ago.

17. See the notice, "Ulrich III" (1077–1121), in R. Hengeler, *Professbuch der fürstlichen Benediktinerabtei der heiligen Gallus und Otmar zu St Gallen* (Zug, 1929), pp. 94ff.

18. Cf. the Bull, *Desiderium quod* (dated from Troja, Italy, 1100), which placed the New Monastery under the protection of the See of Peter: *Locum igitur illum quem inhabitandum pro quiete monastica elegistis. . . ."* Edited in J. Marilier, *Chartes et documents concernant l'Abbaye de Cîteaux, 1098–1182* (Rome, 1961), Doc. 21, pp. 48–49.

Paul the Deacon noted with satisfaction that, thanks to Bishop Chrodegang (742–757), the clergy of the city had been abundantly imbued not only with the divine law but with Roman chant as well.[19] The principle under implementation was to be expressed magnificently well a few decades later in the so-called "Caroline Books":

> No difference in chanting should divide those who share a common faith. United in their manner of reading (and understanding) the one divine law, they should be no less at one in the venerable tradition of a common song; nor should differences in the celebration of the offices separate those united in their dedication to the one true faith.[20]

We of the post-Vatican II age shudder, and are happy to note that neither Pippin nor Charlemagne was wholly successful in supplanting the ancient Gallican liturgy. The only point I wish to make here, however, it this: rightly or wrongly, chronicler after chronicler constantly identified Metz with the importation and propagation of the pure Roman tradition. Thus Paul the Deacon,[21] the author of the *Vita Alcuini*,[22] John the Deacon (†. before 882),[23]

---

19. *Gesta episcoporum Mettensium,* in PL 95:708: *Ipsumque clerum abundanter lege divina, Romanaque imbutum cantilena, morem atque ordinem Romanae Ecclesiae servare praecepit, quod usque ad id tempus in Mettensi ecclesia factum minime fuit.* The passage relative to St Chrodegang may be found with commentary in the Bollandist *Acta Sanctorum Martii* I, 451ff., and in J.-B. Pelt, *Etudes sur la Cathedrale de Metz: La Liturgie,* I (Metz, 1937), pp. 5–6.

20. Mgh, *Leges III: Concilia aevi Karolini II, Supplementum,* pp. 21–22.

21. See above, note 19.

22. Mgh, *Scriptores* XV, 1, p. 189: *Sigulphus . . . puer partes has petierat, Romamque ecclesiasticum ordinem discendum ab eo* (scil., Sigulf's uncle, Autbert) *ductus fuerat, necnon Mettis civitatem causa cantus directus. In quo . . . aliquo desudavit tempore ac multo cum fructu . . . patriam repedaverat propriam. . . .* Printed also in Ph. Jaffe, *Bibliotheca rerum Germanicarum, T.VI: Monumenta Alcuiniana* (Berlin, 1873), p. 16.

23. *Vita Gregorii Magni,* in PL 75:92: *Denique usque hodie quantum Romano cantui Metensis cedit, tantum Metensi ecclesiae cedere gallicanarum ecclesiarum germaniarumque cantus ab his qui puram veritatem diligunt, comprobatur.*

Adhémar of Chabannes (†. 1034),[24] St Gall's great writer, Notker Balbalus, in his *De gestic Karoli Magni* (written c. 883),[25] the compiler of the *Annales* of Lorsch (Einhard ? d. 840),[26] Andrew of Bergamo (c. 877)[27]. . . . It is, of course, easy enough to trip up our chroniclers, to show that they have confused details, or mistakenly repeated about Charlemagne what had originally been written about Pippin. Their accuracy and veracity, however, are beside the point. I simply refer to them as witnesses to the belief that Metz was to be identified with the purest Roman chant.

In returning to the text of our *Prologus*, we learn that the Metz antiphonary proved, upon examination, to be a profound deception. The reality was quite other than what they had heard: *Longe aliter rem esse quam audierant invenerunt.* Bernard derides the antiphonary on the score of both music (*cantus*) and text (*littera*); he finds both *vitiosum* (we would say defective or corrupt), *incompositum nimis* (that is to say, the musical and textual units were so linked as to form an incoherent whole), and finally, *paene per omnia contemptibile* (contemptible in almost every respect).

The moment is a bit dramatic. What did our truth-loving

---

24. *Maius autem magisterium cantandi in Metis civitate remansit, quantumque magisterium Romanum superat Metense in arte cantilenae, tanto superat Metensis cantilena ceteras scolas Gallorum.* The text is cited under Adhémar's name in W. Lipphardt, *Der karolingische Tonar von Metz* [=*Liturgiewissenschaftliche Quellen und Forschungen*, 43], (Münster, Westfalen, 1965), p. 3; the author, however, refers for his source to an article by H. Hucke, "Die Einführung des gregorianischen Gesanges im Frankenreich," *Röische Quartalschrift*, 49 (1954), p. 181. The text is identical with that of the *Annales Laurissenses*, referred to below in footnote 26. Has Adhémar reproduced an earlier text? Or has Dr Hucke, followed by Dr Lipphardt, attributed the text to the wrong source?

25. MGH, *Scriptores* II, 711: *Cantus Metensis . . . per totam Franciam coepit propagari, ut nunc usque ad eos, qui in his regionibus latino sermone utuntur, ecclesiastica cantilena dicatur Metensis, apud nos vero qui Teutonica vel Teutisca loquimur, Mete vel secundum derivationem usitato vocabulo Metisca nominatur.*

26. Text identical with that given above, footnote 24. Einhard's (or Eginhard's) authorship of the Chronicle of Lorsch is strongly contested. Cf. J.-B. Pelt, *op. cit.* (footnote 19), p. 130.

27. MGH, *Scriptores rerum Langob.*, saec. *VI-IX*, p. 224: . . . *tanta quidem dignitatem cantores ibi fuerunt, ut per totam Franciam Italiamque pene multe civitates ornamentum ecclesiae usque hodie consonant. Ibi* refers to Metz.

Fathers do? The Latin is a bit tangled (the manuscripts here present a harmless variant), but the general drift is reasonably clear: "Once they had begun (using it), they used it and retained it up to our own day." (*Quia tamen semel coeperant, sed usi sunt eo, et usque ad nostra tempora retinuerunt.*)

Puzzling. How could our Fathers, with their passion for the authentic, accept an admittedly corrupt version of the chant? Some writers have stated simply that St Stephen, for reasons best known to himself, imposed the adoption of the antiphonary against the will of the brethren.[28] One writer, anxious to demonstrate our Fathers' concern for values of simplicity and prayer, states simply that St Stephen, "instead of involving Cîteaux in a series of re-searches that would have taken the monks into regions of anti-quarianism rather than prayer, . . . was content to accept the imperfect text. . . ."[29] Several writers, finally, have decided that the Metz chant must have been the real thing, but simply not recognized as such by men whose musical formation received in the schools had given them only an artificial, distorted understand-ing of the traditional music of the Church.[30]

I myself would like to suggest that, viewed against their general background, our Fathers' adoption of the allegedly corrupt anti-phonary was not so unreasonable. I think that William of Malmesbury's pen-portrait of St Stephen deserves much closer attention than it has heretofore received. Some Cistercians do not hold William in very high regard because of the nasty things he has to say about St Robert;[31] and it is also quite true that, like every historian, William has his prejudices, and is not immune to error. But I think that William's description of St Stephen and the early

28. Thus Fr Marosszeki s o cist, *op. cit.,* p. 8, followed by Dom Jacques Hourlier osb, in his recension of Fr Marosszeki's thesis, "Les Réformes du chant cistercien," in *Revue Grégorienne,* 31 (1952), p. 3: *L'Abbé imposa la copie, ils obeirent.*

29. Thomas Merton, *The Waters of Siloe* (New York, 1949), p. 14.

30. E. Vacandard, *Vie de St-Bernard,* II (Paris, 1895), p. 104; Dom Jacques Hourlier osb, *art. cit.* (see note 28), pp. 3–4.

31. Cf. Fr Seraphin Lenssen ocso, "St. Robert Fondateur de Cîteaux I" in *Collectanea O.C.R.* 4 (1937), pp. 9–10.

Cistercians, written sometime before 1124, and slipped into Book
IV of his *Chronicle of the Kings of England*,[32] bears every mark of a
personal encounter described with objectivity, and marred only
by the sort of slips which even the best intentioned journalist is
liable to make.[33] In describing the beginnings of the Cistercian
reform at Molesme, William quotes Stephen in a rather long,
densely worded and obviously rhetorical presentation of his views
about those observances not specified by the *Holy Rule*.[34] Stephen
insists on the divine reason (*ratio*) which is at the heart of all God's
works. He says that the Holy Rule is divinely inspired (*divinitus
processit*)—which was the common doctrine in the Middle Ages—[35]
and that the purpose of the Rule is to call back (*revocare*) our nature,

32. PL 179:1286–1290. On the basis of internal evidence, the first edition
must have been issued between the summer of 1124 and the spring of 1125,
according to the excellent edition by W. Stubbs, *De Gestis Regum Anglorum
libri quinque* . . . I, London, 1889, pp. xliii–xliv, where the editor of this Rolls
Series edition adduces the evidence in favor of this dating. From details
mentioned in the chapter about the first Cistercians, Jean-A. Lefevre, in his
article, "Saint Robert de Molesme dans l'opinion monastique du XIIe et du
XIIIe siècle" in *Analecta Bollandiana,* 74 (1956), p. 70, suggests that the material
on which William bases his account must have been gathered around
1122/1123.

33. For a reasoned and reasonable evaluation of the text, Jean-A. Lefevre,
art. cit. (note 32), pp. 70–71, including note 2, p. 71.

34. PL 179:1287c–1288a.

35. The Second Council of Douzy (874) is typical. "In harmony with the
Sacred Scriptures, and the teaching of the holy Fathers, Benedict, blessed
both in grace and in name, inspired by the Holy Ghost, states in his Rule. . . .
Through Benedict the Holy Ghost published the Rule for monks by the same
inspiration in which the sacred canons were previously composed. . . . For the
rest, it is decreed that this same Rule, promulgated by the Holy Spirit and by
the authority of the Blessed Pope Gregory [the Great] is to be reputed as
among the Canonical Scriptures and the writings of the Catholic Doctors. . . ."
Translation taken from Dom Maurus Wolter OSB, *The Principles of Monasticism,*
trans. Dom Bernard Sause OSB (St Louis-London, 1962), p. 6. In two
sections of the Introduction, "Decrees and Documents of the Church,"
pp. 5–9, and "Writings of Saints and Doctors," pp. 9–35, dozens of similar
texts are to be found, investing the Rule with an authority and inspired
quality which many a modern might feel borders on the blasphemous. In
judging the options of our Fathers, however, we might do well to remind
ourselves of their cultural milieu and their particular viewpoints.

which is slipping off in the wrong direction (*fluxum naturae*), back to reason. Stephen then touches on the question of reason and authority (*auctoritas*). Authority, he tells us, cannot be contrary to reason: *Ratio. . . . et auctoritas divinorum scriptorum quamvis dissonare videantur, unum idemque sunt.* Therefore, if authority imposes an exigency which seems difficult to reason, it is nevertheless reasonable to acquiesce to authority. He applies this principle specifically to the Rule. Even if he is unable to understand the reason behind certain prescriptions of the Rule, he is nevertheless willing to abide by the Holy Rule in virtue of its authority: *In qua* (i.e., *Regula*) *etsi habentur quaedam quorum rationem penetrare non sufficio, auctoritate tamen acquiescendum censeo.*

I believe that the Metz antiphonary was in an analogous position. Defective though it seemed to be, it also enjoyed the prerogative of being an authoritative witness to the pure Gregorian tradition.

The early Cistercian hymnal raised a similar problem. In this instance we are fortunate enough to have still extant a single copy of the act of promulgation destined originally to serve as a preface to the hymnal.[36] Redacted towards the beginning of St Stephen's abbotship,[37] the document tells in its narrative section how the hymns comprised in the hymnal had been brought to New Monastery from Milan. Why Milan? Because Milan used the hymns composed (allegedly) by St Ambrose. But why the hymns composed by St Ambrose? Because these were the hymns prescribed

36. Nantes, Bibliotheque municipale, MS lat 9, f. 144r. The MS consists chiefly of Rufinus' translation of homilies by Origen. Our hymnal-notice helps fill up a stray extra half-column at the end of the homilies. It is followed by a sermon, *De sacramento altaris,* preached in the Clairvaux chapter-room by the Premonstratensian, Richard of Wedinghausen, and still extant in another MS definitely from Clairvaux (Troyes, Bibl. mun., MS 302, 12th c.). It seems likely that our MS, before being at Nantes, was at the nearby Abbey of Melleray, a daughter-house of Clairvaux.

37. No mention is made of daughter-houses, which suggests that the letter must have been redacted a bit before 1112/1113, when Cîteaux first began its expansion program.

by St Benedict, according to their exegesis of the Rule,[38] which is in essential agreement with commentaries by Smaragdus,[39] Hildemar, and Paul Warnefrid,[40] to mention only commentators writing prior to the Cistercian reform. It must have taken great faith to accept the tiny corpus of thirty-three hymns. Only a few of the texts and melodies were in use outside the area of Milanese influence; and many of the melodies had a structure and a style utterly foreign to anyone exposed from childhood to the hymns which passed as standard north of the Alps and westward. The limits of the new repertory were such that there was only a single Vigils hymn for every day of the year, including Easter and Christmas![41] Yet, St Stephen and his brethren adopted the hymnal by common decree and counsel of all the brethren of New Monastery, out of fidelity to the Rule as they understood it. The text deserves to be quoted in full.[42]

38. In several places in the Rule, St Benedict seems to equate *ambrosianum* and *hymnus*. Thus, in the Hanslick edition (CSEL 75):

Cap. IX, 4 (p. 54): *Inde sequatur ambrosianum* . . . (a number of the variant readings explicate by adding *"ambrosianum hymnum"*)

Cap. XII, 4 (p. 60): . . . *responsorium, ambrosianum, versu* . . .

Cap. XIII, 11 (p. 62): . . . *responsorium, ambrosianum, versu* . . .

Cap. XVII, 8 (p. 67): . . . *responsorium, ambrosianum, versu* . . .

It should be noted that the terminology *ambrosianum* is found only anent Vigils, Lauds, and Vespers. Quite possibly the holy legislator *was* thinking of precise Milanese (Ambrosian) hymns for these Hours.

39. *Commentaria in Regulam Sancti Benedicti*, PL 102:834 (Comm. on Ch. 9): *Indesequatur Ambrosianus. Id est hymnus. Ambrosianum dicit, vel divinum, vel coeleste, id est divinitus vel coelitus inspiratum. Alii Ambrosianum ab Ambrosio hymnorum magistro dici volunt.*

40. Smaragdus' exegesis is that of Paul. Cf. Pauli Warnefridi, *In Sanctam Regulam Commentarium* (Typis Abbatiae Montis Casini, 1880), p. 232. Hildemar repeats Paul, without adding anything significant.

41. See Peter Abelard's indignant remarks about the style and poverty of this hymnal, in his fiery Letter 10, written to St Bernard sometime around 1131, and dealing with the novel Cistercian usages in liturgy. The passage touching on the hymnal is in PL 178:339.

42. The text has been often re-printed since it first appeared in an unsympathetic, scholarly article by Dom Pierre Blanchard OSB, "Un monument primitif de la regle cistercienne" in *Revue bénédictine* 31 (1914), pp. 35–44. These editions have always been faulty to varying degrees, since the editors

INCIPIT EPISTOLA DOMNI STEPHANI SECUNDI CISTER
[*CIENSIS*] ABBATIS: DE OBSE[R]UATIONE HYMNORUM

3 Frater stephanus noui monasterii minister secundus, successor-
ibus [suis] salutem:
Mandamus filiis sancte ecclesie: nos hos hymnos quos beatum
6 ambrosium archiepiscopum constat cumposuisse, in hunc
nostrum locum, nouum uidelicet monasterium, de mediolan-
ensi ecclesia in qua cantantur detulisse, cummunique fratrum
9 nostrorum consilio ac decreto statuisse, ut amodo a nobis
omnibusque posteris nostris, hii tantum nullique alii canantur,
quia hos ambrosianos beatus pater et magister noster bene-
12 dictus in sua regula, quam in hoc loco maximo studio decreui-
imus obseruandam, nobis proponit canendos.
Quapropter auctoritate dei et nostra, uobis iniungimus,
15 nequando integritatem sancte regule quam in hoc loco haud
paruo sudore a nobis elaboratam et statutam conspicitis,
uestra leuitate mutare aut euellere presumatis; set magis
18 predicti patris nostri sancti propositi amatores et imitatores ac
propagatores existentes, hos hymnos inuiolabiliter teneatis.
EXPLICIT EPISTOLA FELICITER. AMEN.

In brief then, I suggest that, as with the hymnal, so with the Metz
antiphonary: it was the particular concept of authority which was
the determining factor in the adoption of these books.

There came a time, however, when a new generation of monks
could no longer abide the wretched antiphonary from Metz. Since
abbots were among the discontents, and since their number seems
to have been legion, it was simple enough for the annual General
Chapter to take action: *Tandem aliquando, non sustinentibus iam
fratribus nostris abbatibus ordinis, cum mutari et corrigi placuisset.* . . . A
reform of the antiphonary was decided upon, and the supervision
of the work was entrusted to St Bernard: . . . *curae nostrae id operis
iniunxerunt.* Accordingly, Bernard called to Clairvaux those of the
brethren most skilled in the theory and practice of chant: *Ego vero,
accitis de ipsis fratribus nostris* (*fratribus* seems to have for its antecedent
fratribus nostris, i.e., Bernard's fellow abbots), *qui in arte et usu*

---

have wrongly transcribed several of the scribe's punctuation marks as *et*. The
present transcription is my own, based on a microfilm of the MS. A trans. by
M. B. Pennington can be found in Cistercian Studies, 4 (1969), pp. 144f.

canendi instructiores atque peritiores inventi sunt.[43] And how did they go about shaping up their reformed antiphonary? They gathered their material from many different sources: . . . *de multis et diversis novum antiphonarium in subjectum volumen collegimus.* The result, Bernard felt, was an antiphonary irreprehensible as to text and to melody, as any well-trained singer could tell. *Denique cantator ipsius, si tamen gnarus fuerit, hoc probabit.*

Finally, we have the *dispositio* of the text, that is to say, the object of the act, in which Bernard expresses the will of the General Chapter. From now on the revised texts and melodies must be used without alteration, and this in virtue of the unanimous decision of the entire Chapter: . . . *volumus in nostris de cetero monasteriis tam verbo quam nota unique teneri, et mutari omnino in aliquo ab aliquo, auctoritate totius capituli, ubi ab universis abbatibus concorditer susceptum et confirmatum est, prohibemus.*

One last sentence points to the chant "treatise," *Cantum quem Cisterciensis*, where, Bernard tells us, those interested can find the reasons for the various revisions of the texts and melodies.

The Case against the Bernardine Reform

I said earlier that, not very long ago, there were a number of us who were (and still are) convinced that St Bernard's chant reform had been a horrible mistake. The chief source from which we drew

43. Even a summary treatment of the problems connected with the identification of Bernard's "equipe" of specialist would be too involved in a paper of these modest dimensions. Here I can only state that, according to my understanding of the complex problem, the identification of the reformers has been among the less satisfactory points treated by Mabillon (PL 182:1117–1119); Fr Maur Cocheril ocso, *arts.* "Guy de Cherlieu," in *Encyclopédie de la musique* II, (Paris, 1959), p. 372, and "Guy de Longpont, (d'Eu)," *ibid.,* pp. 372–375; Fr Marosszeki, *op. cit.,* Ch. II, "La seconde reforme et ses auteurs," pp. 10–14. Perhaps it will be possible to treat the problem in detail in some future article. From my own study of the source material, I presently tend to believe that "Guy de Longpont" never existed; that the identification of Guy de Cherlieu as one of the reformers seems quite likely; and that the convergence of circumstances points to Richard of Vauclair (monk of Clairvaux, then Abbot of Vauclair, then recalled to Clairvaux, where he served as Cantor, and finally sent to England as Abbot of Fountains) as a likely member of the reforming committee.

our ammunition was precisely this *apologia* for the revised anti-phonary. If a pre-Bernardine antiphonary had been available, we could have compared it with the later, reformed version, and have shown (we thought) the merits of the former over the latter. As it was, we had only many copies of the reformed antiphonary, plus a number of copies of this short treatise of Cistercian chant theory, and also a number of manuscripts of the so-called *Tonale*, a kind of catechism of Cistercian chant.

Our line of attack was usually the same. We would draw up a list of the principles of chant theory described in the treatise *Cantum quem Cisterciensis*, find passages in our repertory where the principles had obviously been applied, and then, groaning at the deformed, mutilated mleody, make it clear that the corresponding Solesme or Vatican version was evidently the only version which could be considered as acceptable.[44] To us it was blindingly clear that Bernard's chant reform had been chiefly the work of "hyper-logicians," who systematically mutilated traditional melodies in virtue of artificial theories in profound contradiction with the true nature of the chant.[45] Thus, when Dom Gabriel Sortais one day

44. Fr Marosszeki, following (with modifications) the outline proposed by Fr Delande OP, in his study, *Le Graduel des Precheurs* (Paris, 1949), reduces the more important principles to four chief ones:
  (1) Principle of modal unity (with avoidance of all ambiguity).
  (2) Restriction of the range:
    (*a*) within a 10-note ambitus,
    (*b*) and to the exclusion of compenetration of plagal and authentic.
  (3) Exclusion of B-flat where possible.
  (4) Simplifications, suppression of repetitions, cuts.
In Chapters VI–IX of his *Les origines . . . ,* he studies these principles and their application.

45. There can be no doubt that the theorists, in general, failed in their attempts to reduce the incredibly rich phenomenon of "Gregorian" chant to categories of a particular system of musical theory. Their writings often helped to foster and further new developments which enriched our musical patrimony, but their attempts to explain the Gregorian phenomenon fall painfully short of their object. With regard to a single typical example which throws light on a much larger area, see the excellent study by Dom Eugene Cardine OSB, "Theoriciens et theoriciens: a propos de quelques exemples d'elision dans la melodie gregorienne" in *Etudes Grégoriennes,* II (1957), pp. 27–35.

asked one of us what is specifically Cistercian about our chant tradition, the reply was simple, "Reverend Father, all the mistakes."

In general, however, I do not believe that the method described was the least bit bad in the circumstances. Further, I think that it is patently evident that the chant theories adopted by our twelfth-century editors were quite bad ones, and that the resultant melodies, compared with those of the better modern editions, are often quite bad. At the same time, I believe that all this touches on only *part* of the picture.

Toward Recovering the Pre-Bernardine Antiphonary

My own work in this area began in earnest five or six years ago, when I had the good fortune to identify at Westmalle (Belgium) a virtually complete Cistercian antiphonary (unbound, but arranged in two volumes), compiled from at least five or six pre-existing manuscripts, the bulk of which are manuscripts ante-dating the Bernardine reform, but re-worked, scraped, and over-written so as to make the earlier version conform with the revised version of ca. 1147.[46]

The proto-history of this manuscript (or rather, manuscripts) is obscure. The original hands vary from a mixed Metz-notation to Norman, with variations in between; and the several correctors adopt just as many different styles of notation in their corrections. The manuscript, then, is in a sense something of a nightmare; in another sense, a paleographical paradise.

Before arriving at Westmalle in 1955, our manuscript had spent a good half-century with the brethren of our Alsatian monastery of Oelenberg. Until sometime after 1906,[47] it had been with the

---

46. Fr F. Kovacs s o cist had already identified a single folio from a similar MS., described in detail in his article, "Fragments du chant citercien primitif" in *Analecta S.O. Cist.* 6 (1959), pp. 140–150. Unfortunately, neither he nor anyone else exploited this important find to its fullest possible measure.

47. My two sources of information—one at Oelenberg, the other at la Fille-Dieu—are somewhat at odds. The convent was affiliated with the Strict Observance only in 1906, with the Abbot of Oelenberg for the Fr Immediate. The MS. passed to Oelenberg at some date after this *terminus a quo,* and before the death of the Abbess, Mother Lutgarde Menetrey, in 1919.

P

Cistercian nuns of la Fille-Dieu, Switzerland, for many centuries. For precisely how long? Impossible to say. Founded around 1268, but officially affiliated with the Order only at a later unknown date, the convent probably received the tomes from their Father Immediate, the Abbot of nearby Hautcret. I have already suggested that the manuscript is a makeshift affair, the sort of thing to be used only in a pinch. Now, the corrections are, for the most part, quite ancient (though a few folios have been corrected by the nuns as late as the fourteenth/fifteenth century). It is only a hypothesis supported by no evidence, direct or indirect; but I suspect that the fruitful abbey, Cherlieu, must have supplied its daughter-house, Hautcret, founded in 1143,[48] with a quick copy of the reformed antiphonary. The patch-work manuscript would have been laid aside as soon as a respectable antiphonary had been transcribed; but dusted off, many decades later, and sent off to la Fille-Dieu when the Abbot of Hautcret found himself obliged to supply his new charges with Cistercian choir books.[49]

No matter what its history or precise origin, however, it is certain that the bulk of the manuscript pre-dates, in its original form, the Bernardine reform. Unfortunately, the scribes responsible for re-working the manuscripts were magnificently expert. Specialists have declared infra red rays or ultra violet rays incapable of making visible the original texts and melodies.

Actually, we have no need of such equipment.

48. And not earlier. According to Janauschek, *Originum Cisterciensium Tomus I*, Vindobonae, 1877, no. CLXXVI, pp. 71–72, the date of foundation is sometimes confused with the date of donation of the property to Guy, Abbot of Cherlieu (and probable protagonist of Bernard's chant reform).

49. The mother-house was obliged to supply the daughter-house with the necessary choir books, according to the ancient Cistercian statute "De construendis abbatiis," included in the earliest known redaction of the "Institutta Generalis Capituli," in Cod. 1711 of the Biblioteca Comunale, Trent, and adopted sometime prior to the redaction of the Trent MS. (sometime between 1130 and 1134, according to Fr Bruno Griesser s o cist, "Die 'Ecclesiastica officia Cisterciensis Ordinis' des Cod. 1711 von Trient," in *Analecta S.O. Cist.* 12 [1956], p. 174). The text may be found in *Documenta pro Cisterciensis Ordinis historiae ac juris studio collecta a J.-B. Van Damme* (Westmalle, 1959), p. 26. I do not know to what extent this obligation extended to the Fr Immediate of the nuns of a newly affiliated convent.

After studying the manuscript carefully, I concluded that the corrected folios could be classified according to three degrees of violence done to them.

1—There was only a single folio in which the corrector had simply barred a few antiphons eliminated from the revised antiphonary. Here we have no difficulty in recovering the original texts and melodies.

2—A goodly number of folios, and even entire sections, called for such extensive revisions, that the scribe simply scraped the entire parchment and rewrote from scratch. Such folios are of no more help to us than folios written fresh many decades after the reform.

3—Other folios—and these are in the vast majority—have been only partially re-written. Sometimes an entire antiphon has been scraped away and re-written. But, on the whole, corrections are confined to occasional notes and neums. It is with the help of such folios that I began my detective work.

But first I have to tell you about three other manuscripts important to our work of reconstruction. The first and least important is an ancient pre-Bernardine Cistercian breviary, written (if we are to judge according to the Epact Table of the calendar) sometime around 1132. Discovered by Fr Konrad Koch, s o cist, in the Preussische Staats-Bibliothek shortly after World War II, this manuscript—usually referred to (wrongly, I think) as the "Stephen Harding Breviary"—is now in the final stages of publication.[50] I

---

50. The first editor, Fr Koch himself, died shortly after beginning work on his transcription of the MS. Fr Bruno Griesser s o cist., whose memory is recalled with love and veneration by all who knew him, had finished the bulk of the editorial work when death overtook him in 1967. The project will soon be published under the aegis of Fr Kassien Lauterer s o cist., monk of Mehrerau. An account of the finding of the MS. may be read in Dr P. Konrad Koch s o cist, "Vollständiges Brevier aus der Schreibstube des hl. Stephan" in *Analecta S.O. Cist.* 2 (1946—though not really printed till 1950), pp. 146–147. The same author has studied the calendar of the breviary in a rather poor article, "Das Kalender des Stephan-Breviers" in *Cist.-Chronik* 57 (1950), pp. 85–96. For a description of the lectionary of the breviary, see Fr Bruno Griesser s o cist, "Das Lektionen-und Perikopensystem im Stephans-Brevier" in *Cist.-Chronik,* 71 (1964), pp. 67–92.

prefer, rightly or wrongly, to refer to the manuscript as the Marburg Breviary, since it is now in the possession of the West German Marburg Library.[51] Evidently, the manuscript is priceless in that it gives us the *texts* of our Order's early breviary. I had already collated this breviary manuscript with breviaries of the Bernardine version, isolating the texts altered by the reformers, when I came across the Westmalle antiphonary. I was immediately able to verify that, so often as the Marburg version had been changed, there was a corresponding correction in the Westmalle manuscript. But, as I have already said, this is the least important of the three manuscripts I have used in connection with the Westmalle manuscript. After all, though it suffices by itself to give us the early texts (though there are occasional scribal blunders which can be controlled by the Westmalle manuscript), it is of no help in the case of the melodies.

My other two manuscripts are marvelous things. They come from Metz; and I shall have to say a good deal now about Metz before we can return to our Westmalle antiphonary.

It will always be a source of puzzlement to me that the same scholars who have written and spoken at length about early Cîteaux and the chant of Metz, have never *studied* the extant manuscripts from Metz. It is true that the bulk of the important manuscripts perished during the horrors of World War II,[52] but much important material is nevertheless extant in the form of photocopies and microfilms.

Within the limits of this paper I could not even begin to describe the small library of material from Metz which I have studied— ordines, customaries, breviaries, processionales. . . . Most of this material is, for our purposes, quite late, as late as the fourteenth and fifteenth centuries. In its own way, however, this late material helps establish a point I wish to dwell on, that is to say, the essential homogeneity of the Metz tradition, *even* at so late a date. We can

---

51. Westdeutsche Bibl. Marburg a.d. Lahn, MS. lat. in octavo 402.

52. As a result of the bombing of Mont Saint-Quentin, September 1, 1944. The occupying army was in the process of transferring close to 3,000 books and MSS. from Metz to Germany.

and should ask ourselves: "Precisely *where* in Metz did our Fathers go? To the Cathedral, with its Roman cursus? or to one of the many Metz abbeys, such as St Arnould's[53] or St Vincent's?" My answer is that, in the final analysis, it makes little difference, since my collation of material from the three places just named, as well as from other sources in Metz, shows that they all shared in basically the same tradition.

I wish I did not have to make a special point of this, but I fear that you might read something just the opposite in one of the forthcoming volumes of Dom Hesbert's monumental *Corpus Antiphonalium Officii*. Dom Hesbert has made a partial collation of my two precious Metz manuscripts, and—unless he has recently changed his mind—will indicate in his classification of manuscripts that they belong to two separate traditions. The two manuscripts, still extant in microfilm and photocopies, are Metz, Bibliotheque Municipale, MS. 83—an early thirteenth-century antiphonary for the temporal cycle only, written for St Arnould's Benedictine abbey; and manuscript 461 of the same library—a late thirteenth-century winter season Cathedral breviary with full musical notation. I say the two manuscripts are substantially the same; Dom Hesbert says, if not the opposite, at least something quite different. How can we disagree?

The answer is simple. Dom Hesbert has compared his hundreds of manuscripts with only a relatively few points of references—the Advent responsory lists and the Advent responsory versets. In the case of the Metz manuscripts, he finds that the responsory versets differ radically, with the Cathedral tome maintaining a staunch Lotharingian position against the French-inclined monastery tome. Splendid. But a comparison extended over a larger area could show that, at some undetermined date, there was a systematic revision of responsory versets at St Arnould's, while the vast bulk of the material remained untouched. St Arnould's avant garde monks also adopted a special Johannine series of Lenten Thursday antiphons, such as were being adopted in the twelfth century at

53. Spelled variously as St Arnoul, St Arnould, and St Arnulf.

Cluny[54] and even at Clairvaux;[55] they also picked up the expurgated version of the famous Christmas responsory, *Descendit*,[56] while the Cathedral remained faithful to the more ancient and also more "difficult" text. I can cite instances in the music, too, where the early thirteenth-century monastic antiphonary sloughs off a traditional reading still retained in the more conservative late thirteenth-century Cathedral breviary.[57] All of this evidence, however, merely proves that two manuscripts derived from essentially the same tradition belong to milieux evolving at a different pace. *Concordantes discordant.*

I have already mentioned several times that my prize Metz manuscripts belong to the thirteenth century. Is it safe to use them when we are concerned with a period earlier by a century? I must admit, too, that a great musicologist who has recently written an important study of a ninth-century Metz *Tonarium*[58]—Walter Lipphardt—throws discredit on both our manuscripts. He admits that he examined photocopies only towards the end of his work,[59] admits, too, that the manuscripts proved useful in clearing up a few difficulties;[60] but on the whole, he tells us, his examination of the manuscripts showed that he was right to have not taken them too seriously earlier in his work.[61] Fortunately, Dr Lipphardt has shown

54. Cf. Dom G. Charvin OSB, *Statuts, chapitres generaux et visites de l'Ordre de Cluny*, I (Paris, 1965), p. 35, Statute 59. This statute belongs to a collection spanning the years 1132–1146.

55. The Bernardine series (not found, of course, in the Marburg MS.) is similar to, but independent of the Cluny antiphons.

56. Cf. Dom D. Catta OSB, "Le texte du repons 'Descendit' dans les manuscrits" in *Etudes Grégoriennes*, III (1959), pp. 75–82, where the author describes Agobard (d. 840) and his fierce polemic against the original text—a tirade which helped produce a number of subsequent watered-down versions, such as we find in the St Arnould MS.

57. E.g., the initial punctum *la* of the traditional first mode responsory verset, attested to by the vast quantity of the better MSS., appears consistently in Metz, MS. 83, as a podatus, *re-la*, indicative of a later evolution.

58. Walter Lipphardt, *Der karolingische Tonar von Metz* [=*Liturgiewissenschaftliche Quellen und Forschungen*, 43] (Münster, Westfalen, 1965).

59. *Op. cit.*, Vorwort, p. VIII, footnote 4.

60. *Ibid.*　　　　　　　　　　　　　　　　　61. *Ibid.*

us at least one of his comparative charts which does indeed make things look bad for our two manuscripts. He conducts a brief statistical survey of some seventy-six antiphons indicated in his ancient ninth-century *tonarium*, but found less frequently in later manuscripts.[62] The distance between the *tonarium* and later manuscripts of Metz and elsewhere is then gauged on the basis of the presence or absence of the antiphons in question. My two Metz documents come off very badly, but only so long as one refrains from controlling Dr Lipphardt's statistics. In the first place, it does not seem very scientific to try to find antiphons from the sanctoral cycle in a book containing only the temporal cycle. Again, it would be surprising to find summer season antiphons in a book destined for the winter season only. The antiphons Dr Lipphardt indicates as missing, then, are usually to be found in *other* documents from the Cathedral or St Arnould's Monastery.[63] Further, he apparently skimmed through his photocopies much too quickly, since he passed over a number of antiphons indicated as missing, but actually present.[64] My own impression, based on a correction of Dr Lipphardt's statistics for our two manuscripts, is that they are smashingly in continuity with the ninth-century *tonarium*. Actually, I am not particularly interested in their continuity with the ninth-century

62. *Op. cit.,* p. 212, "Seltene Antiphonen der frühen Metzer Tradition und ihre Verbreitung."

63. Such as the twelfth/thirteenth-century Cathedral Ordinary, giving all pertinent incipits, easily accessible in the edition by Bp. J.-B. Pelt, *Etudes sur la Cathedrale de Metz: La liturgie:* I (Metz, 1937), pp. 235-464. Or the parallel Ordinaries from St Arnould's, i.e. Metz, MS. 132, *Liber de ordinacione et officio tocius anni,* 13th c.; MS. 502, *Ordo de St-Arnould* (catalogue description), 15th c.; MS. 467, *Ordinatio officii* (wrongly catalogued as an *Expositio Breviarii*), 14th c. To say nothing of the several extant breviaries or equivalents, such as MS. 573 (14th c. St Arnould breviary with psalter, wrongly catalogued as a diurnal); MS. 585, another St Arnould breviary, also wrongly catalogued as another diurnale; and MS. 588, a 15th c. Cathedral breviary with psalter.

64. A few samples only, taken from the St Arnould MS. *Alleluia. Mane apud.,* f. 72v, *Cum sol autem* and *Omnes qui habebant,* f. 152v etc. The author makes similar slips by failing to reckon with orthographic variants; thus, the antiphon *Cum venerit,* contrary to Dr Lipphardt's claim, *is* to be found in our MSS., but with the incipit *Dum venerit.*

tonarium, but with their substantial mutual agreement. If, in spite of evolution in independent directions, the books are still so similar in the thirteenth century, they could scarcely have been less so in the early twelfth century. Perhaps I should add that I have collated the twelfth/thirteenth century Cathedral Ordinary with three of St Arnould's *Ordines*,[65] and have found that the monastery depended on the Cathedral even for points of ritual and ceremonial.

I suggest, then, that our two manuscripts can be taken as representative of a rather homogeneous, but evolving Metz tradition. They have certainly served my own purposes, as I shall now show.

A quick glance at either manuscript should suffice to explain the negative reactions of our Fathers—at least in part. The chant we find here is what Dr Peter Wagner called a "chant dialect," that is to say, a variant form of traditional chant bearing the imprint of a particular region.[66] In our own instance, the major difficulty seems to be the chronic difficulty of our scribes to cope with the half-steps, which tend to disappear or else rise to the note immediately above—fa or do. The result for rhythm and for tune is often disastrous. Again, in a number of standard formulas, such as the fourth mode cadence mi-sol-fa-fa/fa-mi, variant forms involving variant pitches are met with; and there are no less than *four* melodic variant versions for what is obviously one and the same versicle-response melody. Again, although the St Arnould manuscript is well written, and gives every indication of care on the part of the scribe, there are many inconsistencies. The cue-notes referring to the reprise of a responsory do not always coincide perfectly with the passage referred to, and incipits referring to pages where melodies are given *in extenso* sometime present a variant version of the melody. All in all, one gets the impression that a half-note here or there does not make much difference. Compared with the Cathedral manuscript the St Arnould antiphonary seems the more unstable. Obviously, if a manuscript cannot agree with even itself, it will not always agree with another manuscript. And it would be simple but

65. See note 63, above.

66. P. Wagner, *Neumenkunde* (Fribourg, Switzerland, 1905), pp. 280–286.

unscientific to draw up a table of variants, without at the same time discerning the *true* variants from those which are merely the result of our scribes' charmingly amorphous approach to chant. I cannot help but think of John the Deacon's malicious description of the Metz cantors of the ninth century, whom, in fact, he intends to praise. He explains that the imperfections of Metz chant are, after all, only what one should expect from characters so naturally uncouth: *Metenses vero sola naturali feritate paululum quid dissonare pervidit.*[67] They are built big as Alps (*alpina siquidem corpora*); they have voices that roar like bursts of thunderclaps (*vocum suarum tonitruis altisone perstrepentia*). Of course, their raucous singing is in part explained by their hard drinking (*bibuli gutturis barbari feritas*); and the general effect is comparable to a convoy of wagons clattering down a staircase (*quasi plaustra per gradus confuse sonantia*).[68]

We ought not to take John's description too seriously. But it *is* true that ethnic and regional considerations affect musical style. The chanting at Maria Laach is not the chanting at Solesmes. Moreover, we should appreciate the difficulties involved in musical notation. The musical phenomenon in general was simply too rich for one to reduce to a four-line staff. Compromise was inevitable; and sometimes particularly difficult melodies emerged as partially reworked in the effort of notation. My sympathy is with the men at Metz.

We can now return to our Westmalle antiphonary. Our restoration process is simple.

1. We transcribe the two Metz manuscripts separately, indicating differences between them.

2. We transcribe the Westmalle version, indicating the parts where the reviser seems to have been at work.

3. We collate all three manuscripts. Inevitably, the *un*corrected portions of the Westmalle manuscript agree with the Metz manuscripts. Inevitably, the *corrected* portions disagree. The earlier Cistercian version, then, is found in the Metz manuscripts.

67. *Vita Gregorii Magni,* PL 75:91. John begins by pointing out that the Metz chant differs from that of Rome only slightly, but lets himself get carried away by his mordant wit.

68. *Ibid.,* col. 91–92.

Of course, our two Metz manuscripts do not always agree. This makes the study all the more interesting, since our Westmalle version agrees now with one, now with the other manuscript. Here I can only give you the tentative conclusion I have reached: the manuscript transcribed by our Fathers was a monastic antiphonary probably of St Arnould's and less evolved than the present early thirteenth-century version.

I should also add that the manuscript copied was not slavishly adopted as such. The Cistercian sanctoral cycle, in its choice of texts, is quite archaic. I suspect that they must have studied the more modern early twelfth-century Metz chant tomes against the evidence of much older material, such as the ninth-century *tonarium* referred to earlier. Only material corresponding to the ancient books would have been adopted. Furthermore, the liturgical prescriptions of the Holy Rule were absolutely normative, so that the shape of the Cistercian antiphonary was different in some respects from its probable counterpart at St Arnould's, which had five antiphons at Lauds, dropped the Alleluia with Septuagesima, had proper antiphons for Sunday Vespers in Advent. . . .

Evaluation of the Two Reforms

Our Westmalle manuscript, then, studied with the help of our two Metz manuscripts, allows us to work our way back to the Metz-inspired antiphonary of early Cîteaux. We can now see exactly what our theorist-chant reformers had to deal with, and we can see the extent of their revision, and can tabulate their corrections one by one.

The most startling development appears almost as soon as we begin studying the nature of the corrections made by the members of Bernard's commission: the vast majority of the changes have nothing to do with their rules of chant. Rather, they represent an attempt to make the "chant dialect" of the old Metz tradition take on an accent and intonation more in keeping with the living chant tradition in areas to the south and to the west. The old Cistercian melodies had been peripheral, one might say, to the mainstream, the living tradition which flourished (admittedly with countless minor variants) in the cultural milieu from which the vast majority of the early Cistercians had come. The "corrected" version comes much closer to the common chant patrimony of the Black Monks and of the Church in general.

St Bernard himself had already written explicitly in the *Prologus* that the revised material came from many different sources—*de multis et diversis*. A collation of the corrections with the corresponding melodies of hundreds of extant manuscripts shows how accurately St Bernard spoke. At Solesmes I made good use of the comparative tables used in the preparation of the 1934 Monastic Antiphonary. Each antiphon or responsory or other formula is accompanied by the readings given in dozens of manuscripts. In the greater number of instances, the Bernardine revision parallels the versions transcribed, now siding with one group of manuscripts, now following the universal trend, occasionally presenting a new reading which, in *this* case, is usually explicable in the light of Cistercian theory. This is my conclusion based on the study of all the short responsories, the versicle-response melody, the invitatory antiphons, the greater number of the antiphons, the psalm tones, some seventy-five or eighty solemn responsories: the Bernardine reform ensured a parallel with the Church's common chant patrimony.

No less significant is the identification of the *new* texts and melodies introduced in the course of the reform. The second generation of Cistercians was not particularly afraid of being modern. Thus we find marvelously warm, even passionate melodies and texts, such as our incomparable *Salve Regina*, or the Marian antiphons from the Song of Songs, assigned to the Feasts of the Assumption and the Nativity of Our Lady; we find the Johannine texts for the Thursday antiphons in Lent; we find a proper Office for St Mary Magdalen, whose popularity has been growing so during the early twelfth century.

The reformed hymnal presents a quite parallel picture.[69] The

69. The study by Dom Bernard Kaul s o cist, "Le psautier cistercien— Appendice: Tableau analytique de l'hymnaire cistercien" in *Collectanea*

texts of the Milanese corpus were retained; and the reformers were scrupulous in maintaining the so-called Ambrosian hymns at those Hours to which St Benedict apparently assigns them (on the hypothesis that Ambrosian = composed by St Ambrose), that is to say Vigils, Lauds, and Vespers. But the problem of the single Vigils hymn for the entire year was solved by dividing the Vespers hymn in two, assigning one portion to Vigils, another to Lauds, so that the Vigils fare was now quite varied. Moreover, only a part of the Milanese melodies emerged from the reform unscathed. Some were reworked in part, but others were entirely replaced by new melodies; and a good batch of the new melodies seems to have been composed by one or more of the reformers,[70] since in most instances it is clear not only that the melody first appears in our Cistercian books, but that other versions depend on our version. And what melodies these are! *Magnum salutis gaudium, Optatus vobis omnium, Iam Christus astra ascenderat.* . . .[71] There was, moreover, a bulky importation of shamelessly *non*-Ambrosian hymns such as our favorite *Quem terra, pontus et aethra, Conditor alme siderum, Vexilla Regis prodeunt.* . . .[72] Since respect for the prescrip-

---

O.C.R. 13 (1951), pp. 41–56, remains extremely useful. See also the section, "L'Innario Ambrosiano e l'Innario Cistercense" in *Fonti e Paleografia del Canto Ambrosiano* [=*Archivio Ambrosiano* 7], Milano, 1956, pp. 95–103. The transcriptions and notes in Bruno Stäblein, *Monumenta Monodica Medii Aevi I: Hymnen (I)* (Kassel—Basel, 1956), need careful control.

70. Eight such melodies may be mentioned (though I have doubts about the last two)—melodies attached to the following texts, but occasionally used in the same hymnal with other texts: *Magnum salutis gaudium, Optatus votis omnium, Iam Christus astra ascenderat, Mysterium Ecclesiae* (no longer in our hymnal, but the splendid melody remains in the Transfiguration hymn at Lauds), *Almi prophetae progenies* (now in our hymnal with the text for Sts Peter and Paul, *Aurea luce*), *Iesu, nostra redemptio, Ad caenam Agni providi,* and *O quam glorifica.*

71. In general, the ranges are wide, and the extremes of pitch ranged in quick succession. The style is marvelously akin to St Bernard's zestful eloquence: rich, varied, beautiful, and perfectly balanced—emotion without emotionalism.

72. See Dom Bernard Kaul's analytical tables in the art. cited above, note 69; the pertinent information is given, pp. 50–52: 2. *Hymni ex fundo Gallico additi.*

tions of the Rule forbade these non-Ambrosiana being sung at Vigils, Lauds, or Vespers, they were assigned, *mirabile dictu,* to Terce and Compline. Evidently St Bernard and his co-evals recognized as valid the need of having a form of liturgical prayer congenial to the cultural milieu of the local community.

In no way, however, do I wish to minimize the importance of all the changes wrought in the name of chant theory. Though, here again, we might do well to look a bit deeper into the reasons which led to what most of us can recognize today as being mutilations. It was not a question of chant theory, as our forefathers saw it, but of truth. The several chant treatises connected with the Bernardine reform are rich in theology.[73] The basic intuition is that God has expressed his truth in all that is. Whatever is, must be true to its God-given nature, under pain of substituting for its true nature that which is only a false appearance—*similitudo.* In effect, the chant reform, then, was meant to restore to the deformed chant of primitive Cîteaux its true nature, just as the whole ascetical program of Cîteaux was meant to restore to man his true nature in all its integrity.

The underlying principle is splendid. The application was, at least in part, disastrous. Why? Because the chant reformers thought they could *define* in clear terms a phenomenon as living and elusive as the traditional chant. There was a bit of Abelard in more than one Cistercian—including, I think, St Bernard. There was a tendency to define and articulate the essence of things, with a view to making the concrete, existential reality conform with the ideal definition. This is honest enough. But can music, art, love, poetry, personal experience be reduced to really clear-cut categories? If a definition is imperfect, everything that follows is bound to be a bit off track.

I wish to draw attention to another emergent from my study of

73. Besides the treatise *Cantum quem Cisterciensis,* we have also a similar, but less lengthy, treatise destined for the reformed gradual, badly edited in PL 182: 1151–1154. Another lengthy treatise ascribed to Guy of Cherlieu, and drawn upon by the redactors of *Cantum quem Cisterciensis,* is the tract *Regulae Artis Musicae,* edited in E. de Coussemaker, *Scriptores de Musica Medii Aevi,* Nova Series II (Paris, 1857). This edition is almost too defective to be used.

the Bernardine reform. Until now, we have depended for our understanding of the reform on St Bernard's *Prologus* and writings redacted by the men responsible for the reform. Presumably, they had every intention of giving us an adequate picture of their aims and ideals. But, as I have more than suggested, the actual reform was much more complex than they present it as being. They were so preoccupied with the application of their theoretical principles— in which they knew they were departing from the mainstream —that they forgot to mention that they were also plunging into the mainstream in other respects, that they were aligning themselves with the living tradition of their own cultural milieu. Perhaps this should make us a bit cautious in accepting as definitive *ex professo* formulations of aims and ideals coming even from St Bernard and from the first generation of Cistercians. They were certainly clear in their insistence on the integral observance of the Holy Rule, so clear (I think) that one might be tempted to reduce their reform to this single element. But we would do well to situate this principle within the context of their total experience. Perhaps, too, we should not insist on being *overly* explicit about the precise nature of the aims and ideals of our Fathers, under pain of encouraging a program of renewal based in part on a distorted definition of our Fathers.

The first generation of Cistercians seems to have had an extremely absolutist concept of *authority*. The Rule was authoritative, absolutely normative, and to be followed even when not fully understood. The Metz antiphonary had to be adopted, whatever its apparent defects, because it was authoritative. The Milanese hymnal had to be adopted because of its authority recognized by the Rule. The monks of St Bernard's generation were evidently keenly sensitive in the matter of authority, but they also trusted to human reason to define the nature of such things as the chant. In spite of a certain rigidity in this intellectual approach, however, their experience was too rich to be diked and dammed by their speculation in *re musica*. There were positive emergents from their reform to the extent that they took measures to satisfy the exigencies imposed by their psychology, their cultural milieu, and the nature of their spiritual experience.

Perhaps the tensions provoked by the early Cistercian liturgy would have been avoided had the first Cistercians trusted a bit more in the authenticity of their spiritual experience. They would surely have had a liturgy marked by great simplicity, dignity, warmth, beauty, and in continuity with a truly living tradition.

Do not mistake me. I am not against authority; I am not against reason. And I do not exalt the primacy of the spiritual experience as the supreme value. I believe simply that no *real* liturgy is possible without an authentic experience of Christ in his mystery, at the level both of the individual and the community. To the extent that this experience is deep and authentic, to that extent there is a possibility for real creativity and relevance. And to the extent that such an experience *is* present, we ought not to overlay it by a great deal of artificial baggage imposed from without. The whole thrust of the Church's liturgical reform is in the direction of making it possible for the mystery of Christ to find a living, fruitful expression in and through the Church concretized in the local community. A false concept of tradition, or of authority, or of anything else, will stifle the Spirit in large measure. I might also add that, without a genuine experience of Christ in his mystery, we doom our liturgy reform to failure. We are only talking, talking, talking; and all the liturgical commissions in the world, and all possible programs of reform will produce only what is barren, petty, and without substance. I think that this is what is so wonderful about our Fathers in the area of the liturgy: their life in Christ was so deep, so rich, that their misconceptions at the level of reasoned argument and speculation could not radically affect the nature of their way of life, the nature of their witness to God's presence in his Church.

Let us *live*, then. Let us live in Christ—humbly, gratefully, and according to the grace God gives us. If we do this, no matter what our ideas may be about the early Cistercian reform, we shall be very close to our Fathers of Cîteaux.

Chrysogonus Waddell ocso

Gethsemani Abbey,
Trappist, Kentucky

THE WITNESS OF WILLIAM OF ST THIERRY
TO THE SPIRIT AND AIMS OF THE EARLY
CISTERCIANS

IN AN ATTEMPT to ascertain the witness which William of St Thierry[1] gave, by his life and writings, to the spirit and aims of the early Cistercians, it would seem best to begin by examining his own writings on this topic in order to see what he himself actually says about that spirit and those aims. Then we can expand on this first-hand evidence with the explanations and views of others, both medieval and modern. Once we have a good idea of what William saw the Cistercian ideals to be, we can approach his life and writings from another angle, trying to see how he lived these ideals out in his own life and what kind of fruit they bore for him; in other words, we will be looking for the specific quality of his response to them, his "witness" to them. Having treated these two questions, we may then select several themes which will have emerged and discuss their meaningfulness in relation to our present-day situation, striving to bring William's witness to the spirit and aims of the early Cistercians into sharp relief for monks and nuns of today.

Rather than try to handle the question of the Cistercian spirit and aims[2] first, and then apply conclusions to William of St Thierry,

1. For a rather thorough biographical sketch of William of St Thierry, cf. Louis Bouyer, *The Cistercian Heritage* (Westminster, Md.; Newman, 1958), pp. 67–91.

2. A task which others have undertaken. Cf., e.g., M. Basil Pennington OCSO, "Towards Discerning the Spirit and Aims of the Founders of the Order of Cîteaux," above, pp. 1–26.

we will look through William to the early Cistercians and directly at him, for we are mainly interested in his views and his witness.

A brief explanation of the actual terms of our title might also help to clarify our objectives. Suffice it to say that by "witness" we mean the unique character of William's response to the vision of the early Cistercians, as manifesting that spirit to us in a particular way; by "spirit and aims" we understand something along the lines of ideals and style of life incarnating these ideals. We prefer the somewhat vague "early Cistercians" to the more precise "Founders of the Order of Cîteaux," as it leaves a little more leeway; there is some question as to just whom the latter term refers,[3] and for William the Cistercian ideals were incarnated particularly by the community of Clairvaux and the person of St Bernard.[4] By "early Cistercians," therefore, we simply mean those whom William saw living as Cistercians before he himself became one in 1135.

We may begin, then, with an examination of what William perceived the spirit and aims of the early Cistercians to be.

William of St Thierry's Views on the Spirit and Aims of the Early Cistercians

Sources

The work in which William treats the ideals of Cistercian monasticism most explicitly is his last, that first section of the collective work, *Vita Prima Bernardi*,[5] which he was unable to complete before his death in 1148. Though this is primarily a biography of St Bernard and refers only to the communities of Cîteaux and Clairvaux, we can nevertheless consider it to contain

---

3. Cf. *ibid.,* pp. 15ff.

4. Cf. *St Bernard of Clairvaux*; the story of his life as recorded in the *Vita Prima Bernardi* by certain of his contemporaries, William of St Thierry, Arnold of Bonnevaux, Geoffrey and Philip of Clairvaux, and Odo of Deuil, PL 185:225–266: trans. Webb and Walker (Westminster, Md.; Newman, 1960), pp. 56–57.

5. Cf. PL 185:225–259: trans. Webb and Walker, pp. 9–75.

Q

a real portrayal of William's views on Cistercian life in general, for it was in St Bernard and at Clairvaux that he actually encountered Cistercianism.

A few of his other works, as also his relationship with St Bernard and his actions while still a Benedictine abbot at St Thierry, likewise provide information on this topic. Let us see what insights we may glean from these sources.

The Simplicity of Solitude: an Atmosphere Conducive to Prayer

William speaks of the way of life of the Cistercians as one of poverty, simplicity and austerity in an atmosphere of silence and solitude conducive to reading, prayer and contemplation.

Thus he describes Cîteaux as a place of "dire poverty,"[6] "poor, insignificant and small,"[7] whose monks desired to pass on their "inheritance of holy poverty."[8] The monks who set out to make a new foundation at Clairvaux began to serve God "in poverty of spirit, in hunger and thirst, in cold and nakedness, and in long vigils,"[9] for they had "lovingly embraced a life of poverty in Christ."[10] When William first met Bernard in "a little house . . . outside the cloister and boundaries of the monastery,"[11] where he was convalescing from an illness, he was filled with a desire "to share his life amid such poverty and simplicity."[12]

In speaking of Clairvaux, William tells us that "the simplicity and unpretentiousness of the buildings in the quiet valley betray the lowly and simple life led by the monks for the sake of Christ."[13] He sees Cîteaux as embodying "a stricter form of life,"[14] an "austere life."[15] William praises the poverty, simplicity and austerity of the Cistercian life not as ends in themselves, but rather as basic elements necessary for the creation of an atmosphere of silence and solitude. Thus Bernard chose this simple form of life

6. *Ibid.*, p. 23.	7. *Ibid.*, p. 37.	8. *Ibid.*, p. 34.
9. *Ibid.*, p. 44.	10. *Ibid.*, p. 59.	11. *Ibid.*, p. 55.
12. *Ibid.*, p. 56.	13. *Ibid.*, p. 59.	14. *Ibid.*, p. 23.
15. *Ibid.*

because he had begun "to look round and inquire where he would be most sure to find rest for his soul under the yoke of Christ, with nothing to distract him from accepting this yoke whole-heartedly."[16]

This atmosphere of silence and solitude is mainly interior and spiritual, but is fostered by particular modes of human behavior; thus "among men whose lives are under the stabilizing influence of the rule in silence and unity of purpose, the way of life itself helps to establish an inner solitude in the depths of the heart."[17] William also shows an appreciation of the harmonious blending of the values of community life and personal solitude; speaking of the monks of Clairvaux, he says that "Although they all lived together, it may truthfully be said that they were all solitaries, for although the valley was full of men the harmony and charity that reigned there were such that each monk seemed to be there all by himself."[18] These various aspects of solitude in a Cistercian setting are well summed-up in this description he gives of St Bernard: "If he had a chance to be alone he would use it for prayer, but since true solitude is something of the heart, it hardly mattered whether he was by himself or surrounded by many others."[19]

The desire to pray, to commune with God, is indeed the reason why the early Cistercians wanted to create a climate of silence and solitude. William himself was a man of intense prayer, a fact we can see mirrored in his many writings,[20] and in his treatment of Cistercian silence and solitude he stresses this element of being present to God in prayer. He describes Bernard as being able to open up "the innermost depths of his soul to the action of God's loving grace, and to enjoy in his silence and solitude delights such as are the reward of the blessed in heaven."[21] This is a prayer which is nourished by contact with Scripture: "During the hours that

---

16. *Ibid.*   17. *Ibid.*, p. 60.   18. *Ibid.*   19. *Ibid.*, p. 42.

20. For a complete listing of William's writings and a discussion of their probable dates of composition, cf. Dom André Wilmart osb, "La Série et la Date des Ouvrages de Guillaume de Saint-Thierry," *Revue Mabillon*, 15 (1924), pp. 157–167.

21. Webb and Walker, *St Bernard of Clairvaux*, p. 56.

were not devoted to manual labor, he either read, or prayed, or meditated. . . . It was his great delight to pass hours in reading Scripture;"[22] which impregnates the singing of the divine office,[23] and which gradually comes to saturate the monk's whole life: "his soul was flooded with such powerful grace that, while he gave himself completely to the work in hand, his mind was completely taken up with God."[24]

That William considers a simple, poor, austere way of life the best setting for an authentic monastic life of prayer and love is also seen in the zeal with which he goaded Bernard on to his famous *Apology*,[25] in his description of the contemporary monastic scene in his *Exposition on the Song of Songs*,[26] and in his *Golden Epistle to the Carthusians of Mont Dieu*.[27]

22. *Ibid.*, p. 42.

23. Cf. Robert Thomas ocso, "Oraison Liée à l'Office selon Guillaume de Saint-Thierry," *Collectanea Cisterciensia*, 29 (1967), pp. 220–222.

24. Webb and Walker, *St Bernard of Clairvaux*, pp. 41f.

25. St Bernard, *Apologia ad Guillelmum Sti. Theoderici Abbatem*, PL 182: 895–918: trans. M. Casey, *Cistercians and Cluniacs: St Bernard's Apology to Abbot William* in *The Works of Bernard of Clairvaux*, Vol. 1, Cistercian Fathers, I.

26. "The greater part of the earth is in the hands of religious. In the deserts, one sees them erecting palaces. Of the caves and solitary places they make perfumed cells (aromatic, not eremitic!). Once one has entered religion he no longer deigns to travel on foot or with modest equipage. These monks rejoice to be called Christians and followers of Christ, but they stop short of imitating the example of Christ and His disciples on this point (and I pass over many others!)." *Expositio Altera Super Cantica Canticorum*, PL 180:542B, 543C. This English translation appears in "William of St. Thierry: The Man of Faith" by Dom Etienne Chenevière ocso, translated into English from the French by Fr R. K. Anderson ocso, in *The Works of William of St Thierry*, Vol. 3, Cistercian Fathers, IX.

27. *The Golden Epistle of Abbot William of St Thierry to the Carthusians of Mont Dieu*, trans. Walter Shewring (London: Sheed and Ward, 1930), pp. 63–74. For the original Latin, cf. *Epistola ad Fratres de Monte-Dei*, PL 184: 307–354. While it is true that this letter is written to Carthusians rather than Cistercians, William sees their way of life also as an example of monastic renewal; cf. especially Chapter I of this *Golden Epistle*. We will try to see if he has anything to say about the distinguishing characteristics of these two monastic groups a little later on in this paper.

We notice it also in the fact that during the period between his first meeting with St Bernard in 1118 and his eventual entry into the Cistercian community of Signy in 1135, William did not content himself with merely admiring the Cistercians from a distance. As Fr Louis Bouyer tells us:

> About this time (i.e. from 1124 onwards), we find William taking an active part in spreading among the houses of the Black Benedictines the same spirit which had governed the foundation of Cîteaux and which Clairvaux illustrated. Not only was it he who in the years 1120–1125 persuaded Bernard to write his *Apologia*, but he played a leading part at a meeting of Benedictine abbots when they decided upon a return to the strict observance of the Rule in matters of liturgy, fasts, abstinence and silence.[28]

A Renewal of Monastic Life

This aspect of William's zeal for a fervent monasticism, for a life of prayer in solitude, enables us to perceive another facet of his attraction toward the Cistercians: he is interested in basic monastic values. It is precisely because he believes that the Cistercian spirit of simplicity and of solitude as the climate of prayer represents a renewal[29] of an authentic dedication to God, a service of love, as

28. Bouyer, *The Cistercian Heritage*, p. 81.

29. Fr Claude Peifer OSB, in a recent article on monastic renewal (Claude J. Peifer OSB, "Monastic Renewal in Historical Perspective," *The American Benedictine Review,* Vol. XIX [1968], p. 2), distinguishes between "reform" and "renewal" thus: "By a reform I mean a movement which aims at the re-establishment of discipline, correction of abuses, and restoration of accepted structures. By a renewal I understand a much more comprehensive process which does not confine itself to repairing the existing structure, but re-examines the structure itself and the value system upon which it is based, and undertakes to revise and reformulate the theory and to rebuild the structure in a form which will effectively communicate the theory to the contemporary world." William seems to have seen Cistercian life primarily as an effort at "renewal" (as thus defined), but his stress on the poverty and austerity of the life and the degree of solitude attained by the actual physical remoteness of

seen in the way of life of the early Christians, the monks of Egypt and St Benedict, that he admires them so much. He attributes these qualities both to the communities of Cîteaux and Clairvaux as such, and to St Bernard as the individual whom he considers a Cistercian par excellence.[30]

Thus he sees in Bernard and his companions about to enter Cîteaux a renewal of the spirit of community of the apostolic Church of Jerusalem,[31] while the monks of Clairvaux are renewing in their lives that devotion to Christ in the midst of difficulties reminiscent of St Paul.[32] He speaks of Bernard's efforts to rekindle the spirit of ancient monasticism at Clairvaux,[33] and manifests his own conviction that these efforts were successful.[34] He praises the monks of Clairvaux for being imbued with the spirit of St

---

Cistercian sites indicates that for him certain elements of "reform" (again, as thus defined), were, at that time, necessary ingredients of such a "renewal." Thus, though he describes the monks of Cîteaux as having "hopes of the *new order* living on" (Webb and Walker, *St Bernard of Clairvaux*, p. 34 [italics mine]), he also speaks of "the new foundation made by a *reformed* monastic order at Cîteaux" (*Ibid.*, p. 23, [italics mine]).

30. Cf. Webb and Walker, *St Bernard of Clairvaux*, p. 62: "The monastery of Clairvaux in its beautiful valley could truly have been called a school of the science of souls with Bernard as its teacher. Here one could follow his perfect example of how life should be led in complete and loving conformity with the rule, as he organized his monastery and took part in all its many activities."

31. "As the number of those grew who had agreed to go together into the monastery at Cîteaux, the words found in the Acts of the Apostles about the earliest members of the Church could have been applied to them also, for in the whole group there was only one heart and one soul in the Lord, and they lived together in perfect unity."—*Ibid.*, p. 32.

32. "They helped to plant the Church of God by giving their lives in toil and hardship, in hunger and thirst, in cold and exposure, in insults and persecutions and many difficulties, just like the Apostle Paul."—*Ibid.*, p. 59.

33. "The first-fruits of his youth were devoted to the work of restoring among his monks that fervor for the religious life which was found in the monks of Egypt long ago."—*Ibid.*, p. 66.

34. Of his first meeting with Bernard at Clairvaux he writes: "I remained with him for a few days, and as I looked about me I thought that I was gazing on a new heaven and a new earth, for it seemed as though there were tracks freshly made by men of our own day in the path that had first been trodden by our fathers, the Egyptian monks of long ago."—*Ibid.*, p. 58.

Benedict,[35] as they lived "under the stabilizing influence of the rule,"[36] and Bernard for being a "perfect example of how life should be led in complete and loving conformity with the rule."[37]

We may gain some insight into the depth of his feeling on this topic of monastic renewal by striving to answer an intricate question: Why did William actually change over to the Cistercians? He had entered the Benedictine Abbey of St Nicasius, "a good religious house, stricter than most Cluniac houses of the time,"[38] and upon being elected Abbot of St Thierry he had "won the monks' co-operation in raising the standard of Religious life within its walls."[39] Was he not satisfied in this atmosphere of monastic dedication? His own actions, in requesting admittance to Clairvaux in 1124 and, upon being refused admittance there by St Bernard, his actual entrance into Signy 11 years later,[40] answer this question for us. He was seeking something else.

But though this fact seems evident, it is a little more difficult to determine just what it was that he was seeking. There seem to be several different elements involved, all mutually related to each other and to his decision. Dom Etienne Chenevière paints a succinct picture of this situation for us when he writes that:

> One understands how the bustle of burdensome temporal administration, the lure of Cîteaux, of Clairvaux—especially that of its Abbot; a certain mediocrity, sufficiently pervading and seemingly incurable in the Cluniac Observance; the powerful

35. "The loneliness of this place, hidden among the woods and closed in by the surrounding hills, was comparable to the cave where the shepherds found our holy father St Benedict, so closely did the monks of Clairvaux follow his form of life and style of dwelling."—*Ibid.*, p. 60.

36. *Ibid.*   37. *Ibid.*, p. 62.

38. *The Meditations of William of St Thierry*, trans. a Religious of CSMV (New York: Harper, 1954), p. 6 (which is part of the translator's Introduction.) Actually, as Dom J.-M. Déchanet explains on p. 24, note 1, of his *Guillaume de Saint-Thierry: L'Homme et son Oeuvre* (Bruges: Beyaert, 1942), both St Nicasius and St Thierry were autonomous houses, not actual members of the congregation of Cluny; but both had adopted the usages and customs of Cluny.

39. A Religious of CSMV, *The Meditations*, p. 6.   40. *Ibid.*, p. 7.

attraction for contemplation, especially, perhaps, the very lively and humble feeling of his own insufficiency as a superior, had been for William a permanent temptation to resign in order to come and join the ranks as a humble sheep under the shepherd's crook of St Bernard who fascinated him.[41]

Is it possible to single out one of these elements as the primary one? Dom Jean-Marie Déchanet would point to William's friendship with St Bernard as the decisive cause.[42] But this would seem to have been more important at the time of his request to enter Clairvaux, Bernard's own Abbey, in 1124, than at the time of his actual entrance into Signy in 1135.[43] William himself, in his *Meditations*,[44] reveals doubts as to his ability to continue to render fruitful service as Abbot of St Thierry,[45] but even more so his desire for opportunities for prayer in solitude.[46] Two contemporaneous documents from Signy likewise bear witness to this desire for prayer in solitude: a biography of William written there shortly

41. Chenevière, "The Man of Faith".

42. Cf. Déchanet, *L'Homme et son Oeuvre*, pp. 32–43.

43. Cf. Fr Guillaume De Broucker OCSO, "Une Heure Cruciale dans la Vocation Cistercienne de Guillaume de Saint-Thierry," *Collectanea O.C.R.* 19 (1957), pp. 22–33, for an excellent discussion of this question. De Broucker stresses William's spiritual progress during this eleven year period of waiting, and concludes that what may have been a natural desire in 1124 had become, by 1135, an authentic call from God to a more solitary and contemplative life.

44. *Meditative Orationes*, PL 180:205–248; trans. Sr Penelope CSMV, as *The Meditations of William of St Thierry* in *The Works of William of St Thierry*, Vol. 1, Cistercian Fathers, III.

45. Cf. Sr Penelope, *The Meditations*: "It is a very serious thing for him (a shepherd [i.e. Abbot]) to be in charge of the flock, when he cannot give it profitable service."

46. *Ibid.*, p. 81: "Having endangered both our body and our soul through long service and the wearing out of our strength by the prolonged and toilsome exercise thereof, it is in our opinion lawful for us now to look to the hands of the royal munificence, that it may allow our old age recognition of its deserts, and bestow on it a better thing than that which itself is conscious of deserving." And what, we may ask, is this "better thing" William is seeking? He gives us the answer when he asks of the Lord, "Give me, O Lord, the comfort of my wilderness—a solitary heart and frequent communing with you."—*Ibid.*

after his death,[47] and the *Chronicle of Signy*.[48] This is also the opinion of Dom Jacques Hourlier, who notes that no matter what form of life William were to choose, his desire to live for God in a climate of prayer would never be satisfied until he reached the most complete "Sabbath rest" of all, heaven itself.[49] Dom Justin McCann believes William's "chief motive was the desire for closer union with God."[50] Dom Chenevière speaks of "the perfect solitude which seems to have been for him an irrepressible need of the soul."[51] He gives the reason for this solitude when he says that "It was to love better that he left St Thierry, to find love that he came to Signy,"[52] and he demonstrates this by quoting William to the effect that "The perfect experience of love demands the secrecy of solitude, at least a solitary heart in the midst of the crowd."[53]

This question remains complex and difficult to answer, for no matter how we look at it there are several elements involved and William's decision was a highly personal one. But we may come

47. Cf. Déchanet, *L'Homme et son Oeuvre*, p. 54, note 2, for this reference and quote: *Vita Antiqua*, author unknown, appearing in *Bibliotheca Radoliensi* Reuil), Paris B. N. *MSS. lat. 11782* f° 340–341 and published by A. Poncelet in *Mélanges Godefroid Kurth*, t. 1 (Liège, 1908), pp. 85–96. Cf. p. 90: *Unde et ipse domnus Willelmus sinceritate ordinis provocatus, solitudinis etiam et spiritualis accensus desiderio, onus et honorem prelationis deseruit et Signiaci habitum sancti illius paupertatis suscepit.*

48. Cf. *ibid.*, note 1, for this reference and quote: *Chronicon Signiacense*, Paris B. N. Nouvel acquis. *MSS. lat. 583*; published in t. LV of the *Bibliothèque de l'Ecole des Chartes* (Paris, 1894). Cf. p. 646: *Eo tempore domnus Willermus abbas sancti Theoderici, abbatiam suam deserens, in coenobio Signiacensi factus est monachus, ut divinae speculationi quanto secretius, tanto devotius et ferventius, inhaereret.*

49. Cf. no. 61 of the Series *Sources Chrétiennes: La Contemplation de Dieu*, Guillaume de Saint-Thierry, Introduction, Latin Text and Translation (into French) by Dom Jacques Hourlier, monk of Solesmes (Paris: Cerf, 1959), p. 11 (which is part of Dom Hourlier's Introduction).

50. Shewring and McCann, *Golden Epistle*, note 1 on p. XXIV of the Introduction.

51. Chenevière, "The Man of Faith."   52. *Ibid.*

53. *Ibid.* Dom Chenevière is quoting from *Expositio Altera in Cantica Canticorum*, PL 180:473–546.

closest to the truth by saying that William entered Signy primarily
in order to be able to love God more fully by living a life of more
intense prayer in an atmosphere of greater solitude. And since these
qualities of solitude and prayerfulness are, in his mind, equated with
a renewal of monastic life, we may see in his entrance into the
Cistercians a sign of the intensity of his desire for monastic renewal.

Does William Speak of a Specifically Cistercian Quality Proper to this Renewal?

Now that we have seen that it was their zeal for the renewal of
the monastic life in the simplicity of solitude that made the Cistercians
appeal to William so much, we might ask: Does he see this renewal
only among the Cistercians? Or, if he does see it elsewhere, does he
say anything about distinguishing characteristics of the Cistercian
renewal?

We must answer the first of these questions with a simple "No."
That William saw a genuine attempt at monastic renewal outside
the Cistercians is clearly seen in the enthusiastic welcome and
support he gives to the Carthusians, who established a monastery
at Mont Dieu in 1137, two years after he had entered the Cistercian
monastery at Signy.[54] In fact, he gives a more complete treatment
of the aspect of renewal when writing his *Golden Epistle* to these
Carthusians[55] than when writing of the Cistercians. Not only does
he praise their effort at renewal; he is concerned to show how it is
a genuine evolution of the original monastic ideal, and he endeavors
to give a solid doctrinal basis for this way of life. This will include

54. Dom Justin McCann tells us in his Introduction to the *Golden Epistle*
that "The Charterhouse of Mont Dieu (founded in 1137) was situated some
thirty miles to the east of Signy" (p. xxvii). Thus this new form of monastic
life would have easily come to William's attention, and it was after a visit to
Mont Dieu in 1144 that he wrote the *Golden Epistle*.

55. Cf. Shewring and McCann, *Golden Epistle*, especially c. 1: "A Con-
gratulation on The Renewing of the Fervour of Ancient Religion," and
c. 13: "The Example of Ancient Monks, Hermits, and the Apostles of
Christ and First Faithful Souls."

a detailed development of the aspects of prayer and love in monastic life.[56]

Fr Bouyer, in writing of William's *Golden Epistle* and the spirit it reveals, explains very clearly these attitudes of care to base monastic renewal on a thorough knowledge of the relevant sources, and of zeal for monastic renewal in whatever context it may be appearing. He says that for William:

> This return to primitive monasticism, to a contemplative, or more accurately to a mystical, conception of monasticism, should be accompanied by a rediscovery of what the early Fathers would have called its "pneumatic" meaning. A monasticism such as this could not rest content to be an institution which step by step was organized, established, fixed. It must ever strive to remain a creation evoked by the Spirit.[57]

It is a little more difficult to answer the second question, to say whether or not William considered the Cistercians to have a particular approach to this monastic renewal. He is not very explicit on this topic. It is true that in writing to the Carthusians he treats almost exclusively of the solitary in his cell, and phrases such as "The novice therefore that would be a hermit,"[58] may be taken as expressive of his view of Carthusian life, while on the other hand he pictures St Bernard as zealous for the common life,[59] and the monks of Clairvaux as working, praying and living together.[60] Nevertheless, the very familiarity with which he speaks of Carthusian eremitical solitude, and the intriguing phrase, "Although they all lived together, it may truthfully be said they were all solitaries,"[61]

---

56. Cf. *Ibid.*, especially c. 14: "How the Sensual Beginner, or Religious Novice is to be Taught to Draw Nigh to God by Love and Prayer," and c. 16: "The Third State of the Religious Life, that is the Spiritual."

57. Bouyer, *The Cistercian Heritage*, p. 93.

58. Shewring and McCann, *Golden Epistle*, p. 39.

59. Cf. Webb and Walker, *St Bernard of Clairvaux*, p. 41: "Because he was so desirous of leading the common life to the full," and p. 63: "he scarcely ever excused himself from taking part in the common exercises of the community either during the day or the night."

60. *Ibid.*, pp. 59f.   61. *Ibid.*, p. 60.

that he uses to describe the Cistercians of Clairvaux, should lead us
to avoid an oversimplified contrast of Cistercian cenobitism with
Carthusian eremitism, and the conclusion that it was the cenobitic
aspect of Cistercian life that led William to choose it.[62] The truth
would seem to lie closer to the fact that it was at Clairvaux that
William first encountered a simpler, more contemplative form of
monasticism and the seriousness of this attempt at monastic renewal,
which moved him as early as 1118, eventually led him to join the
Cistercians in 1135. It was only later, "in about 1144,"[63] that he
encountered a similar phenomenon among the Carthusians, while
visiting with them at Mont Dieu. The very enthusiasm with which
he writes of the Carthusian life may well lead us to ask whether or
not he was attracted to change Orders again. In actual fact, he did
not do so, for by now he was "old and infirm";[64] he returned to
Signy, there to spend the remaining four years of his life.

   Thus, rather than try to say anything about what William saw

---

62. Cf. Bouyer, *The Cistercian Heritage,* pp. 101f. for an illuminating
explanation of the apparent paradox that "though towards the end of his life
he had entered the monastic order which was most rigorous in the practice
of cenobitism . . . William should have been so enthusiastic for the restoration
of the anchorite life, i.e. the restoration of eremitism which characterized the
Carthusian movement." The explanation is that "For William . . . monasticism
was not a rigid institution. Its cenobitism was not an end in itself, any more
than was the solitude of the hermit. On the contrary, its cenobitism was the
necessary preparation for burying oneself in the desert. And the desert was
sought only as a means to true freedom, that in which the Spirit of God will
take complete possession of the spirit of man."

63. *Ibid.,* p. 91.

64. Cf. Dom Justin McCann in his Introduction to Shewring and McCann,
Golden Epistle, p. xxviii: "Is it possible that William was genuinely attracted
to the Carthusian life, won by the spectacle of an austerity more complete
even than that of the Cistercians, and therefore wrote with such obvious
sincerity of feeling? It may be so; yet, however much attracted, he did not
seek once more to change his Order, but returned to Signy there to spend the
last few years of his life. In the letter itself he tells us that he is old and infirm
(*senex et deficiens*) for he had now (probably) passed his sixtieth year. With
failing strength he set himself to his last work, the *Life of St Bernard.* Presently
he fell into his last sickness and made a devout end, on the 8th of September
in the year 1148."

as specific in the Cistercian renewal, it may be more accurate to conclude with Dom Jean Leclercq that:

> More than any other he illustrates the fact that Cîteaux shared the spiritual attitudes proper to all religious. . . . This Benedictine become Cistercian late in life, friend of Canons Regular and Carthusian promoter, is the symbol of that which binds the *claustrales* of every observance together: over and above the differences in the manner of living, they share the same manner of loving and serving God.[65]

Conclusion

In brief, we may say that William saw the spirit and aims of the early Cistercians to be a new surge of enthusiasm for prayer and love in the simplicity of solitude, a renewal of authentic monasticism. He found this spirit among the Carthusians as well, but it was in St Bernard and his fellow Cistercians that he first saw it being lived in the concrete, and it was among them that he himself lived it for the last thirteen years of his life.

William's Actual Witness to the Spirit and Aims of the early Cistercians

We may approach William's witness to this spirit of monastic renewal in three stages. First, we will try to see how he himself influenced other Cistercians by stimulating the development of a new element in the Cistercian renewal. Then we can take a look at the spirituality and theology of the monastic life which he worked out in the light of this new element. And finally, we will examine his more specifically Trinitarian doctrine, as seen especially in his *Mirror of Faith*[66] and *Enigma of Faith*,[67] striving to discern the unique

65. Jean Leclercq OSB, pp. 249ff. in *Histoire de la Spiritualité Chrétienne*, vol. 2, Bouyer *et al.* (Paris: Aubier, 1961).

66. Cf. *Speculum Fidei*, PL 180:365–398. For a critical edition of the Latin text, lengthy Introduction, and French translation, cf. J.-M. Déchanet, *Le Miroir de la Foi,* (Bruges: Bayaert, 1946). For an English translation, cf. B. Stenger, *The Mirror of Faith, The Works of William of St Thierry*, Vol. 3, Cistercian Fathers, IX.

67. Cf. *Aenigma Fidei*, PL 180:397–440, trans. J. Anderson, *ibid.*

contribution William has made to the history of spirituality and theology. A treatment of these three themes should enable us to grasp the originality of William's witness to "the whole return to the primitive ideals of ancient eastern monasticism,"[68] characteristic of the twelfth-century monastic scene, as he strives to achieve a "general synthesis of catholic tradition."[69]

The Initiation of a Theological Movement

Our discussion of William's views on the spirit and aims of the early Cistercians has shown that he sees the white monks as agents of monastic renewal and is not concerned to point out anything specifically Cistercian in their renewal. A treatment of his witness to this renewal must also take account of this all-embracing outlook, for, as Fr Bouyer tells us: "For his spiritual testament, in which is to be found all the fruit of his thought and experience, we must turn . . . to the famous *Epistola Aurea* addressed to the *Carthusians* of Mont Dieu. . . . In this letter he was to put aside all spirituality divided into compartments and deliberately ignore the rivalries between orders and observances."[70]

But, if William is free of any provincialism or narrow-mindedness with regard to the various monastic orders and is wholly intent on renewal in whatever context it is appearing, and on basing this renewal on an appreciation of the riches of all the elements of tradition (as we will soon see), the manner in which he draws on the riches of tradition is quite original and has a character all its own. He produces something entirely new, an emphasis uniquely his

68. A. Fiske, "William of St Thierry and Friendship," *Cîteaux*, 12 (1961), p. 6.

69. O. Brooke OSB, "The Speculative Development of the Trinitarian Theology of William of St Thierry in the *Aenigma Fidei*," *Recherches de Théologie Ancienne et Médiévale* (Henceforth: *RTAM*), 27 (1960), p. 209.

70. Bouyer, *The Cistercian Heritage*, p. 91. (Italics of word "Carthusians" mine.)

own.[71] And I think we can say that this new approach, developed in a spirit of dedication to the ideals of monastic renewal which the early Cistercians shared with other reforming monastic groups of that time, not only influenced the other Cistercian spiritual masters of the Order's second and third generations, including St Bernard, but actually gave the impetus toward, and set the tone for, a new element, a theological movement which characterized these same Cistercian Fathers.[72]

What distinguished the doctrine of William of St Thierry was the creative way in which he fused the traditions of East and West. Dom Déchanet has developed this theme at length, stressing the influence of the Eastern Fathers on William's thought.[73] Now this synthesis of Greek and Latin elements may also be said to typify the Cistercian theological movement which Dom Odo Brooke describes thus:

> The search among the early Cistercians for the original purity of monastic life is a familiar theme. What is less familiar is the parallel theological movement to which it gave rise. In response to the call of the last chapter of St Benedict's rule to the sources of

71. Cf. *Ibid.*, p. 85.

72. It may seem contradictory to say that William and the other Cistercians were only interested in a renewal of monastic tradition and yet developed an outlook characteristically their own. I think it is really more an indication of the fervor, the originality, the liveliness with which they went about their renewal. These two elements may be seen in these words of Père Placide Deseilles: "The teaching of St Bernard and the Cistercian spiritual masters of the Order's first two or three generations was intended to be only the living and personal echo of the monastic and patristic tradition. . . . Nevertheless, while the monastic tradition does possess a profound unity, the institutions and spiritual doctrine of the Fathers themselves diverge into several currents, . . . Now the founders of Cîteaux and the first spiritual masters of the Order took up a position of their own in regard to these different currents . . . they worked out a conception of the monastic life which was at the same time both traditional and original." Père Placide Deseilles ocso, *Principles of Monastic Spirituality in the Cistercian Tradition,* translated from the French by M. Cyprian Thibodeau ocso (privately distributed, 1964), p. 1.

73. Cf. especially J.-M. Déchanet, *Aux Sources de la Spiritualité de Guillaume de Saint-Thierry* (Bruges: Beyaert, 1940), and *L'Homme et son Oeuvre.*

monastic spirituality in St Basil and Cassian, these early Cistercians looked also towards the full inheritance of the patristic wisdom, which had inspired that life. This led them to the *Orientale lumen*, the light from the east, finding their theological sources not only in St Augustine and the Latin Fathers, but beyond St Augustine in the Greek Fathers, and especially St Gregory of Nyssa and Origen. Less predominantly Augustinian than the Cluniacs, this movement tended towards a synthesis of traditional patristic thought in the east and in the west.[74]

Dom Brooke goes on to point out that the leaders of this theological movement were St Bernard and William of St Thierry.[75] But I think it can be shown that it was William of St Thierry who actually initiated this movement toward a synthesis of east and west, and that in this regard it was he who influenced St Bernard, rather than vice versa.

Dom Leclercq tells us that "St Bernard had no plan of making a synthesis between Greek and Latin theology."[76] But William did have such a plan, and Dom Déchanet has shown the extent to which his doctrine, in comparison with that of St Bernard, is influenced by the Greek Fathers.[77] Fr Bouyer contends that "reminiscences of Origen form a relatively rare element in the whole of his (i.e. Bernard's) work. . . . On the other hand, Origenism . . . pervades the whole of William's thought,"[78] and Fr Jean Daniélou tells us that "he (i.e. Bernard) owed to his friend William his contact with the rich thought of Gregory (of Nyssa)."[79] Mother A. Fiske also

74. Odo Brooke OSB, "Monastic Theology and St Aelred," *Pax*, 49 (1959), p. 87.

75. *Ibid.*, pp. 87f.

76. Jean Leclercq OSB, "Saint Bernard and the Monastic Theology of the Twelfth Century," *Saint Bernard Theologian: Cistercian Studies*, vol. 1 (Berryville, Va., 1961, privately circulated), p. 12. This is an English translation of the French original, which appeared in *Analecta S.O.C.*, vol. 9 (1953), Fasc. 3-4, pp. 7-23.

77. Cf. Déchanet, *Aux Sources*, pp. 14-24.

78. Bouyer, *The Cistercian Heritage*, p. 79.

79. Jean Daniélou SJ, "Saint Bernard and the Greek Fathers," *Saint Bernard Theologian: Cistercian Studies*, vol. 1, p. 52. This article also originally appeared in French in *Analecta S.O.C.*, 9 (1953).

claims that William is "closer to the Eastern tradition"[80] than St Bernard, and goes on to point out the significance of William's effort "to reconcile the spirit of Eastern Christianity with the letter of Western terminology."[81] In doing this "he was consciously going against certain strong tendencies of his own time, . . . the opposition of conservative monastic forces."[82] And:

> in the . . . conflict between mediaeval augustinianism and the rediscovered elements of eastern thought, his work was a plea for understanding, hence of great importance at a moment that has been called a "nerve center" in the history of Christian thought, a moment in which the eastern and western traditions could have been reconciled, and were not. Few accepted the "novelties" in a spirit of moderation; it would seem that in general the Cistercians were the most sympathetic.[83]

Mother Fiske is here following Dom Déchanet, and goes on to show that it was William who initiated this interest of the Cistercians in the Greek Fathers when, in referring again to one of Déchanet's works, she says: "*Aelred is not named with Isaac of Stella and others who followed William of St Thierry in their devotion to the Greek Fathers*, but Cistercians were usually favorable to them."[84]

A Project in "Re-sourcing"[85]: an Original Synthesis Based on a Creative Fusion of Diverse Traditional Elements

As we begin our study of the monastic doctrine which William worked out in the light of this synthesizing tendency, we again

80. Fiske, "William of St Thierry and Friendship," p. 5.

81. *Ibid.* (and based on Déchanet, *Aux Sources*, p. 73).

82. *Ibid.*　　　　　　　　　　　　　　83. *Ibid.*, p. 6.

84. *Ibid.*, footnote 3. Mother Fiske refers to Déchanet, *Aux Sources*, pp. 28–79. (Italics mine.)

85. A theme developed by Adrian Van Kaam cssp; cf. his *Existential Counseling* (Wilkes-Barre, Pa.: Dimension, 1966), p. 120: "Only the leading thinkers of a religion or culture are capable of returning to the source from which their religion or culture originated. This return to the source enables them to distinguish between what is fundamental and what is incidental in their customs. . . . We may call this procedure 're-sourcing'."

R

encounter his broad-minded outlook, for he develops his spirituality of the monastic life most fully in his *Golden Epistle* to the Carthusians.[86] And though this work is of a more "spiritual" nature, we may also refer to it as "theological," because "for William . . . spirituality and theology mutually control each other. Spirituality should be governed by theological doctrine."[87]

Now the spirituality of this *Golden Epistle* is based on a view of man, a psychology of the body and soul, traced out in William's earlier work *On the Nature of the Body and the Soul*,[88] and heavily dependent on the theories of Gregory of Nyssa and Origen.[89] The chief characteristic of this psychological outlook is "a three-fold division of the soul,"[90] into "its vegetal aspect, in so far as it gives life to the body, . . . its rational aspect, in so far as it belongs to itself and is conscious of itself apart from the body, . . . and its specifically 'spiritual' aspect, in so far as it was made for God and is capable of being apprehended by Him."[91] Origen referred to the three aspects as *psyche*, *nous* and *pneuma;* William as *anima*, *animus* and *spiritus*,[92] and it is important to note that this view represents "different aspects rather than component parts. The spirituality of William developed not so much as a static as a dynamic analysis of the soul. It did not so much aim at balancing the *anima*, *animus* and *spiritus* as at making the soul pass from *anima* into *animus* and from *animus* to *spiritus*."[93]

What characterizes William's development of this progress thru three stages is the way he links it to St Augustine's three-fold division of the divine image in man: memory, reason and love. In this way he revitalizes the Augustinian scheme, which had become

86. Cf. Bouyer, *The Cistercian Heritage*, p. 91.   87. *Ibid.*, p. 110.

88. Cf. *De Natura Corporis et Animae*, PL 180: 695–726.

89. Déchanet, *Aux Sources*, p. 59.

90. Bouyer, *The Cistercian Heritage*, p. 94.

91. *Ibid.*   92. Cf. *ibid.*

93. *Ibid.*, p. 95. (For an interesting similar view of man of a modern-day psychiatrist, cf. Viktor E. Frankl, *The Doctor and the Soul* [New York: Knopf, 1966], p. x: "Man lives in three dimensions: the somatic, the mental and the spiritual." Cf. also St Paul, 1 Thess 5:23.)

ossified by his time, by blending it with Origen's view of man, which entirely dominated his spirituality.[94] He shows how:

> in the very heart of the "vegetal" life, the "renewed memory" of the Creator is awakened in that elementary love which is the attempt to obey. In the "rational" life, love is imbued with understanding and becomes pure love, that is to say conscious delight in God. At that stage of the "spiritual" life it expands into the *unitas Spiritus* the unity of Spirit between ourselves and God, in the Holy Spirit himself.[95]

William goes on, in his *Golden Epistle*, to draw out further implications of Origen's teaching. He utilizes Origen's view of the Eucharistic mystery, which affirms the "real presence of the Body and Blood of Christ in the Eucharist, and no less indisputably ... the mysterious presence of the Sacrifice of the Cross in the Eucharistic Celebration."[96] Nevertheless he stresses that "the Body and Blood of Christ are presented by the Eucharist in such a manner as to signify effectively that the Sacrifice is communicated in such a way that we may make it our own,"[97] in order that he might "represent the whole spiritual life, and in particular the whole monastic life, as a Celebration of the Eucharist."[98]

What is even more important for an understanding of William's originality is an insight into the way in which he elucidates "Origen's crucial contrast between faith ('simple' faith) and *gnosis*."[99] For Origen, *gnosis* is simply the flowering of faith, it is "faith incorporated into our whole life and refashioning it by its influence. It is the shining of faith into a soul which has gradually been made capable of penetrating the mysteries of faith."[100] In a monastic context, William blends this theory of the development of faith with the traditional doctrine of monastic obedience as an exercise of faith to propose his own conception. He teaches that this obedience should gradually lead a monk from a faith received on

94. Cf. *ibid.*, pp. 97–100.　　95. *Ibid.*, p. 98.　　96. *Ibid.*, p. 108.
97. *Ibid.*　　　　　　　　　98. *Ibid.*　　　　　　99. *Ibid.*, p. 102.
100. *Ibid.*, p. 103.

external authority and expressed in obedience to a superior, on through a more interior and loving obedience to a final stage of interior freedom, of being guided by the Holy Spirit himself, with charity as the law.[101] And for an appreciation of William's balance in his teaching on the growth of faith, it is important to note here that, for him, though "the role of external authority decreases in proportion to this inward illumination, . . . it is never wholly abandoned in this life."[102]

But William also develops this theme of the development of faith, and with it hope and love, in a more generic context, in speaking of the Christian life as a journey to union with God, in his treatises *The Mirror of Faith* and *The Enigma of Faith*. These works represent not only a synthesis of Origen and St Augustine, of east and west, of the whole tradition of the Fathers, but an original explanation of how we are united with God. They delineate a real development of the doctrine of the Fathers, and we can now examine it more closely.

A Unique Achievement: a Trinitarian Mystical Theology

In speaking of the theological movement which we may consider William to have initiated among the Cistercians, we mentioned that it was concerned with a synthesis of patristic wisdom. But, as Dom Brooke points out: "It was not simply a synthesis of the Fathers. It was a creative synthesis, bearing the imprint of the twelfth-century Cistercian movement. It was a monastic theology in the sense that its leading theological conceptions grew out of the whole monastic ethos."[103] The main characteristic of the Cistercians in this regard was that "In contrast to those theologians among the black monks . . . whose interest centered on the mysteries of

101. Cf. *ibid.*, pp. 194ff.

102. Odo Brooke, "Faith and Mystical Experience in William of St Thierry," *The Downside Review*, 82 (1964), p. 97.

103. Brooke, "Monastic Theology and St Aelred," p. 88.

Christianity in their objective presentation throughout the wide sweep of the history of salvation, the Cistercian movement dwelt on the reflection of this history within the individual soul."[104] They were concerned with "the assimilation of that history through the connatural experience of the individual believer."[105] This connatural experience is an instinctive or intuitive form of knowledge, differing from purely rational knowledge in that "the intentional identity of knower and known in connatural knowledge is not given through a purely intellectual or rational pattern but demands also a natural affinity of knower and known through sympathy or love."[106] And since this "loving knowledge" is thus "rooted in the 'likeness' of knower and known"[107] it is just as real a form of knowledge as purely rational knowledge.

Now, "In the theological context, this kind of knowledge is grounded in an affinity or likeness to God in the believer, whereby his 'nature' is made like to God by grace. To know God connaturally means to know God through becoming like him."[108] As Dom Brooke goes on to show, "the experience of knowing God connaturally developed in these monastic (i.e. Cistercian) theologians through the renewal of the divine likeness. This experience was the basis for a theological reflection on the meaning of that experience."[109]

Thus we may say that the fruit of the Cistercian proclivity for synthesizing the patristic tradition is this method of developing a theology based on an experience of the mysteries of faith, of our likeness to God, of God himself as he transforms us more and more into his likeness by his grace. Such a method unites theology with

---

104. *Ibid.* For the original exposition of this distinction, and an explanation of how these two trends complement each other, the one being a "logical development, a homogeneous evolution" of the other, cf. Jean Leclercq OSB, *The Love of Learning and the Desire for God,* trans. Catherine Misrahi (New York: Fordham University Press, 1961), p. 219.

105. O. Brooke OSB, "Towards a Theology of Connatural Knowledge," *Cîteaux,* 18 (1967), p. 278.

106. *Ibid.,* p. 280. 107. *Ibid.*

108. *Ibid.* 109. *Ibid.*

mysticism. It "shows us that the dimension of spiritual experience is not a purely individualistic point of contact between God and the soul which takes place somewhere on the fringe of God's Revelation to mankind,"[110] but that it is "rooted intrinsically and essentially in Revelation through the judgment by connaturality in the initial act of faith."[111]

But within this school, or theological movement, each author has his own way of approaching this loving knowledge of God based on our likeness to him. Dom Brooke claims that William's presentation is the most theologically profound.[112] William differs from Aelred, who "develops more closely the intersubjective communion in human friendship,"[113] because he is more intent on explaining connatural knowledge "as a participation in the intersubjective communion of the persons of the Trinity."[114] And he differs also from St Bernard, for:

> St Bernard is interested primarily in the analysis of love. . . . William is concerned above all with the union of the two faculties (i.e. love and knowledge), giving an experience *sui generis* which is really knowledge in the strict sense although it is not knowledge of a rational kind. Moreover in this knowledge through love (*amor-intellectus*) there is a much more explicit relationship to the Trinity than in the mystical theology of St Bernard. The union of the soul with the Word is at the center of the doctrine of St Bernard, union with the Holy Spirit at the center of the doctrine of William.[115]

And Dom Brooke gives us a further insight into William's uniqueness when he points out that:

---

110. *Ibid.*, p. 278. (Dom Brooke here refers to H. U. von Balthasar, *Word and Redemption* [New York: Herder and Herder, 1965], pp. 49–86.)

111. *Ibid.*   112. Cf. *ibid.*, p. 280.

113. *Ibid.*, p. 285.   114. *Ibid.*

115. O. Brooke osb, "The Trinitarian Aspect of the Ascent of the Soul to God in the Theology of William of St Thierry," *RTAM*, 26 (1959), pp. 123ff. (Dom Brooke here refers to J. Hourlier, "St Bernard et Guillaume de Saint-Thierry," *S. Bernard théologien* [*Analecta sacri Ordinis Cisterciensis*, 9 (1953), fasc. 3–4], pp. 223–233).

In the theological explanation of connatural knowledge given by William of St Thierry, knowledge and likeness act in reciprocal causality. . . . The likeness, the *similtudo*, is a created participation in the uncreated *unitas*, the Holy Spirit, who is the mutual union of the Father and the Son. Therefore, in accordance with the principle that knowledge and likeness are proportioned to each other, this "likeness" or connaturalization with the intratrinitarian life implies that we participate in an intratrinitarian mode of knowledge.[116]

And "It is precisely this foundation in William's conception of the Holy Spirit as mutual union of the Father and the Son which gives to his mystical theology its special character of the experience of the trinitarian life."[117]

The general thrust of this trinitarian mystical theology is from a basic scriptural faith, on to a deeper penetration of that faith and finally an experience of the Trinity. It is a deepening and flowering of the life of faith, hope and love. In the *Mirror of Faith* William approaches this theme of faith-understanding-experience from a

116. Brooke, "Towards a Theology of Connatural Knowledge," note 18, pp. 280f.

117. Brooke, "Trinitarian Aspect of the Ascent of the Soul," p. 124. Elsewhere Dom Brooke shows that though this "theory of the Holy Spirit as the mutual . . . union of the Father and the Son," is a "theological opinion dating principally from St Augustine," nevertheless, "William's mystical theology, despite its basis in the Augustinian theory of the Holy Spirit, can throw light on the whole Scriptural and 'Greek' Trinitarian tradition," because "the force of William's trinitarian spirituality lies precisely in the Holy Spirit as the bond of union, in whom we are united to the Father and the Son," and "in the Scriptural or 'Greek' trinitarian economy no less than in the Augustinian theory, the Holy Spirit is the bond of union, whereby we are linked with the other Persons. The only difference lies in why this is so. According to the theology of the Greek Fathers, the Holy Spirit is the last Person in the sequence of the descending movement from the Father through the Son in the Holy Spirit, and is therefore the first Person with whom we make contact and in whom we are drawn in the sequence of the ascending movement through the Son to the Father. As this initial point of contact with the other Persons, the Holy Spirit is the link, the bond of union, in whom we participate in the Trinitarian relations." Cf. Odo Brooke, "William of St Thierry," *The Month*, 28 (1962), p. 351f.

mystical point of view, and is primarily concerned with the actual experience of God. In the *Enigma of Faith* his approach is more metaphysical, an attempt to understand God. Let us examine these two treatments more closely, and also William's attempt to unite the more spiritual with the more intellectual aspects of our ascent to God.

In the *Mirror of Faith* approach, the emphasis is mostly on God's part, on grace freely given. The first stage is that of the gift of faith given to all Christians. It is received, and understood in a certain external sense, always guided by authority.

But as one progresses in the life of faith, he is given by God a deeper and more interior penetration of the truths he already believes in. It is what William calls an *intellectus fidei*, an understanding of the faith, yet it is a gift of God and not the result of human speculation. It is a more direct contact with God, and yet it is still a knowledge of faith, a *cognitio fidei*, God known more clearly but still according to our way of knowing. Once again, this illumination does not lead one to abandon external authority, but is a deeper penetration of what was previously held only on the weight of authority.[118]

The third stage is that of vision, of a knowledge of God as he is in himself; here God is known as he knows himself with a *cognitio amoris* which transcends the *cognitio fidei* of the second stage. It:

> is not a superstructure extrinsic to the life of faith, but an experience to which faith is intrinsically orientated. It grows organically from the life of faith. In William's view of living faith as inseparable from love, faith is directed towards *cognito amoris*, the knowledge through love which is the experience of the trinitarian life.[119]

118. Cf. Brooke, "Faith and Mystical Experience," pp. 95–97. (For a more detailed and technical treatment of the theme of this article, cf. O. Brooke osb, "William of St Thierry's Doctrine of the Ascent to God by Faith," *RTAM*, 30 [1963], pp. 181–204, and 33 [1966], pp. 282–318.)

119. Cf. *ibid.*, p. 98. (Dom Brooke here refers to J.-M. Déchanet's critical edition of the *Speculum Fidei* in *Le Miroir de la Foi* [Bruges: Beyaert, 1946], pp. 48–58.)

This theory is based on William's explanation of how we share in God's knowledge and love of himself:

> According to William's strict equation of knowledge and likeness, we not only become like God through our knowledge of him, but we know him through our likeness to him, and this likeness to the Trinity, the *similitudo*, the perfection of the image of the Trinity, is given through love. Therefore it is through love that we know God as he knows himself. God's knowledge of himself is identically the Holy Spirit as the mutual union, the mutual knowledge and love of the Father and the Son. To know God as he knows himself is to participate through the *similitudo* in the Holy Spirit as that mutual union, knowledge and love.[120]

From William's point of view, this is the spiritual fulfillment, the full interior flowering of our life of faith. In his eyes, "Living faith, the faith which is united with love, is . . . impelled through the exigence of love towards this experience of communion with the Persons of the Trinity and it is given its ultimate meaning in this experience."[121] This is what William means when he speaks of *amor-intellectus*,[122] a love which is knowledge, and for him it is an anticipation of the Beatific Vision.

William's more metaphysical approach in the *Enigma of Faith* also proceeds in three stages. In these stages we may see a close parallel with his treatment of the three spiritual states of sensual, rational, and spiritual,[123] ultimately based on his three-fold treatment of the soul as *anima*, *animus* and *spiritus*. Here again we note the

---

120. Cf. *ibid*. (Dom Brooke again refers to Déchanet's *Le Miroir de la Foi*, pp. 154–165.)

121. *Ibid*.

122. Cf. v.g., *Expositio Altera Super Cantica Canticorum*, PL 180:491d: *amor ipse intellectus est*. Dom Brooke treats the question of the exact nature of this knowledge, which has been the subject of recent debate, and concludes with Déchanet, in contrast with Gilson, that "it is knowledge in a strict and not merely metaphorical sense, though a knowledge which is *sui generis* and transcendent both of sense and of reason." Brooke, "Trinitarian Aspect of the Ascent of the Soul," p. 111.

123. Cf. Shewring and McCann, *Golden Epistle*, pp. 75-120.

unity of William's doctrine, for "This relationship of theology to spirituality and to psychology offers an interesting example of theological method. For it is a theology developing in successive stages, each of which is proportioned in turn to the life of the senses, of the reason and of the spirit."[124] Thus this theology is "grounded in the spiritual life of the soul."[125]

The first stage, that of initial or simple faith, is concerned with an attempt to penetrate the meaning of "the Incarnation and the whole temporal economy"[126] in order to approach through these sensible signs to "the eternal, immutable life of the Trinity."[127]

The second stage is that of what William calls the *ratio fidei*, "the reasoning power of faith,"[128] which "places reason wholly under the dominion of faith,"[129] and in which "The philosophical concepts of person, number, relation, generation are compelled to abandon their purely human connotations and are formed by the *ratio fidei* in the new light of the Trinitarian mystery."[130] This approach has both its weakness and its strength. The weakness is the fact that William "refuses to admit the right of developing a metaphysics in its own right,"[131] so that "it can hardly be said that on the metaphysical plane he equals the best achievement of the contemporary scholastic movement."[132] The strength of this approach is that "William's speculations always explain more exactly just where the mystery lies in every aspect of the problem,"[133] and thus highlight the fact that "the human mind never understands the Trinity so well as when it is understood to be incomprehensible."[134]

In the third stage, William strives to go beyond *ratio fidei*, which

---

124. Odo Brooke, "William of St Thierry" (in *The Month*), p. 346.

125. *Ibid.*   126. *Ibid.*   127. *Ibid.*

128. *Ibid.*, p. 347.   129. *Ibid.*

130. Brooke, "Faith and Mystical Experience," p. 101.

131. Brooke, "The Speculative Development of the Trinitarian Theology of William of St Thierry in the *Aenigma Fidei*," *RTAM* 28 (1961), p. 42.

132. Brooke, "William of St Thierry" (in *The Month*), p. 347.

133. *Ibid.*, p. 348.

134. *Ibid.*

"is limited to thinking about God without knowing God as he knows himself,"[135] and achieve a "union of faith with *intellectus* (understanding), and *dilectio* (delight) fused in an inseparable unity as an image of the Trinity."[136] At this point William is striving to achieve a synthesis of the more mystical with the more intellectual ascent, "to integrate these two movements into one movement, in an ascent from faith through *ratio fidei* into mystical experience."[137] It is one of the limitations of William's theology that, unfortunately, "The synthesis is never completely achieved. . . . The three stages of faith in the *Aenigma Fidei* . . . contain no explicit reference to the trinitarian experience. . . . *Ratio fidei* is closely related to the ascent from faith to mystical experience but never wholly integrated with it."[138]

Conclusion

In this finely polished theology of our experience of the Trinity I think we may see the more objective aspect of William's witness to what he perceived the spirit and aims of the early Cistercians to be. He had seen that ideal to be a new surge of enthusiasm for prayer and love in the simplicity of solitude, a renewal of authentic monasticism. Now the unique contribution he makes to this renewal is to go back to the patristic wisdom which had inspired the monastic life,[139] and to formulate an original development of this patristic heritage and thus give a more profound theological explanation of the way we actually experience the God to whom we pray and whom we love. For "Despite allusions to an experimental knowledge of the Trinity in the writings of the Fathers, there was no fully developed theology of this experience. The great contribution of William of St Thierry is to have evolved a

135. Brooke, "Faith and Mystical Experience," p. 101.
136. *Ibid.*
137. *Ibid.,* p. 102.
138. *Ibid.*
139. Cf. Brooke, "Monastic Theology and St Aelred," p. 87.

theology of the Trinity which is essentially mystical, and a mystical theology which is essentially trinitarian."[140]

The more subjective aspect of William's witness to the Cistercian ideal is his own zeal, his own love, the way in which he developed in the simplicity of solitude into a real man of prayer, an ardent, indeed a passionate, God-seeker. This element of personal growth in union with God is necessarily a little more difficult to analyze, but the intensity of William's desire for God is something that strikes us forcefully when we read his works. If this treatment of William's doctrine has perhaps seemed somewhat dry and speculative, his vision itself is very close to the deepest yearnings of a monastic heart. William is a lover, a man of God, and we may catch some glimpse of the strength of his devotion if we allow him to speak for himself, as he does in his *Mirror of Faith* when he says:

> For a man to find himself in some mysterious way in the very midst of the Trinity, and united to God in the very charity which unites the Father with the Son—such a grace is more than the mind can grasp. Such goodness is unfathomable. To be made holy in the Spirit of all holiness, where Father and Son embrace. . . . O sweetness, O deep security for the loving heart! The experience of such happiness, the realization of such an infinite good, although in this . . . life they can never be complete, are yet enough in themselves to constitute a life of blessedness. And in the future life they will be gloriously fulfilled.[141]

Summary

Perhaps the most fitting way to sum up this study of William of St Thierry's witness to the spirit and aims of the early Cistercians,

140. Brooke, "William of St Thierry" (in *The Month*), p. 351. Dom Brooke goes on to point out that "He (i.e. William) is therefore the initiator of the tradition of trinitarian mysticism, which is to be found especially in the writings of Ruysbroeck, Eckhart, Tauler and Suso." (Dom Brooke here refers to L. Reypens, art. *Dieu* [*Connaissance mystique*], *Dictionnaire de Spiritualité*, III [Paris, 1957], 883–929.)

141. *Speculum Fidei*, PL 180:394bc. The English translation appears in Webb and Walker, *The Mirror of Faith*, p. 67.

of his zeal for experiencing Father, Son and Holy Spirit in the simplicity of solitude, and of the areas for discussion this topic opens up, is to listen to William as he prays, saying:

> We adore you, God the Father, who create us and give us life; we worship you, Wisdom of the Father, whose gift of renewed life enables us to live wisely; we praise you, Holy Spirit, for by loving you, and loving in you, we live happily and will dwell forever in utmost bliss. We bless you, three Persons in one God, by whom, through whom and in whom we exist. Though we turn from you by sinning and lose our likeness to you, you continue to uphold us; for you have made us in your likeness and it is you, the source of our life, who renew that likeness in us. To you be glory for ever and ever. Amen.[142]

Patrick Ryan OCSO

Abbey of the Genesee,
Piffard, New York

---

142. *De Contemplando Deo*, PL 184:380. (Translation mine.) I would like to include here a word of thanks to: Fr M. Basil Pennington OCSO, for his invitation to prepare this paper for the Symposium and for his continual encouragement and consistently helpful suggestions; to Dom Odo Brooke OSB, for his interest and thoughtful advice; and to Br Elias OSB, of Mt Savior Monastery, for his kind assistance in locating source material.

TOWARDS CONCLUSIONS: A PRE-POSITION PAPER

D URING THESE PAST four days we have experienced a presence and action of the Holy Spirit like that which was experienced by our first Fathers. We have felt their presence, too, as we have struggled to formulate a clearer idea of the heritage they have passed on to us. We have also experienced this week the absence and the presence of Thomas Merton. We had hoped that he would be here, however the Lord took him to himself. He was absent in body but he was here in spirit. He was truly very much part of our meeting. His sacrifice, the sacrifice of his life, has already borne fruit in many ways.

This Symposium was conceived and organized as part of our renewal effort to discern the spirit and aims of the founders of the Order of Cîteaux. Before presenting a statement prepared by our Conclusions Committee I would like to make a few preparatory remarks.

First of all our self-study and renewal must be situated within that of the entire Church. Pope John XXIII, inspired by the Holy Spirit, called a Council with this end in view, that the Church might look at herself and undertake a self-study under the Spirit's guidance, in order to respond to the call of the Spirit today. The Spirit is speaking to the Church and to all who are members of it. Pope John XXIII gave his life for this renewal. And now Pope Paul VI is following in his footsteps. In his encyclical, *Ecclesiam Suam*, the present Pope has outlined the program of his pontificate;

it is one of seeking increasing self-awareness, of self-study, for the purpose of renewal:

> Our first thought is that this is the hour in which the Church should deepen its consciousness of itself, in which it ought to meditate on that mystery which is peculiar to it, in which it ought to examine, for its own enlightment and for its own development, a particular doctrine which it already knows and which it has formulated and made known during this past century. That doctrine concerns the origin of the Church, its own nature, its own mission, its own ultimate destiny, a doctrine never sufficiently investigated and understood inasmuch as it contains the publication of a mystery kept hidden from the beginning of time in the all-creating mind of God in order that it may be made known through the Church.[1]

When we monks look at ourselves in the Church we can see that like all the members of the Church we are called to this self-study, under the guidance of the Spirit, in order that we may be what we ought to be in this twentieth century.

As we conclude this Symposium we realize that there are many unanswered questions and many unsolved problems. But we have to learn to live with unanswered questions and unsolved problems. True it is part of modern man's psychology to try with all his might to penetrate into every mystery. The adventures in space, for instance, have fascinated us and we seek to know all of the mysteries of nature. But ultimately man has to bow his head in faith to the impenetrable mystery of God. This is something that should characterize the contemplative, who must live an intense life of faith in which by the activity of the Spirit one penetrates ever more and more deeply into the mystery of God and man.

A Statement

The first part of our conclusion is a statement. This is, of course, a pre-position paper. In it we try to put together ideas gathered from the various conferences and discussions. We have been exposed to vast riches, to a heritage which it takes a lifetime to

1. *Ecclesiam Suam*, no. 9.

absorb. What was learned here we will have to think about and meditate on; we will have to synthesize and live. The important thing it seems to me is to live our life. It is through the lived experience of our life that we will come to an understanding of our Fathers, to what we call the mystery of Cîteaux. We have done our best to present that mystery here:

> The Order of Cîteaux came into being as a fact, a happening, the result of a movement of the Holy Spirit in and through men, the monks of Molesme, who came to Cîteaux to live the Gospel specified for them by the Rule of St Benedict and expressed, as time went on, in their own documents, for example, in the Charter of Charity, which are the fruit of their lived experience. They made specific choices, though perhaps without full knowledge at times (choices, as has been brought out, can be made without full knowledge of all that is involved). The basic and essential matter for them was the response to Christ in love. Certain things that are accidental to Christian life as a whole became essential to the specifically Cistercian form of Christian life (e.g., physical separation from society) and values common to Christians as a whole were given special emphasis (e.g., the eschatological).[2]

That is, rather briefly, what we want to say. It needs to be emphasized, explicated. The basic idea is the Cistercian fact. As you know, a fact or a happening is an on-going, dynamic and living thing. There has been a Cistercian fact right here during these days, a happening which has had at its very heart the same life principle experienced by the first Cistercians—the Holy Spirit.

Eight Elements

The explication of this basic statement takes the form of eight elements which were part of the spirit and aims of our founders: renewal, experience of God, community, the Rule of St Benedict, poverty, solitude, charity and the Church. The final element needs to be stressed more for the ecclesiological dimension was not treated explicitly in the Symposium, though it was implicitly present in much of the discussion.

2. This statement was later modified through discussion; cf. *infra.*, pp. 267f.

Renewal: Our Cistercian Fathers called their monastery the New Monastery just as today we hear of the New Church. Pope John XXIII made it clear to us how the Church is in constant need of renewal. So too, the Order. Such renewal, as was brought out by Dom Jean Leclercq, includes an ability to break with the past when necessary. However, any renewal of external structure must flow from a renewal of spirit and from lived experience. It is important to ask ourselves whether we are more concerned about change and external renewal than we are about interior renewal. Certainly we have to be very careful.

In this regard if we look at the example of our friend, Father Louis (Thomas Merton), we can see that he really was a prophet. Perhaps only now will we begin to appreciate him for what he really was. According to his abbot he devoted about two hours a day to writing but spent the whole of the early morning in silent prayer. He was a man of prayer, a true contemplative. In the East, as you know, he met the Dalai Lama in the Himalayas and spent eight days with him. There is a lovely picture of the two of them, Father Louis and the Dalai Lama, a Christian monk and a non-Christian monk, meeting and finding in one another the same contemplative experience vitalized by the same source, the Holy Spirit. In one of their encounters, expressing his curiosity about the Cistercian monasteries in the United States, the Dalai Lama asked whether the monks were experiencing "achievement" in the mystical life. Father Louis reported: "When I explained the vows to him he still wanted to know what kind of attainment the monk's life achieved and if there were possibilities of a deep mystical life in our monasteries. I told him: 'Well, that is what they are supposed to be for but many monks seem to be interested in something else.' "

Here is the danger: of being sidetracked by the "many things," that is, the activities of Martha. We are human beings living on this earth and we have to be concerned about "many things." We do not live in the clouds. Yet the "one thing necessary" in our life must be this lived experience of God. This brings us to the second element, experience.

S

Experience of God: Fundamental for us is the desire to taste and see how good God is. *Vacate et videte*, or in other words, be free to engage in contemplation of God, to have this experience of God. And this, it seems to me, is the source of the enthusiasm found in the Cistercian Fathers, the enthusiasm which Fr Bernard Johnson pointed out as that of "men possessed by God." This explains the joy and ardor of monks. It was Archbishop Goodier who said in his *Public Life of Our Lord* that joy was the characteristic of the Cistercian life, However, the charism of the Cistercian is not flamboyant, rather it is quiet, simple, integrated into daily life. One can encounter mystical experience whether of God or of the saints in any place. An orientation towards such experience is part of the heritage we receive from our Cistercian Fathers.

Community: While the experience of God is a mystery that must be lived in the soul of each monk and nun, the spiritual riches that flow from this experience are shared in a community of persons. As St Benedict says, together we go to God, together we encounter him by the activity of the Holy Spirit perfecting the faith which he has given us. A living tradition or heritage is passed on. In this regard we could note that the papers of the Symposium have given evidence of personal contact on the part of those who gave them. It was not just historical research or theology. Rather it was evident that in their research, in their study, in their reading, the men who gave the papers had come into contact with the men about whom they spoke: William, Bernard, Aelred and the others. In the discussions it was good to see the nuns getting more attention, they really have something to contribute. We have among the Cistercian nuns a rich tradition which needs to be brought more into the light. All our Cistercian forebears, the women as well as the men, are real persons. They are witnesses of a living heritage, a tradition. History and theology are important, and we have to study them; but unless we experience what is being expressed in the books we are far from the target. Here lies the power of example. What we have experienced here is the example of men who have not just been studying but who have been living our life and are sharing with us its fruits.

I would like to insert a word here on the subject of charism. It came in for quite a bit of discussion and some were hesitant to use the term. But it is a word we have to accept, that has to be used even more. The Catholic Encyclopedia in treating of it says that the theology of charism in the life of the Church must be further studied and a history of it written, that an appreciation of charism leads to an ecclesiology in which the Spirit is seen as the source of all the activity among the People of God. That statement could be related to the whole of the ecclesiology which is emerging today out of Vatican II.

The Rule of St Benedict: The fourth element that emerged, and it is very important for the Cistercian monk, is the Rule of St Benedict. The Cistercians strove to live the Gospel; that is clear.[3] When we speak of their fidelity to the Rule it must be understood that they were faithful to the Rule as a practical interpretation of the Gospel. Rigid, strict observance, with a too literal attachment to the Rule was a result of a later development arising out of polemics and the need of self-defense. This especially emerged in the late Trappist reform. With the early Cistercians the *dura et aspera* or, as Father Lekai called it, heroic austerity was not lacking. But they saw this as a sharing in the Cross of Christ, as part of the Paschal Mystery. The end of the Prologue of the Rule brings this out: by patience we share in the sufferings of Christ in order that we might share in his glory in his kingdom.[4] For them suffering and penitential practices were not a negative thing, but were seen in the context of Christ. All the observances to which they were so faithful, manual labor, solitude, vigils, fasting, were centered in Christ. We should continue to be faithful to these for the same reason. They are means to that purity of heart which is identified by Cassian with charity in that wonderful first conference of Abbot Moses. The asceticism of the Rule of St Benedict is simply a preparation for the experience

3. A good witness to this is the account of the founding of Fountains Abbey. The monks of York were Benedictines. They came into contact with the monks of Clairvaux and Savigny and were very impressed by them. What they said about them was: "Here are men who are living the Gospel. We read the Gospel better in the example of these men." 4. RB, Prol. 50.

of God, as the Rule makes clear. The Prologue, for example, speaks of that sweetness with which we run in the way of the Lord.[5] Chapter Seven brings the steps of humility to the climax of perfect love which casts out fear and which is the work of the Holy Spirit.[6] And finally, in the last Chapter, Seventy-three, St Benedict invites us to pass from these beginnings to the heights.[7] St Bernard speaks of Chapter Seventy-three as being distinctly Cistercian. Dom Leclercq pointed out that *puritas regule* can be linked up with the Gospel reality called purity of heart. It is the beatitude from the Sermon on the Mount: "Blessed are the pure of heart for they shall see God."[8] In other words, all the observances of the monk are a preparation for the vision of God in eternal contemplation, while also making him capable here and now of loving with a universal charity.

Poverty: The Cistercian Fathers had a special regard for evangelical poverty in the deepest sense of the word. Material poverty is important, it is indeed a world problem. But there is a deeper meaning to poverty in our Cistercian Fathers. For them it is the *kenosis,* the self-emptying, making one's self available, free for God and for all our brothers in community. This poverty of spirit leads to simplicity which is characteristic of Cîteaux and should be associated with their spirit of poverty. It is a freedom, freedom from all that is superfluous and triumphal in all the aspects of their life, including the liturgy.

Solitude: A real and effective solitude was sought by the founders of Cîteaux in order to favor contemplative life. We come apart to be free from the pressures of the world and thus be able to give ourselves to the contemplative life. At the same time this solitude is filled with community living, with dynamic personal relationship. Cistercians are not hermits in community, even though Cîteaux was called an *eremus.* This word expressed a certain physical separation from the affairs of the world, but it was intended to indicate an attitude. The Cistercians sought a balance of solitude and community life.

5. RB, Prol. 49.   6. RB 7:67.   7. RB 73:2.   8. Mt 5:8.

Charity: There is no need to labor this. Charity was always at the heart of Cistercian life, both in seeking the experience of God and in community living. We see in the interpersonal relations in community, whether between abbot and monk or monk and monk, that these relations were all governed by the outpouring love of the Holy Spirit.

Church: The Cistercian life was part of the life of the Church, a dynamic part. It seems to me that any study of ecclesiology must take into account the rich theology of the Church in the Cistercian Fathers. At the Second Vatican Council Bishop Guyot of Coutance said that everything that the Council was seeking to achieve was expressed in the Cistercian reform of the twelfth century. There is a very real parallel between the twelfth-century need for reform and the call of the Holy Spirit today to renewal and reform. In some way our life should be a witness to the Church of this.

Conclusion

Those are the eight points. In conclusion we thought that a statement in the paper of Br Patrick Ryan summed up well much of what is contained in these points:

> The way of life of the Cistercians was one of poverty, simplicity and austerity in an atmosphere of silence and solitude conducive to reading, prayer and contemplation . . . to diffuse the spirit of prayer and openness to God throughout the totality of the monk's life experience.[9]

Emerging Themes

The contact we have enjoyed this week with our Fathers has been an enriching theological experience. We would like to point out a few of the emerging themes which seem to have special relevance to our times, or we might better say, have great contemporary significance.[10]

9. Cf. above, p. 226.

10. In regard to relevance Father Merton said something in his second to last talk, the one given in Calcutta, which is worth recalling. He had a prepared

There is the theology of the experience of God, a theme common to all the Cistercian Fathers. Then there is the consideration of the personal relationship with each of the three divine persons. This is especially found in the writings of William of St Thierry.

Another consideration is the development, the cultivation of personality. We see this in Aelred, especially in his theology of friendship. Complementary to this is another element about which much is said today, Christian humanism.[11] Bernard and all his disciples were humanists in the full sense of that word. However, Aelred, as Father Columban brought out, was the most remarkable humanist of that period. With the cult of man being today so prevalent we should bring out this true humanism. The development of man is reaching toward fulfillment but it can only achieve this through the experience of God and growth in brotherly charity in the Church.

I think our modern youth coming to the Cistercian life today will fully appreciate our Cistercian Fathers and the Cistercian spirit if this spirit is expressed in our daily lives by our example, that "prophetic example" of which Pope Eugene spoke, and by a teaching that is set forth in contemporary fashion. Thus one conclusion is that we must live what we have learned. Another is that further study, research and reading of our Fathers is necessary; translations and studies must be published. In sponsoring this Symposium and through its series of books Cistercian Publications is making a significant contribution to this work. And we want to support and encourage it in every way possible.

Edward McCorkell ocso.

Holy Cross Abbey,
Berryville, Virginia

---

paper but he put it on the table saying, "You can read this paper if you want to, but I suspect you have better things to do than to read my papers." And then he gave an extemporaneous talk in which he spoke about our irrelevance, that we monks should not attempt to be relevant.

11. Cf. *Populorum progressio*, no. 42.

DISCUSSION

In attempting to formulate an adequate expression of the conclusions of the Symposium, one of the most difficult problems seemed to be that of the relation of the early Cistercians to the Rule, and the relation of the Rule to the Gospel. It would seem imprecise to say that the Rule was in some way a condensation of the Gospel. But can we say, on the basis of the documentary evidence we have, that our Fathers chose the Rule as a way to live the Gospel, or that they chose to live the Gospel by living the Rule more exactly (*purior*)? Whatever were their explicit intentions, it can be said that in the Rule they did find a practical way to live the Gospel.

There was some concern about the introduction of the concept of eschatological into the basic statement since the word was not used by our Fathers. However, the concept which it expresses was found in their lives, in their yearning for the heavenly life, their desire for God, their emphasis on a greater detachment and freedom in the Spirit. In a very true sense they could be said to be seeking to anticipate the heavenly life as they sought to reduce to a minimum their bonds with the world, the means they employed (poverty) and their human relationships (celibacy), while also seeking to give a definitive personal consent to God on earth as it is given in heaven (obedience).

Some felt there should be a more explicit reference to the nuns in the basic statement. However, it was recognized that the first convent of Cistercian nuns was probably not founded until 1128, and it was much later when they became juridically attached to the Order. However, our studies must consider their origins, and therefore some reference should be made to them in regard to a later development.

It was felt by some that the concept of interiority which was well developed in one of the discussions should be brought out more fully, especially as the discussion seemed to point to this as an area specifically Cistercian. At Cluny there was great liturgical emphasis and in our times also there seems to be among Benedictines more emphasis laid upon the search for God in liturgy and other external community activities in contrast to the Cistercians' greater emphasis on personal prayer as the means toward the experience of God. However, we do not want to project or support the concept of the liturgical Benedictine and the non-liturgical Cistercian.

The statement as it was presented seemed to confuse an historical and a theological approach. While this called for some refinement, it was realized that both are necessary if we are to express the reality. Historical fact and theological reflection are both necessary. This Symposium dwelt more on the historical and it would perhaps be well to give more to the theological in the next.

We did not succeed in establishing clearly to whom the title of founder should be attributed in regard to the Order of Cîteaux. It was clear that in its founding there was no break with the past monastic tradition. There was rather an evolution which left behind certain elements which lacked authenticity or encumbered the monks' free search for God. There was further development, if not an evolution in the full sense, within the Order of Cîteaux itself from the time of the founding in 1098 to the adoption of the *Charter of Charity* by the General Chapter of 1123. The increase of the number of monasteries postulated this, but there also enters into the picture the dynamic figure of Bernard of Clairvaux. It was not thought that here there was any deformation of the primitive spirit, but it was recognized that the prosperity and growth which Bernard brought to the Order did have great effect. Bernard himself might best be seen as a sacramental exteriorization of what the contemplative life of the Order of Cîteaux was to accomplish within the Church. However, it is certain that Bernard would not set up his own way of life as a model for his brother monks.

Several times in the consideration of the conclusions, the question was one of terminology rather than of realities. The Fathers often expressed the same theological realities in different terms. We should be careful in using our terms that we do not predicate of the Cistercian founders our terminology, nor the fuller theological development which it sometimes expresses for us today.

This would be true in regard to the expression of the Paschal Mystery. For them it would probably have been considered first of all as a configuration with Christ. They would not have spoken of, nor perhaps thought of, the co-redemptive aspects in the way that we do today. This is more a nineteenth-century evolution. Yet certainly they were not oblivious of the value of a penitential life lived for others and indeed Aelred, Guerric and William, as well as Bernard, all expressed the importance of the monks' having a universal concern for the world, the poor, the needy, for all of Christ.

There were a number of other elements which the group thought should somehow be brought into the basic statement or its development:

Organization

Something that seemed specific to Cistercians was the conjunction of various elements of monastic tradition in a balanced way, set in the framework of a good organization which would help maintain the balance. This framework was the union of the monasteries, general chapters, visitations, etc. There has always existed a tension between structures and charism. With the charism of government the early Cistercians seemed to succeed in successfully incarnating the charism of the monastic vocation in a satisfactory and helpful structure.

Ready Penance

Our life oftentimes has been considered a life of penance. What precisely does this mean? Is it a part of conversion or does it have a positive element to play in the observance of the Rule of St Benedict? In the course of the discussion great emphasis was laid upon the desire of the early Cistercians to embrace a truly ascetical life according to the Rule.

Mary

It was recognized that very little had been said about the Blessed Virgin Mary in the course of this Symposium. Yet, it has always been maintained that devotion to Mary is one of the characteristics of the Order. Is this true? The historical place of Mary and of devotion to her in the Order and the place which this must hold today are in need of further study.

Division of the Order

It must be painfully recognized that today there is not one Order of Cîteaux, but two Cistercian Orders. As we seek to discern the way of renewal, we cannot simply overlook the seventeenth-century split which was juridically recognized in the last century. We must seek to discern what significance this has for us today; is it well that this division continue or better to seek a way towards union in the near future.

Devotion to Christ's Humanity

This was brought out in the consideration of the nuns. Yet primarily it is a very important part of the spirituality of St Bernard and the other Cistercian Fathers. Our relationship with Christ and with Mary should be bound up with our place in the Church.

Work

It would seem that manual labor, which has been held in such esteem in Cistercian asceticism, should be brought out more fully. Perhaps it should be expressed especially in relation to poverty.

In closing, Dom Jean Leclercq expressed his satisfaction by noting the fact that while we had grappled with many problems we did not involve ourselves, as so often has happened in Symposia, with pseudo-problems. It was rather a struggle with the authentic, a true search for truth, and an emphasis on the positive, with a ready acknowledgment of the work that lies ahead.

The meeting closed with a sincere and deep expression of gratitude to God who had so evidently poured out his blessings upon the meeting by the abiding presence of the Spirit of Love and Truth.

CONCLUSIONS

THIS SYMPOSIUM is situated within the renewal efforts of the Cistercian Order, and as such is therefore situated within the renewal program of the Universal Church. The movement initiated by Pope John XXIII under the impulse of the Holy Spirit, which flowered in the Second Vatican Council, has been unremittedly fostered by his successor Pope Paul VI. In his first encyclical, *Ecclesiam Suam*, the Holy Father outlined his program. We might with due proportion apply the following passage to ourselves as a particular part of the Church: "The first thought is that this is the hour in which the Church should deepen its consciousness of itself, in which it ought to meditate on that mystery which is peculiar to it, in which it ought to examine for its own enlightenment and for its own development a particular doctrine which it already knows and which it has formulated and made known during this past century. That doctrine concerns the origin of the Church, its own nature, its own mission, its own ultimate destiny, a doctrine never sufficiently understood. . . ."

STATEMENT

The Order of Cîteaux, as an historical event, was the result of the movement of the Holy Spirit in and through men, the monks from Molesme who came to Cîteaux to live the Gospel according to the Rule of St Benedict. As time went on, they gave expression to their way of life in different writings and documents such as the Charter of Charity—the fruit of their

lived experience, which was fostered, in a special way, by the
union of their monasteries.
In developing this way of life, when they made specific choices
their ultimate aim was a response to Christ in love. Accordingly,
for the nuns and monks who, like them, follow Christ in this
way, certain elements accidental to other forms of the Christian
life become essential to this specifically Cistercian form of the
Christian life, and certain values, common to Christians as a
whole, are given special emphasis (e.g., prayer and penance).

The Spirit and Aims of the Founders

During the course of the Symposium the following elements
emerged from the various papers and discussions. While they are
not exclusive to the Cistercian Order and, taken individually, do
not specify the Order as such, their balanced and harmonious
blending does seem to characterize the "Cistercian movement."

Renewal

Our Cistercian Fathers were conscious of their continuity with
and relation to all the monastic tradition that went before them.
However, they showed a capacity to innovate and to break with
what was inauthentic in that tradition, and thus, to respond to
a call to true renewal. In establishing structures, their purpose was
to make them serve this renewal of spirit. Like the Church herself
the Order will ever be in constant need of such renewal.

The Experience of God

The Cistercian Fathers continuously expressed an absorbing
desire to taste and see how good God is: *vacate et videte*. Such an
experience of God was the source of their enthusiasm ("possessed
by God"), their joy and ardor. It continuously fostered their ideal
of constant prayer. The Cistercian charism is not flamboyant, but
quiet and simple, well integrated into a daily life of service to the
Brotherhood.

Charity

Love of God and the Brotherhood was the heart of Cistercian life. Cîteaux was a *schola charitatis*. Their well-developed theology of love can contribute to the theological renewal of this present era.

Community

"Prophetic example" (Blessed Eugene III) inspired our Fathers and fired them with that "good zeal" mentioned by the Rule. (C. 72.) While the experience of God was a mystery lived in the depths of the individual soul, the spiritual riches that flowed from this experience were shared in a community. Together, Cistercians go to God; together, they encounter him by the powerful activity of the Holy Spirit. It is thus that, in community, a living tradition or heritage was and is passed on, evidence of which was given during this Symposium. We experience this power of example in our daily life in community.

The Church

The early Cistercians lived in close relationship to the local church as well as to the Universal Church. Drawing upon the mystery of the Incarnation they found the Church to be a visible sign, a sacrament of Christ just as Christ is the visible Sacrament of God. The local Church and the monastery were sacraments of the Church giving witness to what the Church as a whole should be. Part of the discernment of the spirit and aims of our founders is to identify our role in the Church Universal and to relate it dynamically to all the other parts of this Body of Christ. As St Paul expressed it, we all need one another, for we are all members of one another.

The Rule of St Benedict

The early Cistercians strove to live the Gospel. Their fidelity to the Rule was simply an expression of this, for they saw the Rule as a practical interpretation of the Gospel. The *dura* and *aspera*, the asceticism of the Rule was a preparation for the experience of God (cf. Prologue, c. 7 and 73). Thus all the observances to which they were so faithful (solitude, vigils, fasting, manual labor) were so many means to that purity of heart which Cassian, in his first conference, identifies with charity.

Poverty

Special regard for evangelical poverty in the deepest sense of the word characterized the first Cistercians. *Kenosis* or self-emptying made them available, free, at the service of God and of the brethren; this poverty of spirit created that simplicity so characteristic of Cîteaux, a simplicity which sought freedom from all that was superfluous. One of the principal expressions of Cistercian poverty was manual labor by which they strove to support themselves and provide for their guests, rich and poor.

Solitude

The founders of Cîteaux established a real and effective solitude in order to favor a truly contemplative life. Cîteaux was called an *eremus*, a biblical word which expresses primarily an attitude of being alone before God. However, the Cistercians were not hermits living in community. They tried to establish a balance between solitude and community life.

. . . . .

Much of what is contained in these elements is summed up in this statement which is drawn from the paper delivered by Brother Patrick Ryan:

> *The spirit of the early Cistercians was expressed in a way of life, a life of poverty, simplicity and austerity, in an atmosphere of silence and solitude conducive to reading, prayer and contemplation . . . bringing about as its fruit an openness to God throughout the day.*

ANALYTIC INDEX

The following abbreviations are used: abb=abbess, abbey; abp=archbishop; abt=abbot; Ben=Benedictine; bp=bishop; card=cardinal; Cist=Cistercian; Cit=Cîteaux; Cl=Cluniac, Cluny; dt=doctrine; e=emperor; k=king; n=note; p=pope; pr=prior, priory.

Laus tibi, Christe.

CISTERCIAN FATHERS SERIES

Under the direction of the same Board of Editors as the CISTERCIAN STUDIES SERIES, the CISTERCIAN FATHERS SERIES seeks to make available the works of the Cistercian Fathers in good English translations based on the recently established critical editions. The texts are accompanied by introductions, notes and indexes prepared by qualified scholars.